THE RESILIENCE OF CORPORATE JAPAN

Human Resource Management Series:
Foreword

The two integrating themes of this series are organizational change, and the strategic role of the human resource function.

The 1990s have witnessed a further shift in thinking with respect to the organizational role of the personnel function. That shift has been reflected in the change of title – to human resource management – and revolves around the notion that effective human resource management is a critical dimension of an organization's competitive advantage. Personnel or human resource management is thus now more widely accepted as a strategic business function, in contrast with the traditional image of a routine administrative operation concerned with hiring, training, paying and terminating.

The range of issues with which personnel managers must now deal has widened considerably, as has the complexity and significance of those issues. Conventional texts in this subject area typically have the advantage of comprehensiveness, by offering a broad overview of the function, its responsibilities, and key trends. Such coverage is always purchased at the expense of depth. The aim of this series, therefore, is not to replace traditional personnel or human resource texts, but to complement those works by offering in-depth, informed and accessible treatments of important and topical themes, written by specialists in those areas and supported by systematic research, often conducted by the authors themselves.

The series is thus based on a commitment to contemporary changes in the human resource function, and to the direction of those changes. This has involved a steady shift in management attention to improved employee welfare and rights, genuinely equal opportunity, the effective management of diversity, wider employee involvement in organization management and ownership, changing the nature of work and organization structures through process 'reengineering', and towards personal skills growth and development at all organizational levels. Further significant trends have included the decline in trade union membership, the increased interest in 'non-union' organizations, and the potentially shifting responsibilities of the human resource function in this context. This series documents and explains these trends and developments, indicating the progress that has been achieved, and aims to contribute to best management practice through fresh empirical evidence and practical example.

David Buchanan
Series Editor
De Montfort University School of Business, Leicester

THE RESILIENCE OF CORPORATE JAPAN

New strategies and personnel practices

Christian Berggren
and
Masami Nomura

P·C·P
Paul Chapman
Publishing Ltd

HF
5549
.2
.J3
B47
1997

Paul Chapman Publishing Ltd
144 Liverpool Road
London
N1 1LA

British Library Cataloguing in Publication Data

Berggren, Christian, 1950–
The resilience of corporate Japan: competitive strategies
and personnel practices in a new low-growth era. – (Human
resource management series)
1. Personnel management – Japan
I. Title   II. Nomura, M.
658.3'01'0952

ISBN 1 85396 309 7

Typeset by Dorwyn Ltd, Rowlands Castle, Hants
Printed and bound by in Great Britain

A B C D E F G H   9 8 7

CONTENTS

ACKNOWLEDGEMENTS

This original impetus for this book was provided when the Japanese Society for Promotion of the Sciences made it possible for Masami Nomura to host Christian Berggren as a visiting scholar at Okayama University for two months in 1993. We would like to thank them, as well as a large number of Japanese managers and union officers, especially those who patiently and generously shared their time with us in both 1993 and in 1995.

During the progress of the book, with its many reformulations and reinterpretations of the basic issue of resilience, we have benefited from extensive discussions with colleagues in Japan and Sweden. The same holds true for several of the individual chapters. The discerning comments by Professor Fujimoto at Tokyo University during discussions in Tokyo, Stockholm and Paris in 1995-96 have been very helpful for interpreting the new competitive strategies in the automobile industry. The insight and knowledge of Yoshida Nobumi at the Jidosha Keiei Kaihatasu Kenkyu-sho has also been a most valuable contribution to Chapter 6. Bengt Asker, previously at Ericsson, the Swedish telecommunications giant, kindly examined Chapter 9 on computers and software. Professor Lillrank at the European Center for Japanese Studies generously shared work-in-progress on current developments in Japan, especially in the software industry. Paul Lillrank and Carl le Grand at the University of Stockholm (visiting researcher in Kyoto 1996–97) have also stimulated the assessments of American versus Japanese dynamics by their provoking and sharply divergent arguments.

When the first version of the manuscript landed with Paul Chapman, it was a rather unwieldy bundle of paper. David Buchanan at De Montfort University School of Business has offered indispensable support and constructive criticism throughout the journey of transforming the original mess to a coherent structure. For a Japanese and Swedish researcher to jointly write a book in a 'third' language is at times a complicated endeavour. In the final stage we enjoyed the privilege of meticulous copy-editing, for which we are deeply indebted.

ABOUT THE AUTHORS

Both authors are long-time students of the themes focused upon in this book. Masami Nomura's books have all sold well in Japan: his study of the development of Toyota, *Toyotism – Maturity and Metamorphosis of a Japanese Production System* (1993, in Japanese), of Japanese work organisation, *Skill and Division of Labour; Taylorism in Japanese Firms* (1993, in Japanese) as well as of employment practices, *Lifetime Employment* (1994, in Japanese). *Alternatives to Lean Production* (1993) by Berggren is a major study of the Swedish automobile industry, comparing its particular forms of work organisation with the dominant Japanese pattern. Nomura has repeatedly visited Germany as a guest researcher. Berggren was a visiting scholar in Australia in 1991–2, in Japan 1993 and in France 1994. The collaboration between the authors started at a conference organised by Wissenschaftszentrum in Berlin in 1987. Together they have participated in symposia and conferences on the Japanese production system in Italy, Canada, Japan, Korea and Sweden from 1988 to 1994. In 1993, the authors spent two months undertaking fieldwork together in Japan; in September 1995, several of the companies were revisited and new ones were added in a second round of joint field studies (see appendix, 'A note on sources'). Nomura brings an in-depth knowledge of Japanese management and practices to this book, and Berggren the western perspective. In countless discussions over the years, Nomura has sometimes emphasised the weaknesses and Berggren the strengths of Japanese corporate organisation. The final result, it is hoped, is a nuanced synthesis. In preparing the book there has been some division of labour. Nomura is the main author of Chapters 4, 8 and 5 (except for the opening and concluding subsections); Berggren the author of the remaining chapters. The overview on the Japanese economy (Chapter 3) has been written jointly.

LEARN ABOUT THE TERMS USED IN JAPANESE BUSINESS

amakudari Literally, descent from the heaven. After retirement, senior bureaucrats become top executives of companies they once regulated.

chuto saiyosha Mid-career entrant. People who join the company in an irregular fashion (that is, they are not part of the annual April hiring of new graduates).

Denki Rengo Japanese Federation of Electrical Machine Workers' Unions. Federation of enterprise unions in the electrical and electronic industry.

endaka High yen.

endaka hukyo Recession caused by high yen.

fukumieki 'latent capital'. Unrealised capital gains coming from the difference between the booked and the current price of corporate stocks and real estate.

gemba Literally, workplace. Usually, *gemba* means the workplace where goods are produced.

gyaku yunyu Import to Japan of goods produced at Japanese transplants abroad.

haken shain Temporary employees dispatched by personnel agencies.

ippanshoku, sogoshoku After the Equal Opportunity Law aiming to eliminate discrimination against women became effective in 1986, many firms introduced a new hiring system for white-collar workers, which has two different tracks

- *sogoshoku*, (comprehensive workers). These can later be managers, and have to accept transfers to other cities or overseas; and
- *ippanshoku* (general workers) who have restricted pay increases and promotions. Most women including university graduates are hired as *ippanshoku*.

JAW Confederation of Japan Automobile Workers' Unions. Federation of enterprise unions in the automobile industry.

jusen Financial firms for housing loans, founded by banks. According to a directive from the Ministry of Finance in 1990, *jusen* companies were exempted from the limitations on loans to speculative real-estate investment imposed on other financial institutions. A large part of the *jusen* loans were made to corporations associated with politicians, former bureaucrats and criminal syndicates, the *yakuza*.

Kaisha Literally 'company'. In western texts kaisha represents the ideal type of competitive Japanese company.

Kaizen literally 'improvement' signifies continuous and never-ending improvement by small steps.

kana Japanese syllabary. In the Japanese language, there is one system of Chinese characters (*kanji*) and two sets of *kana*, that is, phonetic characters *hiragana* and *katakana* (for western words).

kanji Chinese characters (pictographs).

kanryo Those who are promoted to high-rank positions or who are qualified to be promoted to high-rank positions.

karoshi Death from overwork.

katatataki Literally, tap on the shoulder. Suggestion that he or she should retire from the company.

keiretsu Enterprise groups. Horizontal *keiretsu* is nearly equal to *kigyo shudan* – groups of companies loosely organised around a big bank. Vertical *keiretsu* are vertically related production groups, consisting, for example, of an automobile company and its various layers of suppliers.

kibo taishoku Voluntary retirement.

kigyo shudan Group of companies.

Komeito Political party financed and supported by a big religious organisation, Soka Gakkai.

konai sagyosha Subcontract workers working on the site of the parent company.

kudoka Hollowing out of the national economy.

Minshato Political party founded by the right-wing group of the Japan Socialist Party in 1959.

mochiai Cross shareholding.

muda Waste, that is non-value added activities. According to Ohno Taiichi, the famous founder of the Toyota production system, there are seven forms of muda: overproduction, waiting, transporting, too much machining (over-processing), inventories, moving and making defective parts and products.

nenko Seniority and/or age.

Nikkei: Nihon Keizai Shimbun The largest economic newspaper in Japan.

Nikkeiren Japan Federation of Employers' Associations. One of the four leading economic organisations in Japan.

nenpo sei Annual salary system.

noryoku kyu Pay largely determined by an employee's ability.

ohen Short-term (usually several months) transfer within a firm.

Sakigake Political party founded by 10 spun-off diet members from the ruling Liberal Democratic Party.

senmon gakko Vocational training school.

Shinseito Political party founded in 1993 by 44 former diet members of the ruling Liberal Democratic Party.

Shinshinto Biggest opposition party, founded by Shinseito, Komeito, Nippon Shinto and some other small parties, in 1994.

shukko Transfer of employees to other related firms.

shusa Chief engineer for product development.

shushin koyo Lifetime employment.

soki taishoku Early retirement. One of the measures to cut employment.

yakuza Japanese Mafia.

yuka shoken hokokusho Annual reports submitted to the Minister of Finance by companies whose stock prices are listed in the stock exchanges.

zaibatsu Large and diversified business groups which rose to prominence in the early twentieth century. Normally they were structured around family-controlled holding companies. Mitsubishi, Mitsui and Sumitomo are three famous examples with a long historic tradition. During the American Occupation, the pre-war *zaibatsus* were dissolved, but in the 1950s they reconstituted as *kigyo shudan*. In their new shape, these business groups are less tightly knit together by financial bonds, and they are not centred around family-controlled holding companies any more.

Organisational structure and positions in a typical Japanese firm

torishimariyaku kai (board of directors)
    kaicho (chairman of the board)
    shacho (president)
    senmu (senior managing director)
    jomu (managing director)
    torishimariyaku (member of the board)
jigyo honbu (division)
    jigyo honbucho (division director)
kojo (plant)
    kojocho (plant manager)
bu (department)
    bucho (department chief)
ka (section)
    kacho (section chief)
in the manufacturing sector
kakari (subsection)
    kakaricho (subsection chief)
kumi
    kocho (senior foreman)
    kumicho (foreman)
    hancho (group leader)

In most Japanese firms, there are *bu* (usually translated as department) and at its lower level *ka* (section). In the production area, the organisation is further broken down to *kakari* (subsection) and *kumi*. There are firms such as Toyota that have *han* (sub-group) as the lowest unit, but *han* plays no important role for administration. *Kumi* is the most important unit for production control. At each level of organisation, there is a *cho* (chief), for example, *Kacho*.

1

INTRODUCTION

> Restructuring and voluntary retirements are the last things we would resort to.
>
> (Matsushita, overseas planning office, 1993)
>
> In spite of the pressure to reduce the workforce, there will be no dismissals. This has always been emphasised by top management.
>
> (Daihatsu headquarters, 1995)
>
> Our company has been 80 years in business and has never fired anyone.
>
> (Sharp headquarters, 1995)

The emergence of Japan as an economic superpower in the 1980s produced an entire literature devoted to explaining the miracle and to providing western managers with lessons. Books ranged from simplistic treatises of Japanese management, such as Ouchi's *Theory Z* (1981), to scholarly enquiries into Japan's interfirm relationships, represented by Gerlach's *Alliance Capitalism* (1992). 'Learn from Japan' was a common catch-phrase in American as well as European industries. Since the early 1990s, however, global competitive relations have changed. In many fields US industry has regained a position of pre-eminence, whereas Japan has been mired in a protracted recession. A surge in the exchange rate, combined with a serious slump in domestic demand after the burst of the Bubble Boom in 1991, created a double squeeze on the Japanese economy. Together, these factors have resulted in several years of stagnation and grim prospects for growth. For many large Japanese companies, and even more for small ones, this has been the worst time since the late 1940s. During previous postwar downturns, the oil crises in the 1970s and the *endaka* (recession because of high yen) in the 1980s, Japanese companies intensified their efforts to rationalise production and upgrade products, and soon emerged as even more competitive. The post-Bubble recession has been different in several respects, much longer than previous downturns, and much more serious because of the confluence of several factors: *endaka*, crises in the financial and real-estate sectors and stagnation in domestic consumption. A return to the previous rates of growth seems highly unlikely.

The first purpose of this book is to analyse how Japanese companies in internationally competing sectors adjust to the new situation. What are their strategic responses in terms of product policies, production organisation and international operation? What role will the Japanese manufacturing base play in the future? This analysis involves a re-examination of the literature on Japanese supremacy, which dominated so much of the debate in the late 1980s and early 1990s. Why, for example, did the prophesies of Japanese leadership fail in several industries? What will be Japanese competitive weaknesses and advantages in the years to come?

The second purpose of the book is to investigate the fate of Japan's heralded personnel practices during and after the long recession. In the wake of its international ascendancy in the 1970s and 1980s, the employment policies and system of human capital formation in large Japanese companies attracted the attention of the entire industrial world. 'Lifetime employment', *nenko* (seniority-based wages), one-company careers and enterprise unionism diverged from any simple notion of convergence towards one basic model in the developed capitalist world. These practices were not traditional, 'cultural', features, but developed after the Second World War during Japan's high-growth period, when the continuous expansion was only interrupted by short spells of recession. Indeed, the promises of stable employment and long-term careers seemed to be predicated on constant growth and expansion. The post-Bubble recession and the transition to a low-growth economy provide an acid test for Japan's system of corporate governance and personnel management and a unique opportunity to gauge the depth of the differences between this system and the Anglo-Saxon standard.

According to conventional western wisdom, Japan's personnel policies from its period of high growth are a luxury Japan can now ill afford, and as a result there will be a necessary 'normalisation'. In this view, Japan's previous differences are mainly attributed to macroeconomic factors, such as cost of capital. When these factors are changing, Japan will lose its distinctive features and converge with western (in America interpreted as US) capitalism. A representative case is Jesper Kroll, a chief analyst at S. G. Warburg in Japan. According to him (Kroll, 1993) the Bubble economy of 1986–90 represented the 'final, frantic climax of capitalism without costs'. The low cost of capital in Japan, compared with the USA, 'allowed for much of Japan's superficial uniqueness in the global economy: it allowed for lifetime employment, it allowed for high capital spending to GDP ratio, more frequent scrapping and high private sector R&D expenditure budgets, . . . it allowed for production of better quality products with added functions without raising prices'. With costs of capital and profit requirements now approaching international standards, Kroll argued, Japanese firms have to compete by western terms, and scrap their costly personnel practices (ibid.). This pessimistic outlook is not an exclusive US phenomenon, but shared among important business circles within Japan, which we illustrate in Chapter 3. Is the era of Japanese exceptionalism finally drawing to its close? This book will present the public Japanese debate, and the various reform proposals from the employers' federation and industrial unions. Above all, however, the focus is on real developments within firms. What kind of workforce adjustments have been implemented during the recession? Are Japanese personnel practices being replaced by a more ruthless downsizing, US style? What are the structural implications of the long recession and the bleak growth perspective?

At the heart of this book is a broad analysis of shifts in the employment system (Chapter 5) and four specific industry studies (Chapters 6–9), where Japan achieved, or was supposed to achieve, world leadership in the 1980s: automobiles, consumer electronics, machine tools, and computers and software. These four industries, apart from computer software, figure prominently in Japan's export statistics. In 1992, the automobile industry alone accounted for 20.4% of Japan's total exports (Nippon – a charted survey of Japan, 1994: 78). Leading companies within these four industries (Toyota and Nissan, Matsushita and Sharp, Mori Seki and Okuma, Hitachi and Fujitsu) are all prominent representatives of 'classical' Japanese competitive strategies and personnel practices. Within this set, however, there are important differences. The makers of consumer electronics have a strong international orientation and were pioneers in moving the production of TVs and VCRs offshore. By contrast, the computer and software firms have been dedicated to the domestic market. Another difference concerns the degree and nature of western competition. In machine tools, the Japanese makers of standardised computerised machines have more or less eliminated western rivals. In automobiles a global seesaw game is taking place: Japanese makers were far ahead in assembly productivity and product lead-time in the 1980s; and western firms staged a rapid catch-up in the early 1990s, followed by a new Japanese leap in overall efficiency since the outbreak of the recession. Packaged software represents the other extreme; here Japanese providers are far behind formidable US competitors, and attempts to deploy industrial management skills have been largely unsuccessful. The four sectors have been studied at several levels: at the industry level, at the level of individual firms and at the workplace level.

The 1990s signify a rupture with four decades of high growth and stable politics in Japan. The dominant pattern in the four industry studies, however, is perseverance and resilience. This resilience is found at many different levels. No major firm has withdrawn from any of these industries, and the structure of permanent competition remains a very important aspect of industry dynamics. Further, resilience is a striking aspect of Japan as a manufacturing base. The future expansion in automobiles and machine tools will take place overseas, but at the same time manufacturers are up-grading their competitive position in Japan. The consumer electronics and 'information industries' move production of commodity products offshore but also invest heavily in new facilities for high-tech products in Japan, such as liquid crystal displays, plasma screens, semiconductors and semiconductor-making equipment. Resilience and perseverance are also very much part of the strategies of individual firms, as is illustrated by the cases of Matsushita and Mori Seki in Chapters 7 and 8. Finally, perseverance and resilience apply to employment practices, too. In spite of the protracted crisis, the dominant pattern of workforce reduction has been gradual adaptation using the conventional Japanese repertoire. There is a normalisation process, but not as a convergence to western (US) standards – rather a return to Japanese normalcy, after the detours and excesses of the Bubble Boom. This unfortunately also involves a confirmation of the traditional Japanese system of gender segregation.

Resilience and perseverance are a major theme throughout the book, but there are also a number of qualifications and subthemes. Corporate resilience mainly pertains to large firms. The future of the infrastructure of small subcontractor firms seems to be much more uncertain. This is demonstrated in the account of the two industrial districts, Sakaki and Ohta-ku, in Chapter 4.

The industry studies highlight how much effort Japanese managers spend to safeguard the cherished employment security which is at the core of Japanese personnel practices. However, it is also emphasised that this practice has neither covered a majority of Japanese employees nor prevented several waves of employment adjustment in depressed industries. A common trend in current personnel policies is to make this practice even more exclusivist. Companies honour their obligations to their existing workforce, but devise a variety of means to minimise recruitment of regular employees in the future. The *nenko* system, the seniority-related compensation, which was introduced at the behest of unions in the late 1940s, is surviving, but employers have made use of the recession to experiment with performance-based pay in major companies. The enterprise unions are still an important part of the Japanese social pact, but have to find ways to influence these processes of change or run the risk of becoming entirely marginalised.

Other subthemes come out of the individual industry studies. The automobile industry was already faced with a looming crisis before the burst of the Bubble Boom: labour shortages, exhausted workers, model proliferation and declining profitability. The recession has implied 'a return to normalcy' in several respects, in productivity focus as well as personnel policy. However, there are also important aspects of change. The internationalisation process accelerates. The renewed productivity focus does not imply a return to traditional Toyota-style *gemba* (shopfloor) focus. Previous forms of incremental rationalisation are more difficult to enforce, and process engineering and preproduction planning are becoming much more significant. The consumer electronics firms have already established global systems of manufacturing. At the same time they compete in increasing their Japanese capacity for future growth products, in their established way of technological up-grading and internal diversification. In this sector, too, there are important changes in production organisation. New unstable products do not allow much time for piecemeal, shopfloor rationalisation; advanced process engineering and instantaneous ramp-up of new models are of crucial importance. The machine tool industry represents a paradox. This was the hardest pressed by the business slump in 1992–5, but at the same time enjoyed the strongest position in terms of international competitiveness. Its problem is to find new growth markets. Inside Japan there will probably be some industry consolidation (modifying the pattern of corporate perseverance), but in other aspects change will be of a very gradualist nature. In computers and software, Japan's strength is utterly uneven, which has invited sharply divergent western views on this industry. In several component areas Japanese companies are world leaders, and will remain so. They are gradually internationalizing but will maintain major operations in Japan. In personal computers, Japanese companies are latecomers, which are now quickly catching up after adopting US standards. Software represents Japan's 'soft spot'. Here Japanese companies sought to take advantage of their manufacturing management skills in a most interesting organisational experiment: the large-scale software factories, which did not survive the end of the IBM era. The PC revolution and the new world of open systems are driving fundamental changes in the way Japanese software divisions operate; at the same time Japan faces the challenge of developing an independent software sector, free from the constraints of its powerful industrial groups.

For Europe, the resilience and dynamics of corporate Japan should stimulate some critical reflection. In the 1980s, 'learning from Japan' was a widely diffused but often ill-understood business credo. In the 1990s, the USA has regained its status as dominant model of technological innovation as well as job creation. This is linked to a neoliberal agenda where deregulation and 'unfettered market forces' are seen as major prerequisites for a rejuvenation of European competitiveness. American-style management and forms of labour market flexibility are also gaining currency in continental Europe. The European debate would benefit from a renewed look at corporate Japan and how it distinguishes between flexible deployment and the stable employment of labour, between JIT production and JIT hiring. The Japanese way of labour-hoarding during a recession makes it difficult to instigate quick turnarounds in bleeding companies; on the other hand it also means that companies have resources at hand for a rapid expansion when there is a business up-turn. At the same time, the long-term personnel responsibilities mean that there is a constant pressure to innovate and expand product ranges.

In several respects, this book occupies a middle position, stressing continuity and *gradual* change. Japan's alliance capitalism is not a transitory phenomenon, and its particularity not an issue of low costs of capital! Against the simplicities of both the 'Japan as no. 1' and the recent Sunset literature, our emphasis is not only on understanding the resilience and staying power of Japanese industry but also on highlighting contrasts and contradictions. The composition of the author team, a Japanese and a western academic, has facilitated such an approach. A western student of Japan is often inclined to find clear-cut patterns which are easily contrasted to western practices. In writing this book, there has been an ongoing dialogue, where the Japanese partner has corrected such 'western' simplifications by pointing to important counter-cases. This has contributed to a more nuanced and also more complex account, by which we hope the reader will be informed – and perhaps sometimes also disturbed. Teamwork has allowed for the combination of an insider's insights into the Japanese debate with an outsider's comparative perspective. In Japan there is a strong tradition of crisis consciousness, as demonstrated by the long debate on the risks of hollowing-out (Chapter 4), and a Japanese researcher will thus tend to point to all the edges that are fraying. By contrast, a Swedish researcher, depressed by Europe's dual problems of high unemployment and low innovation, tends to be impressed by the resilience and 'shock-absorbing capability' of Japanese corporations. This book is the result largely of joint fieldwork, but we have preserved our different writing styles since they will alert the reader to these shifts in perspective.

The book also takes a middle position in terms of coverage and depth. It is neither a general treatise on economic and social changes in contemporary Japan nor a specialist enquiry into a particular industry. Recently, several in-depth studies of individual sectors have emerged, for example Martin Fransman's work on Japan's computer and communications industry (1995). When possible, we build on such studies, supplemented by our own fieldwork. This book will not give a complete overview of key industrial sectors in Japan. The international standing and heavy competitive pressure in the four industries selected make them an excellent object for the central themes of the book: endurance and survival strategies, competitive repositioning and internationalisation, and continuity and change in personnel practices.

OVERVIEW OF THE BOOK

The book starts with three chapters on economic, political and industrial changes in Japan. Chapter 2 starts out with the literature of the 1980s and early 1990s, when Japan's superior performance resulted in enquiries into the nature of its competitive dynamics and forms of corporate control. Some of the starkly divergent views on Japan are presented before turning to the US resurgence in the 1990s, and the uncomfortable position of Europe. The chapter ends with a critique of ordering nations into 'No. 1', 'No. 2', etc., and stresses the problems of replacing the simplistic admiration of Japan with an equally simplistic adoration of the USA. The next chapter deals with domestic economic development in Japan. It starts with a brief account of the high-growth period and the particularity of the post-Bubble recession. This is followed by an analysis of the partial 'decomposition of the developmental state', which was brought about by the end of political stability and the demise of the mighty bureaucracies of MITI and the Ministry of Finance. Whereas Japanese corporations displayed confidence, bordering on arrogance, in the 1980s, recent political and economic developments have resulted in a widespread sense of anxiety and insecurity. The chapter ends with a comparison of the attitudes of the business community in 1990 and 1995, which provides a vivid picture of this change. For a long time, the situation of Japanese companies was tightly coupled to the prosperity of Japan's domestic economy. In the 1990s, this identity was being dissolved. Domestic production and employment are slowly contracting in key sectors (such as the automobile industry), while companies are expanding and building new production bases offshore. In Japan, this internationalisation is dreaded as industrial 'hollowing-out' – *kudoka*. Chapter 4 gives an account of this process from a Japanese perspective.

After this overview of economic and industrial development, Chapter 5 focuses on the 'three pillars' of industrial relations in Japan's large firms: lifetime employment, the *nenko* wage system and in-company unions. A critical account of the operation and limitations of the employment system during the previous decades is followed by an analysis of change and continuity in the 1990s. Chapters 6–9 are devoted to the four industry studies. Against a backdrop of new market conditions and competitive strategies in each industry, organisational changes, employment adjustment and personnel policies are analysed. Industry overviews are combined with accounts from plant studies and management interviews.

The concluding chapter, Chapter 10, brings together the central themes of the book. It summarises the efforts of Japan's core industries to regain competitiveness, discusses the implication of Japan's new economic and political regime, and seeks to assess the future of its employment practices. This chapter brings the two themes of the book back to one central question: is the era of Japanese exceptionalism, of unique competitiveness and unique employment policies, drawing to a close? Is Japan finally approaching 'normal' (Anglo-Saxon) capitalism? This question concerning forces for convergence versus forces sustaining diversity is a *basso continuo* running through the book. The currently popular debate concerning globalisation and the alleged withering away of national economies implies a very strong convergence thesis (see, for example, Ohmae, 1990). The answer in this book is that diversity still carries the day. Japan's 'alliance capitalism' is modifying itself, and adapting to new circumstance, in the way it has been doing for decades, but its basic model of corporate governance, competition and employment remains largely intact.

PART 1

ECONOMY AND EMPLOYMENT

2

FROM JAPANESE SUPREMACY TO US RESURGENCE

JAPAN AS NO. 1

In 1980, Ezra Vogel published his famous book, *Japan as No. 1*. According to Vogel, Japan had created a uniquely successful economy but, even more, Japan had 'unlike Western countries, consciously examined and restructured all traditional institutions on the basis of rational considerations' (1980: 4–5). Vogel's prediction of Japan's ascendancy was based on a very confident view of the future: 'As information processing becomes more important, Tokyo has the potential for becoming the information capital of the world . . . the national government's commitment to making Japanese companies superior in computer and telecommunication systems gives it distinct advantages over other countries' (ibid.: 250).

The history of Japanese export successes supported Vogel's contentions. This story started in the early postwar period, when Japanese sewing-machine producers challenged the previous world leader, the US Singer company, and launched a major offensive to Europe. It was followed by other light consumer goods, such as watches, cameras and radios and, somewhat later, by steel, ships and motorcycles. In the years after the publication of Vogel's forecast, the Japanese export machine progressed to world-leading positions in automobiles and machine tools, and further to semiconductors, copiers and laser printers. Even in computers and software, where US companies used to enjoy pre-eminence, Japan made impressive inroads. Analysts sounded grim warnings about Japan's imminent dominance in information technology, a representative example being Forrester's (1993) *Silicon Samurai – How Japan Conquered the World's IT Industry*.

Why were the Japanese so successful in such a broad range of industries? Economists, for example Tsuru (1993), normally stress macroeconomic factors of supply and demand. After the war, Japan was characterised by an abundant and unusually elastic labour supply. Thus the new industries could expand rapidly without requiring any bonus rise in the wage rate. A high savings ratio assured that export industries enjoyed low-cost capital. A continuous increase in world trade and open western economies created dynamic market opportunities, and facilitated a swift catch-up in technology and science. Another explanation is offered by political scientists, who emphasise the role of the Japanese 'developmental state' in targeting industries, securing capital flows, creating a stable and predictable environment, and focusing the efforts of business. Chalmers Johnson (1982) set the standard with his study of Japanese industrial policy during the decades of high growth and the restructuring in the 1970s. Okimoto (1989) demonstrated the importance of ministerial initiatives and government–business networks for the development of the semiconductor industry in the 1980s.

THE POWER OF *KAISHA* DYNAMICS

Another, mesooriented perspective has been offered by enquiries into the competitive dynamics of high-growth industries. A prominent case is Abegglen and Stalk (1987). Since this book focuses on competition and change within four particular industries, a closer look at the arguments of Abegglen and Stalk is warranted. First it must be noted that there is a major difference in Japan between internationally competitive and export-oriented industries, such as automobiles and consumer electronics, and domestically oriented sectors. Ranging from construction to telecommunications equipment, these are normally supported and protected by particular standards and symbiotic ties with government agencies and semi-public customers. Because of the huge difference in productivity and performance between the 'international' and 'domestic' sectors, the Japanese economy, more than that of other nations, is a study in contrasts. Abegglen and Stalk focus squarely on the first sector in their powerful portrait of Japanese '*kaisha* dynamics'.

An illustrative case is the 'calculator war' of 1967–73. In a few years the three early movers, Sharp, Canon and Oki, were joined by another 20 competitors. Sharp initially had the lead. But Casio, then relatively unknown, had the most aggressive expansion plans. As Sharp grew at 100 % per year, Casio grew at almost 200%. By 1973 Casio had achieved the leading position in Japan. While the market doubled each year, Casio enlarged its share from 12 to 36% and increased output more than 96 times! Sharp regained the initiative, however, by using its technological advantage in LCDs (liquid crystal displays) to pioneer advanced palm-top calculators. Later this was followed by the introduction of an automated production process which reduced the price significantly. At the end of the 1970s, Sharp was once more the leading calculator producer in Japan. The intense competition and the eventual decline in demand proved too much for many of the entrants. In the mid-1980s, nine competitors remained, still an impressive number given the mature market situation.

Another case is the motorcycle industry. In the early 1950s, this industry had over 50 participants. Tohatsu, with a 22% market share, was the leading company and Honda was second. At this time, Tohatsu was much more profitable and financially solid than Honda. But Tohatsu chose to be conservative, whereas Honda went for growth. In a market expanding 42% per year, Honda grew at about 66% and within five years emerged as the undisputed leader. Tohatsu's share dropped to less than 4%, Honda soared to 44%. When market growth slowed to less than 10% per year and a dominant product design had been firmly established, this competitive structure with

Honda at the top became permanent. By 1969, the 50 makers of the 1950s had shrunk to today's four: Honda, Yamaha, Suzuki and Kawasaki, an unusual degree of concentration for Japan (Abegglen and Stalk 1987).

Box 2.1 Kaisha *dynamics – the self-charging competitive engine*

1) *A potential growth market emerges, as a result of novel product or production technologies or the new application of existing technologies.*
2) *A few pioneering companies invest heavily in technology and production facilities. Mass production starts to drive costs down.*
3) *Demand takes off as prices are lowered and applications developed. The pioneers are followed by several new entrants. Established rivals from related industries confront entrepreneurial newcomers.*
4) *A race to expand plant capacity unfolds, as each company strives to enlarge its market share. Within a few years, total production capacity is doubled, and then doubled again.*
5) *Prices are set below initial cost levels to trigger demand and to dispose of the increasing output. Price competition and production expansion stimulates further market growth.*
6) *The booming market attracts more competitors, who seek to differentiate by new features and new applications. A new round of output doubling follows.*
7) *Demand growth in Japan slows down. Competition continues in export markets, where western firms are attacked by an avalanche of cost-effective Japanese makers.*
8) *Exports decline, low-end production is transferred overseas. The industry structure in Japan is stabilised. No new firms enter, a few may leave. Remaining companies continue to watch each other closely – and to compete in new markets.*

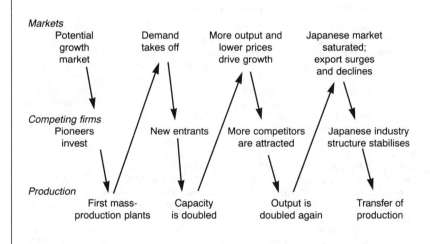

Several factors constitute these *'kaisha* dynamics' (Box 2.1). First, in growth markets Japanese firms set prices as low as possible, often below initial costs, to create demand and expand the market, instead of the western habit of setting high initial prices and then waiting to see how demand develops. Low prices are supported by massive plant investments, a so-called *doubling strategy*. Anticipating a steep demand increase, capacity and output are repeatedly doubled within periods of only two or four years. Such aggressive expansion is needed for maintaining and enlarging market share, and for creating the economies of scale which are required to realise the programmed cost reduction. The intensive competition is further heightened by new entrants, from upstream, downstream or related industries. This entry accelerates the process of cost reduction, capacity increase and market expansion. New models are launched incessantly, and features and options added, which further serve to enlarge the market. When the domestic market is saturated and growth rates stabilise at a single-digit level, competition continues in export markets, or moves on to other markets. The ultimate prize in these competitive battles is always increased market share. *Kaisha* dynamics characterized more or less all of Japan's successful export industries from the 1950s to the 1970s. It is still a powerful mechanism in new growth markets, as the case of lithium-ion demonstrates (see Box 2.2), and we will meet it several times in this book – for example, in the analysis of LCDs and flat-screens in Chapter 7.

Box 2.2　Kaisha *competition in the 1990s – the case of lithium-ion batteries*

Lithium-ion is a new technology for powerful, rechargeable batteries. Compared to the industry mainstay nickel-cadmium (nicad), lithium-ion batteries boast a threefold increase in storage efficiency (energy per weight unit) and deliver three times the normal voltage of a nicad battery (3.6 compared to 1.2 V). In 1995, the market for lithium-ion batteries, estimated at US$300 million, was almost owned by the Japanese. The unfolding of kaisha *dynamics in this field could be summarized as follows.*

- *The diffusion of power-devouring portable electronic gadgets (video cameras, mobile phones, computers) create a surging demand for low-weight rechargeable batteries.*
- *Sony misses out in the development of nickel hydride technology, predicted to be the main successor to nicad batteries. Instead the consumer electronic giant focuses on lithium-ion, more difficult to manufacture than nickel hydride, but more powerful and easily rechargeable. In 1992, Sony successfully launches a camcorder powered by lithium-ion. For three years Sony enjoys a virtual monopoly in the new market and rapidly increases production at its Koriyama plant. Of the 12 millions units delivered in 1994, Sony produced 80%.*
- *As overall demand for light-weight rechargeables continues to grow, and the price of lithium-ion batteries goes down, the market surges: from 12 million units in 1994, to 35 million in 1995, 120 million in 1996, and an estimated 400 million units in 2000. The booming market attracts a swarm of competitors: Toshiba, Matsushita, Sanyo, Hitachi Maxell, Nippon Mori (controlled by NEC), Mitsubishi, Yuasa Batteries . . .*
- *Sony invests feverishly to expand production. Capacity at its first plant in Koriyama is doubled and a new plant is constructed in Tochigi, increasing Sony's output from 5 million units in 1993 to 30 million in 1995. In spite of this doubling strategy, the pioneer loses market share when the new entrants start mass production. By the end of 1996, total monthly output in Japan is expected to reach 22 million.*
- *Sony charges ahead in developing new applications. A potentially enormous market is rechargeable batteries for electric vehicles, where lithium-ion could replace the heavy and ineffective lead technology. Both Toyota and Nissan introduced cars powered by lithium-ion batteries from Sony in 1997. NEC, the telecom and computer company, expands the market in other directions by including the new type of batteries in laptops and mobile phones. Competition continues, market saturation is far away . . .*

Sources: Nikkei Weekly, 21 August 1995; 19 February 1996; Business Week, 15 February 1993.

Why are Japanese companies so focused on market share? Revisionist writers, such as van Wolferen (1989), who argue that the Japanese economy and society are qualitatively different from the west, contend that the ultimate motive is about power: 'Enlarging one's market share, like enlarging the territory one controls, depends on the desire for greater power, a political motive' (1990: 22). Abegglen and Stalk (1987) offer a simpler, but more convincing motive: in a high-growth economy, such as Japan, where industrial production expanded 18 times between 1950 and 1969, maintaining market share is a matter of sheer survival. If a firm keeps it sales volume stable by charging premium prices, while the overall market expands tenfold, it will soon suffer from a fatal diseconomy of scale compared with its competitors. High growth intensifies competition for market share. At the same time, the fierce competition, the continuous cost reductions and the incessant introduction of new models accelerate growth. In the economic history of western countries, one or a few companies have tended to dominate new markets after only a short phase of unfettered competition. That was the case in the electrotechnical industry at the turn of the century; and in the US automobile industry in the 1920s and in the computer industry in the 1950s. In postwar Japan, competition has typically tended to be a much more permanent feature, which Michael Porter has emphasised (1990: 412–13).

This is not a cultural phenomenon. In the prewar period, the large *zaibatsu* conglomerates tended to specialise in certain industrial fields. During the occupation these groups were dissolved. When they reorganised and regrouped in different forms during the 1950s, a new competitive pattern emerged, the so-called 'one-set' principle. Every major group and large integrated firm now strove to possess 'one set' in each major industry. This resulted in a much higher competitive intensity than before the war. In the high-growth markets, competition was further amplified by new and innovative entrants, such as Honda in the automobile industry, Sony in consumer electronics and Mori Seiki in machine tools.

The dynamics of '*kaisha* competition' in the 1950s and onwards resulted in a vibrant atmosphere of innovations, in a way similar to the early American automobile industry, where a multitude of entrepreneurs competed against each other as well as established firms from other industries. In the US case no dominant design had emerged, and for a few decades there was a stream of innovations in both product and process. Being a late developer, however, postwar Japan encountered dominant product designs in all major fields, and had to develop by borrowing, adopting and improving, step by step, western technology. In a pattern typical for late developers, Japan's export industries focused on the manufacturing process, in order to compete on cost, and increasingly also quality (Amsden, 1990). These efforts generated a hot-house for organisational improvements and innovations: new forms of shopfloor management, supplier relations, materials control, as well as skill development. In the 1980s, exports of Japanese consumer electronics and automobiles started to be complemented by 'exports' of these manufacturing innovations, principally in the form of Japanese production transplants. In spite of the initial scepticism of many observers, the majority of these plants quickly approached the productivity and quality levels of their parent companies. The cultural hypothesis, that Japanese manufacturing efficiency was embedded in and dependent on a unique Japanese culture, was falsified. Studies of Japanese management, presenting lessons for western management, entered a second boom period.

A SUPERIOR BRAND OF CAPITALISM?

The Japanese achievement in the 1980s also stimulated a new interest in the old debate about divergence or convergence between Japan and western countries. In the wake of the collapse of State Socialism, this discourse addressed theoretically much more significant issues than the majority of the management and 'Japan as no. 1' literature had. At the heart of this capitalism debate was a fundamental question: are different forms of capitalist dynamics and corporate control sustainable in a global economy, or could they be only transitory phenomena?

An important contribution was Michael Gerlach's *Alliance Capitalism* (1992). According to Gerlach there is a profound difference between Japan and the USA concerning the very heart of capitalism – corporate ownership and control. In the USA investment funds are the major owners, whereas in Japan other corporations are the principal shareholders. Corporate stock-ownership in Japan differs from the US system of corporate control in four important aspects: a high degree of concentration, stability, reciprocal relationships and multiplexity – meaning that there is an inter-related set of relations between a firm and its shareholders. An industrial bank, which normally owns minority interests in the core firm of its group, is not only or primarily interested in dividends on its shares. More important is the growth and prosperity of the client firm, since this will contribute to the growth of the bank's own business, the number of accounts and the volume of its loans. The virtue of this system, according to Gerlach, is the way it generates stable and predictable business relationships, making it possible for managers to focus on investments, product development and growth, instead of share prices and the threat of hostile takeovers. Further, the Japanese system of corporate cross-ownership has contributed to the evolution of stable internal labour markets, lifetime employment commitments and long-term career orientations. To summarise, Gerlach presents Japan as a superior brand of capitalism, which has reduced uncertainty and increased reliability in business relations, thereby lowering transaction costs and promoting strategic behaviour instead of the opportunism and short-term horizons typical of much US capitalism.

Carl Kester (1996) compares Japanese and US patterns of corporate governance from the perspective of transaction cost economics and agency theory, and argues that each nation has evolved a system that is at once highly developed along one particular dimension of these problems while undeveloped along another. Japanese corporate governance emphasizes the reduction of the transaction costs associated with self-interested opportunism and investment in relation-specific assets. The Anglo-Saxon system is focused on the agency costs associated with the separation of ownership from control – the problem that agents hired to do a job cannot always be counted on to act in the best interests of the principals. This problem is particularly salient in the USA because of its class of largely specialised stakeholders. Kester links the system of corporate governance to the dominant nature of contracting in each country. In Japan, the typical contracting between, for example, a supplier and an automobile assembler is implicit and informal. This is strongly related to corporate personnel policies, 'lifetime' employment and long-term careers, which

> inevitably result in the creation of an extensive network of enduring personal relationships among individual managers inside and outside the company. These are crucial to the efficacy of implicit contracting [quoting a senior manager]:— 'If you treat someone badly either inside or outside the company by taking advantage of them to profit for the moment, it will not soon be forgotten. This is because people remain with the same company throughout their entire careers'.
>
> (Kester, 1996: 112)

The role of equity in Japan's system of relational corporate governance is to act as a financial glue that holds various parties together in long-term trading relationships. The line between ownership and management execution within the Japanese corporate groups is blurred. Their efficiency is vitally dependent on a high competitive intensity between groups, since there is no effective ownership control of managers. To sum up, Japan's 'alliance capitalism' has a true systemic character, where the elements of corporate governance, interindustry (horizontal) competition, internal labour markets and permanent employment, and long-term supplier relationships, are all closely related.

'Alliance capitalism' is basically a postwar phenomenon. Before the war, large Japanese firms were controlled by equity owners, in a way similar to Anglo-Saxon companies. Their boards of directors were dominated by large shareholders, and dividend payout ratios were high, 69% in 1931–5. During the war this changed profoundly. At the end of the 1940s the boards of large firms had become completely controlled by inside directors, promoted from the ranks of career managers (Okazaki, 1994: 350–75). During the 1950s, the elevation of salaried managers to commanding positions was buttressed by the development of cross-ownership between firms. Since that time the basic pattern of corporate control has remained stable.

The particular forms of corporate governance in Japan's alliance capitalism are closely related both to the competitive behaviour of its firms and to the relations between management and core workers. In a system of shareholder control, capital is in principle mobile, and investment in one market easily accompanied by divestment in another. In Japan, however, capital is to a large extent controlled by management. And in the kind of labour market that evolved for large firms in Japan from the late 1940s, managers as well as workers are also essentially immobile. Their 'community of fate' within the firm increases the severity of competition between firms, and renders divestment and industry consolidation by mergers and acquisitions very difficult. Firms tend to be very reluctant to withdraw from any significant market, even when the period of rapid expansion is over, if there are no related growth markets available. Large-scale downsizing and unrelated diversification, of the kind so popular in the USA, where electrotechnical companies merge with media groups, are practically unknown in Japan. The structure of unusual competitive intensity in successful Japanese industries is one of Porter's major observations, but he does not link this feature to the system of corporate ownership and control and stable internal labour markets (Porter, 1990).

This particular pattern of perseverance is evident in the industries studied in this book. In the automobile industry there are six independent passenger-car producers and two semi-independents (Subaru and Daihatsu) – more than in any other car-producing country. The deep post-Bubble recession has only resulted in minor modifications, such as Toyota increasing its share in the group company Daihatsu. In the machine tool industry there are eight major makers, incessantly competing for market share, and more than 100 smaller producers. The long recession in the early 1990s has not resulted in any major consolidation. The same is true of the TV industry. Matsushita, Sony, Hitachi, Sharp, Sanyo, Toshiba and Mitsubishi are all continuing their operations in spite of several years of poor profitability and flat sales.

In a 'Confucian perspective on economic issues', Ronald Dore (1987) has taken a view on Japanese interfirm relations similar to Gerlach. According to Dore, a frequent pattern in Japan is that production is neither co-ordinated through the hierarchy of vertically integrated corporations nor through the market in the sense of a continuous pursuit of the best buy. Instead, co-ordination takes place through relational or obligational contracting, a flexible yet stable relationship, which both sides recognise an obligation to maintain. Relational contracting reduces the risks of opportunism, where one partner in a contract takes advantage of the vulnerability of the other partner, and thus transaction costs tend to be lower in Japan than in an Anglo-Saxon free-market capitalism. This is, of course, difficult to substantiate and, in contrast to Gerlach, Dore does not argue on the basis of systematic statistical comparisons. His argument is on a different level. According to him (ibid.: 181) the Japanese

> have never really caught up with Adam Smith [and his belief in the pure self-interest of the invisible hand]. They have always insisted that the butcher and the baker and the brewer need to be benevolent as well as self-interested . . . It is that sense of duty – a duty over and above the terms of written contract – which gives the assurance of the pay-off which makes relational contracting viable.

Dore contrasts the pure allocative efficiency of the market mechanism with a more important *dynamic efficiency*: continuous improvement of a manufacturing process or relation-specific investments in a supplier–assembler network. In his view dynamic efficiency presupposes a sense of fairness in the social and economic arrangements. This sense of fairness cannot be achieved if each actor in the market is encouraged to increase his or her own short-term benefits irrespective of others, but requires a need for compromise and restraint in the use of market power. According to Dore the Japanese inter and intrafirm relationships are highly effective in developing mechanisms for compromise and fair shares, and he calls upon his western audience to liberate itself from 'the imprisoning rigidities of the marketist ideologies which make hungry self-interest not just an instinct but a duty' (ibid.: 227).

The virtues which, according to these authors, flow from Japan's alliance capitalism are manifold: patient capital, persevering and committed management and workers, and a strong focus on incremental improvement in existing or related businesses instead of quick fixes and quick quits. This orientation cultivates a capacity for mastering new technologies, increasing production yields and lowering prices, through cumulative efforts. Companies take long-term responsibilities for regular workers, and external shocks are absorbed with a minimum of social disruption. Alliance capitalism also has drawbacks, however. Its system of preferential trading within the corporate groups has contributed to Japan's enormous trade surplus and the resulting *endaka hukyo* (recession because of high yen) in the mid-1980s and 1990s. Further, the strong group structure, involving banks, insurance companies, trading houses as well as manufacturers and suppliers, has impeded the development of a venture capital market, rendering high-technology start-ups more difficult. Moreover, the cohesion of the groups has tended to fragment important markets and obstructed the diffusion of general standards and applications across groups.

WESTERN VIEWS ON JAPAN: A NEVER-RECONCILED DIVERGENCE

These problems were seldom discussed in the late 1980s or early 1990s. At that time an overwhelming literature, both popular and academic, supported the general view of 'Japan as no. 1'. In 1990, the MIT researchers Womack, Jones and Roos published a best-selling tribute to Toyota, arguing that its system of lean production would become the standard production system in all industries in the twenty-first century. Writing just one year before the burst of the Bubble Boom, Womack et al. asserted that the production and sales systems of the Japanese automobile industry had eliminated the risk of overproduction and solved the classical western problem of market cyclicality. Other automobile industry studies supported the thesis of Japanese superiority. Clark and Fujimoto (1991) compared product development performance within Japanese, European and US automobile makers. The Japanese companies came out as top performers in terms of engineering productivity, lead-times and quality conformance, although the total quality and product integrity of the European specialist producers were also acknowledged. The particular form of subcontracting in Japan's automobile industry was another object of interest and admiration, from Michael Smitka's *Competitive Ties* (1991) to Toshihiro Nishiguchi's *Strategic Industrial Sourcing – The Japanese Advantage* (1994). The latter book was promoted as the standard text on Japanese supplier relations. The author summarises its basic argument as follows: 'The Japanese subcontracting system has undergone a long evolutionary process . . . The result is a distinctive mechanism in which the problem solving-oriented commitments by customer and subcontractor are reinforced from within by means of institutional arrangements that promote the continuous and flexible output of high-quality, low-cost products' (Nishiguchi, 1994: 214–15).

Michael Cusumano progressed from an acclaimed study of the Japanese automobile industry (1985) to Japanese software factories. He found the same management skills and quality systems here as in the car plants and addressed the factory approach to software development as a 'challenge to US management' (1991). Other authors focused on the industrial relations and employment system within Japanese core companies. Here the Japanese researcher, Kazuo Koike (1981; 1982), was particularly influential in promoting the view of Japanese practices as rational investment in human capital aiming at long-term skill formation. Also within Japan, there was an increasing sense of superiority. The translation of Ezra Vogel's book in the early 1980s was a best-seller, but its content was never really discussed. All the time, however, there has been a counter-current of sharply critical literature, from dissidents in Japan to revisionists and 'bashers' in Europe and the USA. Whereas Dore (1987) portrayed a system of compromise and fairness, mutual obligations and benevolence, van Wolferen (1989) presents a sinister image of ideological coercion and control, a 'house-broken press', a 'subservient education system' and a 'truncated power structure' without any accountability. The conditions of labour have been particularly contested. Womack, et al. (1990) argued that under the Toyota production system, flexibility is free, and work challenging and rewarding. Further, the spread of this lean production would result in easy and inexpensive automation of basically all repetitive tasks. Redesigns of the assembly line to enrich and enlarge assembly tasks, of the kind developed by Swedes and Germans, were dismissed as completely unnecessary: 'Lean production is a superior way for humans to make things . . . Equally important, it provides more challenging and fulfilling work for employees at every level, from the factory to the headquarters' (ibid.: 225). A study of the lean electronics plants in Wales in the early 1990s provided a picture of the Japanese factory regime far from this glowing vision. On their assembly lines, work was intensive and surveillance tight. Managers emphasised that each individual should be aware that management knows every time he or she has made a fault. Staffing policies were tight, since all slack labour was seen as waste. Peer pressure and public displays of individual records were used to enforce strict discipline and keep absences at an absolute minimum. Smoking, drinking and eating were banned from production areas. Bell-to-bell working was enforced without any allowance for washing or relaxation before the end of the work day. The pressure on management was also relentless: 'much busier, much more expected of you, much more get the job done . . . much longer hours than anywhere else I've seen' (Morris et al., 1993: 75). Similar descriptions of the factory regime have been presented by studies of Japanese automobile transplants in Europe and North America (Fucini and Fucini, 1990; Garrahan and Stewart, 1992; Robertson et al., 1993). But there are also highly positive accounts of the way the same automobile plants 'harness the workers' knowledge as a source of value directly at the point of production . . . [and move] decision-making down to the shop floor' (Kenney and Florida, 1993: 39).

The assessments of Japan's economic performance and prospects are also starkly divergent. Ezra Vogel (1980: 248) conveyed an image of an economic and social system that was recession proof: 'The Japanese for the last two decades have been caught up in a series of crises, shocks, disasters and so-called "depressions" when growth rate goes down as low as five percent. Each time there was a wave of panic, and each time Japan rallied to astound the pessimists.' Indeed, the shock-absorbing capacity of Japan's manufacturing industries after the crises in the mid-1970s and 1980s was impressive, and seemed to warrant such a view. Other observers, however, have focused on Japan's financial system: the speculative rise of land price during the 1980s, the exorbitant price/earnings ratios of Japanese shares, the weak profitability and minimal cash reserves of Japanese banks. From a focus on these aspects, Brian Reading (1992: 291, 294) predicted the coming collapse of Japan:

In the mid-1980s the Japanese believed correctly that absurdly high asset prices would only go absurdly higher . . . It was a fool's paradise. The 1990 stock market crash put this process into reverse. Higher land and share prices will work only while they continue to rise, thus a system in which the shareholder and landowner expects to be rewarded by an endless stream of capital gains is fatally flawed. The next bubble, like the last, is bound to burst. The collapse in the Japanese financial system is inevitable, only the timing is uncertain – Japan's economy is doomed.'

The position of Japan relative to the USA has been equally disputed. As late as in 1995, two journalistic accounts presented completely polarised views, the first announcing that Japan was far behind the USA, the other that Japan was on the way to complete superiority:

There are many reasons for the low productivity of Japanese workers compared to American workers. Some have been considered in this chapter: emphasis on non-productive teamwork, working long hours in a state of fatigue, little support in capital outlays and consensus decision making . . .'

(Eberts and Eberts, 1995: 272)

Seen from a Tokyo vantage point the degree of self-delusion prominent

Americans displayed in underestimating Japan's strength in the early 1990s was clear evidence that the United States is incapable of taking even the first step toward restoring its ability to compete with Japan.

(Fingleton, 1995a: 8)

This medley of divergent views has not been presented in order to evaluate the evidence or to compare the calibre of the contributions – on both sides there is a mixture of serious research and lightweight journalism. It would be easy to criticise Brian Reading concerning the 'coming collapse' of Japan, for example. Admittedly, the disarray in the financial sector is a serious problem. Japan's taxpayers will directly or indirectly have to pay a heavy tribute in order to save its battered banks, perhaps as much as 5–10 % of the GDP, in relative terms double the amount paid by the US government to its bleeding banks in the 1980s (Larsson, 1995). The traditional policy of the Ministry of Finance – 'the armed convoy' policy – which protected all banks from bankruptcy, was abandoned during 1995. A few individual institutions have collapsed. This will hardly break Japan's financial system, however. After a few years of politically protected interest rate earnings, the banking sector will be able to dispose of its non-performing loans (see further Chapter 3). Fingleton could be rebuked for not observing that the USA has been rebuilding its competitive strength at an impressive rate since the mid-1980s. The various arguments are not always well informed; interesting, however, is the very phenomenon that polarised views on Japan have such a long history and keep pouring out. How difficult it seems to accept the complexities and contradictions as well as the dynamics of the Japanese economy and industry! In the 1980s, linear extrapolations of Japanese economic growth seemed to confirm the 'no. 1' hypothesis, and supported a stream of literature in this direction. In the first half of the 1990s, the Japanese challenge has been replaced by a reinvigorated USA. The previous exaggerations of Japanese strength are increasingly giving way to views of the opposite extreme, of supreme US power. To this we will now turn.

THE NEW US CHALLENGE

The contrast could hardly be more stark: Corporate America versus Japan Inc. In the US, rising productivity, soaring profits, and growing international revenues are sharply boosting the market value of companies . . . But the superstrong yen and weak financial system are hammering corporate Japan, sending profits and market capitalization plunging. [Japanese companies] struggled with a mediocre 5% return on equity far less than the average 20% for US companies.

(*The Business Week Global 1000*, 10 July 1995)

In the 1980s, the USA was seen as an industrial has-been, outdistanced by the surging Japanese economy. Studies of national competitiveness and how the USA should regain its competitive edge abounded, a prominent example being the report of the MIT researchers, Dertouzos et al. (1989). In the 1990s,

the relations of economic power have shifted. Far from continuing its alleged decline, the US economy has resurged. While Japan was caught in a
protracted recession with zero growth from 1992 to 1994, the US economy
registered robust growth and productivity increases year after year, albeit
starting from a level of very weak productivity growth in the 1970s and
1980s.

The US resurgence is reflected in an increasing lead in high-tech sectors
such as biotechnology, computers and software, as well as in dramatic turnaround in traditional manufacturing sectors which were under heavy siege
during the 1980s. In 1980, Japan passed the USA as the world's leading
automobile manufacturer. A few years later, it repeated the feat in semiconductors. In 1993 however, the USA regained the position as the dominant
global semiconductor producer. An even more spectacular comeback took
place in automobiles. In 1994, the USA replaced Japan as the world's premier car producer. One explanation for the reversal is the Japanese transplants in North America. But the most important factor is the turnaround in
Detroit. In the 1980s, Japanese brands increased their penetration of the US
market every year, and in 1991 their share exceeded 30%. That was the peak.
In 1993–4 the Japanese share of the passenger car market stabilised at
around 29%. Cars constituted a stagnating segment, however. The growing
truck and van market, which in 1994 became nearly equal in size to the car
market, was practically owned by the US companies. Together the Big Three
controlled 86% of this profitable segment (*Automotive News*, 9 January 1995).
The fate of the joint ventures is a symbolic case of the changing times. In
1991, Mitsubishi acquired Chrysler's part of the joint Diamond Star operation in Indiana. Two years later, the tide had turned. Ford bought 50% of
Mazda's ailing Flat Rock plant outside Detroit, and took effective management control. And in 1995, the Rockefeller Center, once the ultimate US
trophy for the Mitsubishi Estate Co., was transformed into 'a white ele-
phant', and Mitsubishi's two subsidiaries that owned and operated the
buildings had to file for court protection under Chapter 11 (Mitsusada,
1995c).

The US industry made a strong comeback in steel, too. In 1993, the US
steel industry, helped by the general economic recovery and high capacity
utilisation, became the most productive in the world, measured as hours
worked per metric tons shipped. As in computers, the toughest rivals of the
big steel companies, US Steel, Bethlehem and Armco, are not the Japanese
producers but the new fast-growing, non-union, US entrepreneurs investing
in mini-mills (Baker, 1994). Further, the USA maintains a superior competitiveness in other important sectors. Processed foods is a large manufacturing
industry in both Japan and North America. According to a widely cited
report, Japanese productivity in this sector is only 33% of the North American figure (McKinsey Global Institute, 1993).

At the same time US industry increased its early lead in the field of
biotechnology. This sector illustrates the strength of the USA's venture
capital market and academic science base. In the early 1980s, 1,200

doctorate-level scientists and engineers were working in US biogenetic engineering, while only 160 similarly trained personnel could be found in Japan's industrial laboratories. From 1977 to 1983, more than 100 new specialised US biotechnological firms were started to exploit scientific advances in the 'life sciences', and established chemical and pharmaceutical firms also entered the field. Equity markets raised US$1.5 billion for the start-up firms, and the established firms invested heavily (Alexander, 1994). In spite of minuscule profits and frequent bankruptcies, venture capital continued to pour in and start-ups to proliferate. By the early 1990s, more than 400 new US biotech companies were estimated to be in business. As Sharp (1995: 400) has remarked, the new biotechnology firm was largely a US phenomenon: 'The small-firm sector has been and remains very active in the US, is of growing importance in the UK, but remains negligible in other European countries . . . and remains negligible in Japan.'

For several decades the rising technological strength of Japan was reflected in a formidable increase in patents registered in the USA. From 1960 to 1982 Hitachi's annual number of new US patents increased from 2 to 544, and Toshiba's from 3 to 301 (Abegglen and Stalk, 1987: 124). However, recent R&D and patent figures suggest a deceleration in Japan's technological race. According to an EU study in 1994, Japan's R&D expenditures in real terms decreased for three consecutive years. For the first time in the postwar period Japan's patenting activity in the USA had fallen. By contrast, the economic recovery in the USA was reflected in increasing R&D expenditures and number of patents granted. In transport equipment, for example, Japanese patents accounted for 37% and US for 31% of the total number of US patents in 1990. In 1993, the relations were reversed; now US patents accounted for 37% of the total and Japan for 30% (EU, 1994: 57, Table 1.9F).

The broad shift in competitive relations features as a recurrent theme in the Japanese business press, including the leading *Nihon Keizai Shimbun* (*Nikkei Weekly* is the weekly English edition). In a roundtable discussion in 1994 with participants from various industries, a *kacho* (a mid-level manager) in the semiconductor industry formulated the general opinion:

> In our company, everyone tended to think we could no longer learn from the US. We discussed scrapping a program whereby researchers were sent to the US for study because we thought it was meaningless. But in late 1992 we began sensing a change. We realized that US manufacturers were still ahead of us in terms of basic design of high-tech products . . .
>
> (*Nikkei Weekly*, 21 January 1994)

At the time when the shift in competitive relations started to become known, reports in the US business press could not conceal their triumphant mood. The question 'Japan – how bad?' covered the front page of *Business Week* on 13 December 1993. The same day the cover of *Newsweek* exclaimed: 'Japan. The system has crashed'. In another *Newsweek* article (Samuelson, 1993) the conclusion was expressed in the heading 'Japan as number two'.

EUROPE – NO REASON FOR JOY

In the late 1960s, the French politician Jacques Servan-Schreiber sounded the alarm about the threat to Europe posed by US multinational firms. According to Servan-Schreiber (1969: 212), this

> American challenge is not ruthless, like so many Europe has known in her history, but it may be more dramatic, for it embraces everything. Its weapons are the use and systematic perfection of all the instruments of reason. Not only in the field of science, but also in organization and management, where Europeans used to be irrational – the fetishism of precepts passed down from father to son, burdened by routine

Europe had not much time to shape up and respond to the challenge: 'There are only a few years left, and if we take electronics as a gauge, very few.' (ibid.).

This forecast of US hegemony was forgotten in the 1970s. The US military was bogged down in Vietnam, and its economy plagued by economic recession, aggravated by the war and the oil shocks. In the 1980s, there was a new threat, but now coming from Japan. The 1990s, however, was thought to be the decade of a unified Europe. The fall of the Iron Curtain and the anticipated realisation of the single market in 1992 gave birth to a veritable 'EU-phoria'. Military and economic developments, however, brought Europe back to reality – and to a new US challenge. Entrepreneurialism, competitive markets, an open economy plus hard and long working hours (too long according to many students) combined to give the USA a distinct advantage in productivity and innovation. This was brought out by the EU study on science and technology (1994: 58, 104):

> [Overall] the gap between the EU's labour productivity in manufacturing and the US labour productivity has increased further, particularly over the last five years.
> Only in motor vehicles does the EU, like the US appear to have narrowed the productivity gap with Japan. In computers and pharma, the EU's productivity gap *vis-à-vis* the US has widened over the last decade, in electronics, instruments and electrical machinery the productivity gap *vis-à-vis* Japan has increased significantly.

With the exception of aerospace, the EU's share of US patenting was falling across all industry sectors. From 1981 to 1993, the EU's total share fell from 23 to 17%, whereas the Japanese overall share increased from 15 to 24% (slightly less than the peak at 26% in 1992). The European inferiority was most pronounced in electronics. Of its three subsectors (telecommunications equipment, components and consumer electronics), Europe had a strong position only in the first, but was increasingly falling behind in the others. The reason did not seem to be a lacking commitment to scientific research; as a proportion of GDP, Europe spent much more on academic research than Japan. Nor had Europe a lack of advanced technology users. In information technology, western Europe was ahead of Japan, and in some cases more advanced than the USA. In 1995 Sweden, for example, was one of the first countries in the world where sales of PCs for home usage overtook the sales of television sets. A key problem in Europe, however, is 'the missing link' between university research and industrial innovation. Europe neither possesses Japan's manufacturing prowess nor its competitive structure of internally diversifying corporations, with their capacity for building new businesses from core competencies. On the other hand, Europe lacks the unfettered US free-market dynamics, its multitude of high-tech start-ups and hard-driving entrepreneurial spirit.

WHAT IS 'NO. 1'? THE US AMBIGUITIES

If Japan is not and will not be 'no. 1' in the way Vogel predicted, and the 1990s will not witness the success story of a unified Europe, the natural answer is that the USA has regained the title as the model nation. However, at this point it is pertinent to ask about the meaning of such a position. What about the welfare and quality-of-life content in the measures of GDP and productivity growth? Such issues were posed in Japan in the 1970s, when the 'growthmanship' of the previous decades of high growth was brought into question. The well-known Japanese economist Shigeto Tsuru summarised the GDP components with a questionable welfare content under four headings (Tsuru, 1993: 143–5):

1) 'The cost of life'-type. For example, high commuting costs without compensating advantages made necessary by urban sprawl.
2) 'Interference of income'-type. This Schumpeterian term refers to 'services which are made indispensable through built-in institutional arrangements in the society concerned'. A classical US case is the ubiquitous necessity to use lawyers. A case in postwar Japan is the expansion of tutoring schools at all levels, from kindergarten to college, to prepare for entrance examinations. In many households the cost of these schools is surpassing expenditure on food.
3) 'The institutionalisation of waste'-type. This component refers to the deliberate obsolescence of consumer durables, in order to promote sales of new models.
4) 'Depletion of social wealth'-type. The most important case here is environmental destruction, a hotly debated issue in Japan in the early 1970s.

These arguments qualify the social welfare content of GDP and productivity growth at a general level. In the USA the ambiguities of economic growth as a measure of progress have been glaringly exposed in the 1990s. On the one hand there is an impressive economic record: robust GDP growth, annual productivity improvements at more than twice the pace of the 1970s and 1980s, corporate earnings and technology investment at record levels and regained or enlarged global competitiveness and leadership in a wide range of areas (Farrell et al., 1995: 38–46). On the other hand, this 'era of productivity' is accompanied by political involution and social regression. A general

distrust of politicians has paved the way for a spread of populist dema-
gogues. Right-wing talk-shows are usurping the public arena, threatening
the viability of the democratic dialogue. Political participation as measured
by voter turnout in elections is at a record low. Since the mid-1960s, the
trend in electoral participation has been steadily downward, from 60 to
slightly above 50% in presidential elections, and from 50 to only 35% in mid-
year, congressional elections (Vital Statistics on American Politics, 1993).
Newt Gingrich's aggressive Republican agenda gained its majority on the
basis of only 20% of the electorate!

On the social level, economic inequality has reached a level that makes the
USA a unique case among OECD countries:

> No country without a revolution or a military defeat and subsequent
> occupation has ever experienced such a sharp shift in the distribution of
> earnings as America has in the last generation. At no other time have
> median wages of American men fallen for more than two decades.
> Never before have a majority of American workers suffered real wage
> reduction while the per capita domestic product was advancing . . . the
> top 20% of the labor force has been winning all of the country's wage
> increases for more than two decades.
>
> (Thurow, 1995: 8)

The US economic polarisation is reaching such a state that 'the winner-take-
all society' has become an established way to describe its new market dynamics (Frank and Cook, 1995). This development is the very antithesis of
the restraint in use of market power and the importance of social fairness
urged by Ronald Dore in his study of Japan's economic morality. Developments in the 1990s aggravate the US national predicament of being an un-
easy combination of first-world and third-world communities. In the 1960s,
the US people enjoyed more equality and were more supportive of inclusive
policies, manifested in the idea of the Great Society and 'war on poverty'. In
the increasingly unequal 1990s, the war on poverty has been replaced by a
war on the poor. In economic power and dynamism, the USA is unequalled
within the group of advanced nations. In terms of basic life quality the
picture is different: the USA is ahead in GDP per capita, but also in terms of
marriage breakdowns, infant mortality and homicide (Fassbender, 199: 6).

At the workplace level, US firms are more productive than ever before,
but half a decade of mergers, downsizing, outsourcing and 'business reengineering' has generated widespread feelings of anxiety and distrust
among its workers. This problem is discussed in two reports from a large
survey commissioned by the President's special commission into labour–
employer relations. The researchers, Freeman and Rogers, found that many
employees are 'worried about their future and not confident they can trust
management with it' (1995: 5). Of all workers surveyed, 63% had low trust
that their company will keep its promises to the employees. An overwhelming majority wanted more influence for employees as a group, but at
the same time they did not believe management to be prepared to accept

more employee influence. A very sizeable minority would support a union if local elections were held. However, the report found 'management extremely hostile to efforts to establish independent employee organizations' (Freeman and Rogers, 1995: 19). Overall, the study disclosed a major 'representation and participation gap' in US workplaces. In the present political atmosphere, there are no prospects of closing this gap in any significant way. High-performance organisations without high trust seems to be a very real possibility. Anxiety and opportunity appear to be the drivers for hard work rather than commitment based on a sense of participation and membership in the enterprise. This flies in the face of many accounts of the roots of Japanese productive performance, (for example, Lincoln and Kalleberg, 1990). Does this make the Japanese experience devoid of value for the late 1990s? The discussion above suggests that the performance of nations cannot be compared to the way tennis players are ranked on the global scoreboard. Industrial competitiveness is not played out in just one field, but in many. The Japanese and US industries have different competitive profiles. Further, both of them – and it is hoped, also their European counterparts – are highly dynamic phenomena. When debunking the extrapolations of the previous decade, one should avoid making new ones. Despite high costs and a super-strong yen, Japanese manufacturers are rapidly expanding in high-growth segments, in the consumer electronics and computer components industries, for example, as we will see in Chapter 7. In the automobile industry they are waging a comeback, taking advantage of a widespread network of offshore production plants. The proximity and close relations to the expanding Asian economies constitute a long-term benefit.

In the USA, market and labour flexibility has contributed to a new dynamism, but also to increasing inequality and anxiety at the workplace. So far, Japan's large corporations have maintained their different tack. A recurrent theme in the book is the future of its employment practices, when they are not supported by high growth and generally expanding markets. Does alliance capitalism still make a difference? Before answering this question, we will first look at domestic economic development.

SUMMARY

The chapter started with an analysis of the roots of Japan's postwar industrial successes. In particular, it focused on the mesolevel of corporate competition and struggle for market share. This famous Japanese 'kaisha dynamics' was characterised by rapid launch of new products and capacity expansion, dramatic lowering of costs, repeated output doubling to maintain and expand market share, and a relentless search for new applications. Japan's postwar growth is associated with the forms of corporate governance and control established in the 1940s. This system of 'alliance capitalism' with interlocking stock-ownership and career managers in control of companies plays a vital role in maintaining permanent competition as well as permanent employment. 'Alliance capitalism' has also contributed to the pattern of corporate perseverance, so evident in recession times. Companies rationalise and streamline, but do not withdraw and do not consolidate. The chapter's discussion of the roots of economic power was followed by a review of the persisting differences in western views on Japan. The divergence of opinions partly reflects the choice of sector for study: export-oriented manufacturing with its fundamental strengths, or the financial sector, which will need a long time to recover and reform.

After the discussion of Japanese successes, we turned to the US resurgence in the 1990s: the remarkable comeback in old sectors such as automobiles, and the increased US lead in new high-tech fields. For Europe, the unseating of Japan as 'no. 1' has been no reason for joy, since the old continent is lagging in both productivity and innovation. 'Learning from Japan' has been replaced by US recipes for deregulated labour markets and cutbacks in social welfare. The US performance is a paradox, however, combining economic power and social decline, increasing productivity and heightened job insecurity. This cleavage has been exasperated by the ruthless downsizing and labour-shedding of the 1990s. The European debate on productivity and innovation would benefit from a second look at Japanese developments. In spite of the problems of Japan's political economy, its large corporations have been remarkably successful in combining stable employment with productivity growth and continuous innovation. These accomplishments are discussed in further details in Chapters 6–9. Chapter 3 will give an overview of economic and political changes in Japan.

3

THE END OF ENDLESS GROWTH

FROM THE HIGH-GROWTH ERA TO THE BUBBLE BOOM

From the 1955 to the first oil crisis in 1973, Japan enjoyed an average growth of 10% per year, a rate unparalleled in the western world. The national mobilisation to compensate for the lack of natural resources and the devastation of the war included hard work and low wages, high savings and investment ratios and close collaboration between business and government to promote targeted sectors and to protect 'infant industries' which could exploit the open western markets. The oil crisis resulted in a deep, but short, recession. Previous high-growth sectors, such as textiles and shipbuilding, were officially designated as 'structurally depressed'. As a whole, the Japanese economy soon recovered and entered the 1980s under the MITI vision to build a 'creative, knowledge-intensive industrial structure' (Komiya et al., 1988). Major firms in home appliances and consumer electronics ushered in mass production of new consumer durables such as VTRs and camcorders, as well as professional electronic equipment. Automobile manufacturers expanded their model ranges and accelerated the renewal tempo in a fierce competition to increase their shares in the domestic market. In the second half of the 1980s Japan enjoyed a new period of high growth, peaking at 5.6% in the fiscal year 1990. This extraordinary growth in an advanced economy, later referred to as the Bubble Boom or, more officially, the Heisei Boom, impressed western pundits profoundly. With hindsight it is evident how deeply many best-selling studies on Japan were influenced by the atmosphere of the Bubble Boom. The assertions of Womack et al. (1990) that the Japanese automobile industry faced no risk of overproduction and had solved the classical western problem of market cyclicality are just one example of these extrapolations. Because of the academic time-lag, studies imbued by the confidence of the Bubble Boom kept pouring out well in the 1990s, a recent example being Nishiguchi (1994).

Many of these studies overlooked some basic macroeconomic facts – for example, how dependent the Japanese industry had become on a continuous expansion of the home market. After the appreciation of the yen in 1985, exports dropped in the automobile industry, but this was more than compensated for by brisk domestic sales. This demand expansion, however, was fuelled by asset and real-estate speculation, hence the name 'Bubble

Boom' driven by the myth that land prices could not drop (see the discussion of the *fukumieki* phenomenon later in this chapter). Another basic factor driving the high growth of the 1980s was the low capital costs, which meant that companies could expand capacity and product range with scant regard for profit margins. A third basic factor explaining the high growth rate was the exceptionally long working hours, in manufacturing as well as service industries. The long working hours contributed to high capacity utilization, to high service levels and an extraordinary pace of new-product development. According to the Economic Planning Agency, engineers in Japanese R&D departments worked on average 56 hours per week in 1991, compared with 46 hours in the USA and 45 hours in Germany (EPA, 1992: 228). Another survey by the EPA attempted to measure the real working hours, including service overtime and other forms of unpaid work not registered in the official statistics, and found that the average Japanese man worked a total of 2,500 hours in 1992. One out of six had a total work time of 3,100 hours! (Iida, 1994). Japanese unions tried to reduce the excessively long working hours by raising overtime allowances, but lacked the power to enforce their demands and not even the spectacular *karoshi* cases, 'death from overwork', changed this basic pattern (National Defence Council for Victims of Karoshi, 1990). Japan needed a prolonged recession to reduce overtime and overwork!

AFTER THE BUBBLE – A DIFFERENT RECESSION

In 1991 the boom came to a halt. The recession became serious in 1992, when growth decreased to 0.8% and worse in 1993, when GDP declined by 0.5%. In 1994–5, the surge in the value of the yen repeatedly frustrated prospects of recovery. In 1996, at last Japan was coming out of the recession and GDP was expected to grow by around 2% (Ikeya, 1995b). From a Japanese perspective this is a very low figure. The slow recovery is one feature of the post-Bubble recession that stands out; another is the length of the recession.

Between 1990 and 1993, manufacturing output steadily declined. Because of previous investment decisions, however, production capacity continued to increase in most industries. As a result the operating rate fell sharply. If 1990 equals 100, the overall operating rate in manufacturing in 1994 stood at 88; in transportation equipment it was down to 77 and in general machinery it was as low as 69 (MITI, 1995). At the same time, the growth in labour productivity, previously a key source of Japanese competitiveness, ceased and instead there was negative growth. If the performance of 1990 is indexed at 100, productivity had fallen to 95.6 three years later, and recovered slightly to 98.4 in 1994 (Japan Productivity Centre, 1996). To a certain extent this decline is an aspect of the traditional Japanese labour-hoarding in recessionary times. Thus the official unemployment ratio increased only slowly, reaching 2.7% in 1993, and 3.4% two years later. For Japan, this was a record level, the highest ever since the government started to publish unemployment figures in 1953. From a European perspective it was hardly an alarming figure. Total employment in Japan actually increased, from 63.8 million in 1990 to 66.2 million in 1993, with a further slight increase in 1994. This seems to testify to the robustness of the Japanese labour market and employment system during the protracted recession.

It can be argued, however, that the official Japanese statistics underestimate real unemployment, and especially the extent of latent unemployment (Taira, 1983; see also Chapter 5). A well-known fact is that when female workers are made redundant, very few of them report as unemployed (Dore, 1986). Women are not 'bread-winners' in their families, and after a job loss they are seldom eligible for unemployment benefits. Traditionally, this made the female workforce an important buffer on the labour market. In the post-Bubble recession, much of this elasticity seems to have disappeared. If companies pruned female workers on a large scale it should be reflected in a declining labour force participation ratio. Labour force participation has been very stable, however. Between 1991 and 1994 the rate of male participation increased slightly, from 77.6 to 78%. During the same years the female rate decreased, but only by 0.6 percentage points, from 50.7 to 50.1% (the same level as in 1990). Among employed women, the proportion 'engaged mainly in work' increased during the 1990s, whereas the number of women 'engaged partly in work besides house-keeping' actually decreased from 8.5 million in 1990 to 7.4 million in 1994 (*Monthly Report on the Labour Force Survey*, January 1990; 1995; *Statistical Yearbook of Japan*, 1995.) In Chapter 5, we will return to the issue of change and continuity in the position of Japanese women on the labour market.

The oil shocks of the 1970s were caused by one strong, external factor. Japan responded by diversification, and rapidly expanded production and exports of new consumer goods and advanced machinery. The post-Bubble recession was different. First, there was a simultaneous slump in the financial, real-estate and manufacturing sectors. A Japanese economic best-seller was accordingly entitled *Hukugo Hukyo* (*Complex Recession*) (Miyazaki, 1992). The land and asset speculation during the Bubble Boom resulted in a situation of massive 'bad loans' for Japanese banks and other financial institutions such as the infamous *jusen*, the house-loan institutes which were exempted from normal restrictions on real-estate loans by the Ministry of Finance (on the difficult *jusen* problem, see below). The crisis revealed that a broad section of the society's élite had been implicated in dubious operations, and this made the sorting out of the financial sector's problems a particularly slow and cumbersome process (Fulford, January 1996). The stains in Japan's financial system were symbolised by the 'Japan premium', which emerged in 1995, following the collapse of regional financial institutions and suspected irregularities in relation to Daiwa bank's US$1.1 billion trading loss in New York. This premium meant that Japanese banks had to pay an additional interest charge for obtaining funds on the international market compared with US and European banks (Ishibashi and Iida, 1995).

Another difference from earlier crises was the difficulties of Japanese manufacturers in pinpointing new growth products and 'driving industries'

Table 3.1 Production of consumer electronics and automobiles, 1986–93 (calendar year)

	1986	1990	1993
Colour television sets (millions)	13.8	13.2	10.7
VCRs (millions)	31.3	27.9	15.8
Camcorders (millions)	3.3	8.8	7.7
Passenger cars (millions)	7.8	9.9	8.5
NC machines (1,000s)	216.0	343.0	167.0

Source: MITI, 1993; 1995.

which could play the same role as consumer electronics and automobiles did in the 1970s and 1980s. In the meantime, the production volume of the success stories of the previous decade was rapidly falling (Table 3.1).

A third difference was the strong yen, which made exports increasingly difficult for many industries. The *endaka* in the 1980s, when the yen–dollar exchange rate surged from 264:1 in 1985 to 145:1 in 1987, only caused a mild recession in Japan. The second *endaka*, in 1994–5, was much harder to accommodate. This time the yen reached 80 yen per dollar, before stabilising at around 105–10:1 in 1996. Export difficulties as well as increasing cost competition on the domestic market spurred a new round of overseas investment and transfer of production offshore. In 1993, for example, Sony unveiled plans to raise overseas production from 30 to 50% of total within three years. Nikon intended to produce half of its camera output in overseas factories in the fiscal year 1996, compared to 7% in 1992 (Kato, 1993b). These and similar moves triggered a widespread fear of 'hollowing-out' in Japan, which we will return to in Chapter 4.

The consequences of rising costs are not evenly distributed across industries, however. Despite the new *endaka*, exports of semiconductors, components and advanced manufacturing equipment from Japan are thriving, whereas production of cars and television sets is rapidly being moved offshore. Small manufacturers are most seriously affected by the restructuring of their corporate customers. Firms with fewer than 300 employees per establishment employ three quarters of all manufacturing workers, in total 14 million people. According to a white paper on small business published by the Small and Medium Enterprises Agency in 1994, they will never again be able to rely for contracts and support on their large corporate customers the way they used to (Sumiya, 1994b). Several factors are aggravating their situation. Only a small fraction develop their own products. Few of them have the resources to venture overseas. Further, the *keiretsu* system has fostered a climate of dependency:

> . . . most managers [in these small and medium-sized firms] are reluctant to step outside the keiretsu network on which they have depended for so long . . . Not only does their dependency stifle existing businesses, it also affects the climate in which creative new businesses are

formed. People don't want to set up new small businesses in such a risky environment'

(Sumiya, 1994b)

In the USA, the prospects of a future non-inflationary growth in the economy have become more and more optimistic during the first half of the 1990s. This optimism is based on three powerful productivity drivers in the US economy: international competition on cost and quality in an increasingly open economy; far-reaching deregulation; and the dynamics of new technology, especially the massive spread of information technology. These three factors are much less powerful in Japan. Its lack of economic openness is becoming a drag on future growth. The predicament was spelled out by Yuki Okamoto in his 'Tokyo Report 1995': we will be solving the trade issues, but 'not through an expansionary spiral – not America or Europe exporting more to Japan – but Japan exporting less to these countries' (Okamoto, 1994). A low-growth era is widely expected in Japan after the end of the recession. If it comes true, this, much more than the recession, will signal the end of the Japanese 'miracle'. According to Toshiaki Kaikimoto of the Japan Research Institute, the economy is entering a third stage. In the first, from the early 1950s to 1973, the economy grew at least 10% per year. In the second stage, lasting until 1991 growth averaged 4%. In the third stage the growth rate will be halved again to 2%, Kaikimoto predicts. The Mitsubishi Research Institute, another prestigious private think-tank, forecasts the same low level of real growth (Oishi, 1994). This will not be enough to maintain previous levels of low unemployment. In order for service industries to absorb new workers growth has to be 2.6–3% per year, according to the Ministry of Labour. If not, there will be real problems of unemployment in the future.

JAPAN'S INTERNATIONAL ASYMMETRIES

The new *endaka* was a consequence of Japan's huge trade surplus. From US$70 billion in 1990 it increased to a record of US$136 billion in 1992, and then fell back somewhat to an expected US$111 billion at the height of the new *endaka* in 1995 (Ikeya, 1995c). In contrast to the 1970s, the enormous surplus made a general export-driven expansion policy impossible, even if it would be economically viable at firm level in several industries, for example semiconductors and machine tools. From being a European and US obsession, which never prompted the Japanese government to take effective action, the surplus finally became a *Japanese* problem, emanating from structural characteristics of the Japanese economy: its combination of competitive export industries and highly protected, inefficient sectors (agriculture, construction, services). Another factor is the group structure of industrial organisation. 'Alliance capitalism', with its strong patterns of preferential intragroup trading, may be good for companies within the groups but has detrimental macroeconomic consequences, one of them being the way this structure makes the Japanese market so difficult to penetrate for competitive foreign products. When the current account and trade surplus started to decline substantially in the second half of 1995 and first half of 1996, this process was mainly driven by *kudoka*, i.e. production relocation and re-exports to Japan from Japanese plants overseas rather than a real opening-up of the economy (see Chapter 4).

Japan's trade imbalance is only one aspect of the many asymmetries in its international economic relations – a fact strongly emphasised by Edward Lincoln. The trade surplus is shadowed by a rapidly growing investment disparity. By the end of 1991, the cumulative value of Japanese investment abroad was 22 times larger than that of foreign investment in Japan. The year before, Japanese firms acquired 460 firms abroad while foreign companies only acquired 17 firms in Japan! (Lincoln, 1993: 70, 74). Japan's difficulties in developing economic relationships of mutuality and balance also show up in its technological trade. Being a late developer, Japan started out as a massive importer of technology, which was reflected in a deficit in its balance-of-payments statistics on patent royalties. In the 1980s Japan rapidly progressed to an advanced industrial status and increased its revenues from technology exports, but its overall technological trade did not move towards surplus. Instead the deficit actually increased throughout the decade, reaching US$4.1 billion in 1992, a startling contrast to the large US surplus on royalties and fees. Nearly half of Japan's technology export is directed to Asia, where the majority of its revenues are coming from Japanese manufacturing transplants. The imbalance in relation to Europe and the USA continues. As Lincoln (ibid.: 95) observes, this 'indicates a continuation of a system designed primarily for absorption of technology from other advanced nations. Changing the system to enhance the outflow of technology through patent licensing or participation of foreigners in domestic research and development may be slow and difficult'. This protectionist pattern contributes to the continual trade friction between Japan and the western economies.

Historically, so-called 'structurally depressed industries' in Japan have demonstrated a formidable capacity for survival and perseverance. In the periods of restructuring following the two oil crises in the mid-1970s and early 1980s several industries were designated as 'depressed industries' and received special government support to smooth the restructuring process. One of them, the aluminium refining industry, was nearly extinguished during the round of structural adjustment, 1982–7. Other 'depressed sectors', such as shipbuilding and petroleum-based industries, for example synthetic fibres, stabilised amidst slowly increasing imports. In most sectors, the number of employees was reduced significantly, but production levels were maintained or increased. Apart from aluminium, imports did not increase significantly (Sekiguchi, 1994). Rationalisation in Japan does not mean abandonment of a basic industry. This was demonstrated by the attitude of the steel industry during the *endaka* in the middle of the 1980s, as epitomised by Yoshihiro Inayama, former chairman of Nippon Steel and chairman of

Keidanren: 'We built these steel plants with the sweat of the Japanese people . . . To say it is better to get rid of them because foreign products are a little cheaper is ridiculous' (quoted in Tabb, 1994: 166). Much of the same spirit of determination prevails in the industries studied in this book. After several years of recession and losses hardly any firm has withdrawn from any of these four industries; there have been no mergers or consolidation. Admirable as it may be, this spirit and structure contribute to the macroeconomic imbalances of Japan. The labour market seems to be characterised by a similar capacity for endurance and perseverance, which is reflected in the low official unemployment figures. According to the Ministry of Labour, the service industries will be able to absorb workers spun off by the manufacturing sector. This will continue to keep unemployment low – provided there is a decent growth of around 2.6–3%. Multimedia, telecommunications, health care and caring for the elderly, waste disposal and recycling are designated as future growth sectors. The problem for the restructured employees, however – and this is also a classical US dilemma – will be to find new jobs with comparable pay and benefits (Ikeya, 1995a).

An important geoeconomic factor that might brighten Japan's economic outlook considerably is its proximity to the booming countries in east and southeast Asia. Here the island country has a distinctive advantage to the western economies. In 1994, Japan's cumulative direct investment in east Asia totalled US$64 billion, against US$26 billion from the USA and US$7 billion from Germany. Asia bought more Japanese exports than the USA and had become the largest source of Japan's trade surplus (Neff et al., 1995). Japanese companies are attracted to southeast Asia for several reasons, the most important being growing markets, low costs and handsome returns on investment. On average Japanese companies enjoy much higher profit margins in Asia than in the west. Consequently, several major Japanese firms are engaged in building regionally integrated trade and production networks, which will be almost impenetrable for western competitors. However, relations with Asia are not without problems. One is the imbalance in trade and Japan's structural surplus – the problem of asymmetry is recurring once more! Another is the perceived closedness of Japanese companies. This is spelled out by the chairman of Acer Group, Taiwan's leading PC maker: 'Of course we try to learn from the Japanese style in thinking long term in quality and in teamwork . . . [but we don't want to learn] unwillingness to transfer technologies, tight control over subsidiaries by parents and lack of incentives on employees caused by lifetime employment' (Isaka, 1995a). The same criticism is echoed by Chinese managers from Malaysia: '. . . accepting other Asians does not fall within the Japanese perspective . . . [thus] The top local talent tends to opt for American and European corporations, where they see more promising futures' (Sato, 1995b).

Increasingly, the east/southeast Asian economies are powering themselves with strongly increasing intraregional flows of trade and investment. Japanese companies will be important partners of this development, but it will not necessarily benefit the domestic Japanese economy to the same extent. History and international politics complicate Japan's relations with east Asia. A former colony of Japanese imperialism, South Korea always criticises Japan as having not apologised for the past colonialism, and there is no mutual trust between the two countries. The relationship between Japan and China is also fragile. The Chinese government utilises the unhappy past to extract economic concessions from Japan. Taiwan is an exception to this pattern, since Japan's historical reputation in Taipei is generally favourable. Unfortunately, Japan has no formal diplomatic ties with Taiwan. The image of Japan in southeast Asia is much more positive than in China or Korea, but here Japan is in a difficult political position between Asian nationalism, typically presented by the Malaysian Prime Minister Mahathir, and the universalism pressed for by the USA. The former is organised in ASEAN, and the latter in APEC. Though Mahathir calls for an enlarged ASEAN, including Japan, to become a solid base for economic co-operation, Japan cannot join it for fear of US reactions. Japan is expected to be a partner of the USA and at the same time to be a leader in Asia, which is hardly compatible. For all these reasons it is difficult to evaluate the impact of Asian economic expansion on Japan's domestic growth. The Asian pull has not been a factor in the discussion of Japan's economic prospects above.

CHANGING POLITICAL PARTIES AND THE BUREAUCRACY UNDER ATTACK

To understand Japan's economic situation after the Bubble Boom, it is also necessary to give a brief overview of the changes in the political arena. In a remarkable way, the 'end of endless growth' coincided with the end of the stable politico-bureaucratic regime that characterised Japan for four decades. The new instability, along with the openly exposed divisions within the bureaucracy, have made it more difficult to solve urgent economic problems, the crisis in the financial sector in particular, and this has hurt overall growth. We will come back to this at the end of the section but first we will give a brief overview of important changes within the party system.

The split of the LDP and confusing political constellations

The year 1993 is a historical turning point in Japan's postwar political history. Since the merging of the two conservative parties in 1955, the Liberal Democratic Party (LDP) alone has ruled Japan. In 1993, however, the LDP lost its majority in Parliament when critical groups left the party. After the election of the Lower House in June 1993, seven parties, including new conservative parties, agreed on forming a non-LDP coalition government. The LDP became an opposition party for the first time in its history.

It was not accidental that the LDP lost their power immediately after the cold war came to an end. In 1955, two rivalling socialist parties united into a new Socialist Party of Japan (SPJ) which was regarded as an ally party of the USSR and Mainland China. The unification of the two socialist parties triggered the formation of the LDP by the two conservative parties which feared strong socialist influences. In a sense, the confrontation between the LDP and the SPJ was a cold war within Japan. Since then, the LDP has stayed in power for 38 years. The SPJ, as the biggest opposition party, raised objections against the LDP on almost all major political issues.

The immediate causes ending the LDP rule in 1993 were money scandals of leading LDP politicians and power struggles within the LDP. In the early 1990s, the LDP began to decline in numbers. Critical members left the party one after another. In June 1993, the biggest group in the LDP split and 44 lawmakers left the party, which finally made the LDP a minority in the Lower House. After the general election to the Lower House, where no single party received a majority, the first non-LDP coalition government was formed in August 1993 under Prime Minister Hosokawa. Seven parties including the SPJ joined the coalition. In January 1994, a new election law aimed at fundamental changes of the Japanese election system was passed. A few months later, Prime Minister Hosokawa suddenly resigned, however, due to his own money scandal and policy differences within the coalition. A second coalition government was formed under Prime Minister Hata, once a leading politician of the LDP. This coalition was expected to be similar to the first one, but the SPJ declined to join due to mistrust of the Shinseito Party, established by spun-off members from the LDP. This second coalition government was, from the beginning, a minority in the Lower House. Two months later, the cabinet failed.

After the second coalition government crumbled, there were many possible party combinations. Finally, the LDP, the SPJ and the Sakigake (spin-off group from the LDP) parties agreed to nominate the chairman of the SPJ, Mr Murayama, as a candidate for prime minister. Left-wing groups of the SPJ, which criticised the LDP most harshly when the SPJ was an opposition party, wanted a coalition with the LDP, while right-wing groups preferred a non-LDP coalition. This showed symbolically that the postwar system had definitively ended. The third coalition government under a socialist Murayama was formed in June 1994. Under his leadership the SPJ changed its principal policies one after another. The SPJ declared the Self-Defence Forces legal, acknowledged the Treaty of Mutual Co-operation and Security between Japan and the USA as necessary, and accepted the rising-sun flag as the national flag. After Murayama resigned in January 1996, a fourth coalition government was formed under Prime Minister Hashimoto of the LDP with the same coalition groups as the third one (see Figure 3.1.)

Thus, political constellations in Japan are far from stable. First, the new election system for the Lower House will reorganise political parties fundamentally. The new system is a combination of single-seat and large constituency systems. Smaller parties will find it more difficult to survive under the new election system. Even the SPJ will possibly diminish. Secondly, the Shinshinto, the biggest opposition party established by Shinseito, Komeito, Minshato and other small parties in 1994, will possibly split. It is not likely that either the LDP or the Shinshinto could form a single-party cabinet.

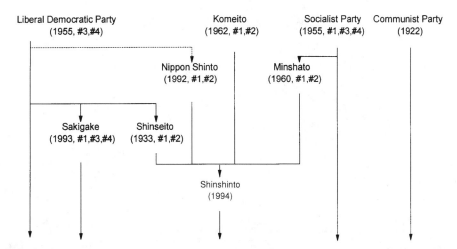

Figure 3.1 Political parties and government coalitions in the 1990s (the year is the year founded; # signifies participation in coalition governments)

Because there are no big differences in policies among parties, except the Communist Party, any kind of coalition is thinkable.

The end of the power triangle?

Until single-party rule by the LDP broke down in 1993, there had been a stable power structure within the political establishment (Figure 3.2): a triangle of the LDP, *kanryo* and big business (on this triangle, see Wolferen, 1989, Chap. 5):

1) *LDP and* kanryo. *Kanryo* is defined as those who are promoted to high-ranking positions or who are qualified to be promoted to such positions. The highest *kanryo* position is to become administrative vice-minister. From the time the graduates from élite universities are recruited to this track, they are treated as *kanryo* and their career path is established. The LDP tried to control *kanryo* in two ways. First, the LDP could influence promotion and personnel reshuffling of the top *kanryos*, though they had a great deal of autonomy in personnel policies. Secondly, the LDP could determine which bills proposed by *kanryo* should be passed. On the other hand, *kanryo* supply human resources to the LDP. About 30% of Lower and Upper House members come from this category. Further, *kanryos* have in-depth information and know-how in policy-planning (see also Johnson, 1995).

2) Kanryos *and big business. Kanryos* control big business by using industrial policies, administrative guidance, subsidies and regulations. Big business accepted retired *kanryos* as top managers in their own companies (*amakudari*) and thus were in close contact with the bureaucracy. Top managers of big business were nominated to become advisory committee members of the government.

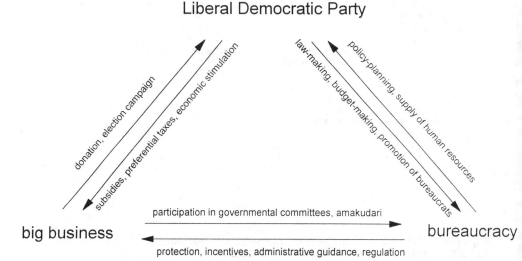

Liberal Democratic Party

big business

bureaucracy

donation, election campaign

subsidies, preferential taxes, economic stimulation

law-making, budget-making, promotion of bureaucrats

policy-planning, supply of human resources

participation in governmental committees, amakudari

protection, incentives, administrative guidance, regulation

Figure 3.2   The power triangle in Japan
Source: Nakano, 1993: 139

3) *Big business and the LDP.* Big business supported the LDP in several ways. First of all, big business offered money to the LDP, which unfortunately often resulted in scandals for politicians. Secondly, big business delivers votes to the LDP. Asked by the LDP, individual big firms organise election campaigns for its candidates. Firms ordered not only their employees but also their main suppliers to vote for the ruling party. The LDP, on the other hand, took the interests of big business into consideration in its policy-making and in its dealings with the bureaucracy.

This stable power triangle will not work in the 1990s. First, the end of single-party rule inevitably changed the relationship between political parties and bureaucracy. Secondly, after-effects of the Bubble Boom are so serious that a traditional political style cannot cope with the problems. When the first coalition government was formed in 1993, it seemed that the bureaucracy would be independent and more influential in policy-making because of a weak coalition, the complicated process of policy-making within a coalition, and the low skill of politicians on policy-planning. The relationship between political parties and *kanryos* is, however, not so simple. Two powerful ministries, MITI and Ministry of Finance (MOF), are finding it difficult to adapt to the new political situation.

Coalition governments and the demise of MITI

The public problems of MITI have already started with the first non-LDP coalition. In this government, Mr Kumagai of Shinseito was nominated the minister of MITI. The new minister told MITI's Director of the Industrial Policy Bureau, Mr Naito, to resign from his post implying that the atmosphere at the ministry was negative due to his presence. The minister further pointed out that Naito misused his position when he previously promoted a son of the former MITI administrative vice-minister to a higher position after the son had announced his LDP candidacy for the Lower House election. In the postwar history of the bureaucracy, of course, conservative politicians sometimes intervened in the personnel affairs of top *kanryos*, but usually only to influence promotion issues. The Naito case was the first in which politicians demanded the resignation of a high-ranking *kanryo*.

This was the beginning of the struggles between MITI and coalition parties. Naito rejected the accusations of the minister by arguing that it had been a normal practice of MITI to promote a *kanryo* before he ran for political election. He further pointed out that Kumagai, a former *kanryo* of the MITI, was promoted to a higher position when he ran for election to the Lower House. The press reported that Naito was to be promoted to administrative vice-minister, with the support of some influential politicians of the LDP. Because of a strong rivalry between the LDP and the Shinseito, Kumagai decided to dismiss Naito. Thus Shinseito tried to establish a principle of supremacy of politics over bureaucracy. The MITI was split. The administrative vice-minister supported Kumagai, while not a small number of high-ranking *kanryos* criticised the minister, alleging that the intervention of politicians in the personnel affairs of *kanryos* would endanger the neutrality of the administration. High-ranking *kanryos* were involved in this affair and the normal activities of MITI ceased. Six days later, Naito announced his resignation. At a press conference he said that it was difficult to accept the demands made by the minister, but he would resign to normalise MITI activities.

The unhappy story between MITI and the political parties did not end with the resignation of Naito. The first coalition government fell apart in April 1994. The second coalition government lasted only two months. The third coalition was formed by the LDP, the SPJ and the Sakigake. The LDP had returned to power. In this coalition government, the MITI minister came from the LDP. The new minister forced the administrative vice-minister who had supported Kumagai's dismissal of Naito to retire. Naito was recalled to become a semi-governmental agent for MITI. The incident damaged the authority of MITI. As political groupings are uncertain, similar incidents may occur again. Previously, under the stable rule of the LDP, top *kanryos* had close connections only with the LDP. Now they must rethink their relationship with political parties.

These troubles gave the public an image of confusion and weakness within MITI. Why has MITI weakened? Previously, MITI was seen to be a rival ministry of the powerful MOF. The declining influence of MITI seems to come from more profound problems concerning its *raison d'être*, namely, industrial policy. Industrial policy is often identified with policies used to stimulate the development of specified industries. In this sense, industrial policy played an important role between 1960 and 1975 (Ono, 1992: 144). A popular book by Chalmers Johnson about the history of MITI (1982) argued the importance of strong industrial policies until 1975.

After the recession in the mid-1970s, MITI began to abandon its 'picking winners' industrial policy. Instead, MITI regards the market mechanism as the most important economic system and limits its use of industrial policy to areas where the market mechanism does not work well, such as the prevention of pollution, international co-operation and energy policies. Also important for MITI is to work towards future visions of Japan. This new industrial policy was clearly declared in the strategic paper, *Visions of International Trade and Industry in the 1980s* (MITI, 1980). This philosophy continues also in the 1990s (MITI, 1990). From the viewpoint of supporters of a traditional industrial policy, this new industrial policy means 'the end of MITI' (Namiki, 1989).

However, the changing of industrial policy from 'picking winners' to infrastructure-making does not necessarily mean 'the end of MITI'. The basic problem is that MITI cannot easily create new visions and find effective methods for implementing its grand plans. In the strategic paper of 1980 on industrial policy, MITI formulated national goals for the 1980s:

1) Contributing to the international community as an economic power.
2) Overcoming limitations of scarce natural resources.
3) Creating a society in which vitality and the enjoyment of life can coexist.

Ten years later, MITI presented three national goals for the 1990s:

1) Contributing to the international community and promoting self-reform.
2) Realising an enjoyable and affluent society.
3) Securing infrastructure for economic development in the long term (MITI, 1990: 15).

It is easy to see that there are no substantial differences in national goals between the 1980s and 1990s. Thus, one can conclude that MITI did not realise its national goals in the 1980s and that its industrial policies during that decade were ineffective. This is the fundamental reason for the declining stature of MITI.

The Ministry of Finance and the collapse of the financial system

While MITI had troubles with coalition governments, the MOF still seemed to be the ministry of ministries. But soon it turned out that the MOF would have its own difficulties with the political process. The first stage opened with a plan for tax reform designed by the MOF. In the first non-LDP coalition government, the administrative vice-minister of the MOF quietly negotiated with Mr Ozawa, the most influential leader in Shinseito, to introduce a new welfare tax. Prime Minister Hosokawa abruptly announced the plan at a midnight press conference. Even the Chief Cabinet Secretary, who came from the Sakigake Party, knew nothing about it until the press conference. The plan was severely criticised by the public and soon abandoned. This incident caused mutual mistrust within the coalition, which finally lead to the downfall of the non-LDP coalition. Politicians as well as the public began to think that the MOF was now so arrogant that it believed it could manipulate politicians and ignore open discussion in Parliament. In the second stage, the third coalition government tried to reorganise special public corporations in an attempt at administrative reform. The MOF resisted the merger of special banks in which the presidency was secured for retired MOF *kanryos*. Finally, the dispute was settled in a compromise. Political parties, particularly the LDP, regarded the MOF as the main barrier to administrative reform.

Bankrupt financial institutions accelerated the ill-will of the public against the MOF. Three bankrupt credit unions were managed completely arbitrarily by the chief directors, lending money without examining the value of mortgages and even worse, lending money to their own families. Why should these three bankrupt credit unions be saved by using public money? After they went bankrupt, it was revealed that several top MOF *kanryos* received big money from the failed credit unions. Further, they were introduced to call-girls by chief directors of these credit unions.

The Daiwa Bank scandal in 1995 disclosed the hidden relationship between banks and the MOF. A trader of Daiwa's New York retail bank illicitly covered up trading losses totalling US$1.1 billion over a 12-year period. After headquarters was informed of the huge losses, top managers consulted Mr Nishimura, the director of the banking bureau of the MOF during a dinner at the Daiwa's guest-house. Nishimura neither accused Daiwa Bank nor informed the US authorities about this fraud. Daiwa Bank interpreted Nishimura's attitude as an implicit agreement that the MOF would tolerate and accept a further cover up of the scandal. According to US laws, this is a crime, and it was supported by the MOF. In 1996, Daiwa Bank agreed to pay a US$340 million fine, a record for such a US criminal case, and shut down all branches in the USA.

The most serious case is the huge amount of bad loans made by housing-loan firms, which is discussed in the next subsection. In the rapidly prevailing atmosphere of MOF bashing, the administrative vice-minister Saito, who was a big name among *kanryos*, had to leave the MOF one month before the scheduled date. Mr Shinozawa became his successor in May 1995, but stayed in the position for only seven months, the shortest length of service in postwar history. He explained that he would retire from the MOF to clean up the sour atmosphere at the MOF.

The *Jusen* problem and the MOF

In the post-Bubble recession, seven out of eight housing loan firms (*jusen*) fell into a fatal crisis. The MOF submitted a list of their bad loans to the Lower House in early 1996. Of the total 4.4 trillion yen in outstanding loans to the top 50 borrowers, 4.2 trillion is considered non-performing. The total value of the collateral for the loans is estimated at 1.1 trillion, which represents only 24.4% of the total outstanding loans.

To liquidate seven *jusens*, the coalition government submitted a special bill to the Lower House in February 1996. According to the bill, the Deposit Insurance Corporation, a semi-public safeguard system for depositors, would set up a special debt-collecting company (Jusen Disposal Organisation). The DIC is to be staffed by personnel from legal authorities including public prosecutors and police officials. It would investigate the parties or individuals in question. If the Jusen Disposal Organisation faced difficulty in recovering *jusen* debts, or if it uncovered criminal behaviour, it would take the necessary steps to secure an indictment.

The government decided to spend 685 billion yen from public money for covering the losses from the *jusen* mortgage lending fiasco. But this amount of money is not sufficient to cover the total loss. Even if the Jusen Disposal Organisation is set up, it will be very difficult to collect on the claims. First, ownership of collateral is quite ambiguous. Each building or lot is claimed by many creditors, making orderly liquidation of the loan impossible. Secondly, *yakuza*, Japanese gangsters, are mixed up in many defunct property schemes. It would be dangerous to collect money from them. In 1994, two bank executives were murdered, supposedly by *yakuza*. The government gave a preliminary estimate that so-called secondary losses will total at least 1.2 trillion yen. Final losses are reported to grow to 3 trillion yen in the worst-case scenario. If the government spends 2 trillion yen to liquidate *jusens*, this means that everyone living in Japan will be forced to pay 16,600 yen. The government deplored the 'painful decision' but legitimated it as necessary and unavoidable for saving the financial system as a whole.

The *jusen* problem outraged the public. Citizens were angry at the government and the MOF. Why should taxpayers have to pay for incredibly irresponsible firms? Though the decision to spend public money was made by the coalition parties, there are several reasons why the MOF is being severely criticised by the public.

First, MOF investigated *jusens* from September 1991 to August 1992. If the MOF had taken appropriate measures at that time, the amount of bad loans would have been much smaller. The MOF's crisis management ability is being questioned. Secondly, there has been little disclosure about the whole affair. Though the government insists that a 685 billion yen outlay in public money is necessary, it has not presented data to prove that founding banks and farm banks cannot cover these losses. Furthermore, the MOF has not revealed the total bad loans of financial institutions. The *jusen* problem is only a part of the serious bad loans. The MOF once said that the total in bad loans among financial institutions amounts to at least 37 trillion yen, which is hardly believable to the public. Thirdly, *jusens* accepted retired MOF *kanryo* as top managers (*amakudari*). The public believes that because of this human network the MOF had tolerated the reckless management of the *jusens*.

The MOF has lost the public's trust. Not only the press but also leading politicians within the coalition have begun to demand the division and reorganisation of the MOF. The influence of MITI is already declining. The

MOF must also seek a new role in politics. The post-Bubble recession has brought hard times not only on business but also on ministries and politicians.

Economic implications of the confused political scene

The confused political scene will influence corporate competitiveness in several ways. The political turbulence has delayed a reform of the financial system, and prolonged the financial crisis. It could end the traditional methods of corporate financing which have been so effective in securing cheap money for manufacturing firms. Japanese banks cannot supply money as easily as before. The future of the financial system is uncertain, because neither political parties nor the MOF have a clear vision. Further, the collapse of the financial and real-estate sectors have retarded the recovery of the national economy. In this recession, Japan experienced the bankruptcy of several banks for the first time since the war. It has shaken depositors' and consumers' confidence. Finally, though Japan's manufacturing industries are not dependent on the industrial policies of MITI in the way they were in the 1960s and early 1970s, political confusion and bureaucratic paralysis affect public confidence and the general business climate. It has become more difficult to restart domestic growth because there is less of a common vision and orientation within the business community.

THE NEW 'WEAKNESS DEBATE' IN JAPAN

In the Bubble Boom of the late 1980s, many Japanese believed that Japan was no. 1 in the world and would remain in that position. Two facts encouraged this mood: the competitiveness of manufacturing industries and the strong Japanese yen. Only scant attention was paid to the fact that not all manufacturing industries were competitive, because the success of the two leading industries, automobiles and consumer electronics, was so impressive. After the burst of the bubble, however, the social atmosphere of Japan changed from boundless optimism to deep pessimism. In the press and in books, one could see many depressing captions and titles, such as 'The collapse of the Japanese-style enterprises', 'Japanese personnel management has ended', 'Destruction of employment' and 'Sin and punishment of MOF'.

To understand what in mainstream opinion has changed, we take two editions of a book entitled *Contemporary Enterprises. An Introduction* (Nikkei, 1990; 1995). The book is written and published by *Nikkei*, the biggest economic daily newspaper in Japan. *Nikkei* is often called 'the newspaper of Japan Inc.' and reflects the mainstream opinion of the business world. The book is important not as a study of actual changes, but as a reflection of dominant business attitudes. The first edition was published in 1990, immediately before the burst of the bubble, under the copy: 'Why are Japanese enterprises Number 1 in the world? What are the driving forces of their competitiveness?' This book analyses their secrets from the widest viewpoints, including production engineering, decision-making, personnel management and marketing strategy.'

Five years later, *Nikkei* released the second edition. In the preface, *Nikkei* struck a different note:

> The first edition of this book was published in July 1990. Already five years have passed. At that time, Japan was in the middle of the bubble boom. Japanese firms were absolutely confident. The bubble boom fever seized managers. An atmosphere as if prosperity would last forever prevailed. Caught up in this mood, the first edition of this book emphasized Japanese management as the source of strength for Japanese firms, and was seen as transferable all over the world. But the prolonged *Heisei* recession revealed that Japan's successful post-war economic system is hardly transferable and that Japanese management is only one of a number of management methods, not THE management method. The environment of the Japanese economy has changed rapidly. The cold war has ended. The yen appreciated highly and the Eastern Asian economies were developing fast. The post-war economic system is characterized by one-country prospering with maximum exports and minimum imports. Now, the time has come for this system to end its historical role.'
>
> (Nikkei, 1995: I)

As the Preface of the second edition suggests, the second edition evaluates Japanese management very differently from the first edition.

Lifetime employment and loyalty to the company

First edition: Japanese firms regard their employees as 'value creators'. They prefer maintaining employment to paying dividends to shareholders. Employees look at their firm as a family. This strengthens loyalty to the firm, which is a main source of the strength of Japanese firms (pp. 14–23).

Second edition: From the viewpoint of costs and adaptability to changing industrial structure, social and economic conditions determine if loyalty to a company can contribute to the competitiveness of a firm. Lifetime employment and the *nenko* system have merits only for developing firms. There are critical views if Japanese management has indeed been 'human centred' and 'long-term oriented'. Though Japanese firms say that lifetime employment is ideal, they have cut down employment by using 'voluntary retirement' when business has slackened. It is realistic to say that there will be lifetime employment in booms and no lifetime employment in recessions. There is no substantial difference between 'voluntary retirement' and dismissal by nomination. For voluntary retirement, the management makes a list of those who should leave and, if necessary, solicits the co-operation of its enterprise union. Managers persuade listed employees to apply for 'voluntary retirement'. There are cases in which Japanese firms have dismissed employees more readily than US firms (pp. 57–60).

Globalisation and multinationals

First edition: The consumer electronics industry and the automobile industry are the most competitive industries of Japan. For the time being, strong export firms in these industries have no competitors in the world. Increasing overseas production should have resulted in overcapacity in Japan. But an expanding domestic market enabled these high-tech firms to convert domestic capacity for new or high value-added products. Other leading Japanese companies have also made strategic investments in the USA, such as Sony's acquisition of the famous movie company, Columbia Pictures, in 1989 (pp. 373–5).

Second edition: Sony, Matsushita and Mitsubishi Estate are the big three, stamped as having failed in direct investment in the USA. There are many Japanese firms that are struggling hard for survival in the USA. Even Honda is not accepted as a US company either by US authorities or by US car makers, though its sales in the USA are bigger than those in Japan. In the late 1980s, Asian transplants were thought of as small and independent operation bases. They are now to be mass-production plants under the direct control of the head office. Domestic plants have suffered not only from the changing economic structure of Japan since the *endaka* but also from the increasing capacity of these transplants. It is this process that is known in Japan as hollowing-out (pp. 356–82).

Cross shareholding and corporate finance

First edition: The Japanese interfirm groups are called *kigyo shudan*. Within the group, group members share each other's stocks. This *mochiai* enables the firm to be independent of individual shareholders. Under the *mochiai* system, firms have huge *fukumieki*, assets that come from the difference between the present price of stocks and the booked price. This *fukumieki* drives the stock price, which creates more *fukumieki*. By issuing stock at market price, firms can receive very cheap money (pp. 275–6).

Second edition: After the Bubble Boom, Japanese firms have to use *fukumieki* to cover huge losses in operations and bad loans. This further led to the deterioration of the stock market and further declining of *fukumieki*. Japanese-type capitalism based on *fukumieki* will diminish (pp. 213–19).

Marketing and price competition

First edition: Japanese society and consumers are not so sensitive to price because they are accustomed to the philosophy of control by the government. Due to this idea, the market mechanism has not worked well. Even if competition is tough, price does not lower, as shown in the case of cars and consumer electronics. Compared to the USA, Japanese automobile makers have a strong control on price (p. 360).

Second edition: 1994 will be a historic year in marketing as the first year of price reductions. From beer to automobiles, the price of all products began to fall, not because of the post-Bubble recession but because of a complex combination of hyper-*endaka*, deregulation, information revolution and other causes. Further, low-wage countries such as former socialist countries, China and India are entering into the market of capitalism. Mega-competition has begun.

The future vision of firms

First edition: Japanese firms are characterised as 'company capitalism', while Anglo-Saxon countries are characterised as 'capitalist capitalism', which seems to be declining even in the USA and the UK. Japanese people regard firms as value-creating social organisations, whose final goal is to exist for ever. Japanese firms treat their employees as value-creators and develop their skills and abilities. Recently, however, there have been several phenomena indicating an interest gap between firms and their employees. First, the upwardly soaring land prices and stocks make firms much richer, but the standard of living of employees has not improved. Secondly, in a considerable number of firms, the top manager positions are monopolised by a single family. Furthermore, there are many top managers who do not give up their position, though they are old enough to retire. Thirdly, it is expected that employees who were peripheral in traditional Japanese firms will increase, such as foreign workers, young employees who have another life value and female employees. Japanese firms have to adapt to this new situation. (pp. 576–87).

Second edition: The three-year-long zero growth damaged Japanese firms. Many top managers feel acutely that the success of the past does not secure the success of tomorrow. Japanese management used to be synonymous with lifetime employment, the *nenko* wage system, *keiretsu*, *mochiai* and so on. These have lost their certainty completely. Separating from past management styles, firms of the twenty-first century should prepare for restarting from scratch. There are three problems they will have to consider: global environmental problems, management under an international horizontal division of labour, and strategies for an information society (p. 522).

The comparison of the two editions shows clearly how deeply mainstream opinion has changed in five years (a summary is given in Table 3.2). Lost confidence and dark pessimism are hanging over Japan. Japan is searching for a new paradigm. In the Bubble Boom, Japanese firms were arrogant, as if there was nothing to learn from foreign countries. Now, they acknowledge Japanese firms are no longer no. 1. It is a time for learning from each other.

Japanese business people have a long tradition of crisis consciousness. Especially important were the first oil crisis in 1973 and the *endaka hukyo* in 1986. By overcoming these recessions, they finally started to believe that Japan was no. 1. The burst of the Bubble Boom destroyed this confidence.

Table 3.2 A comparison of the 1990 and 1995 editions of *Nikkei's Contemporary Enterprises*

	1990 edition	*1995 edition*
Aim of the book	why are Japanese firms no. 1 in the world?	the time of the Japanese system has ended its historical role
Lifetime employment	lifetime employment strengthens loyalty to the firm, which is the main source of strength of Japanese firms	lifetime employment in booms and no lifetime employment in recessions
Globalisation	expanding domestic market compensates overcapacity caused by overseas production	Japanese firms are suffering from both unexpected shrinking domestic markets and increasing overseas production
Cross shareholding	*mochiai* enables higher stock prices and huge *fukumieki*, and thus cheap investment money	*fukumieki* is used to cover losses and bad loans, which deteriorates the stock market
Price competition	price-insensitive consumers and strong manufacturers lead to high prices	mega-competition began due to *endaka* and deregulation
Future vision of firms	Japanese firms are characterised as 'company capitalism' and Anglo-Saxon as 'capitalist capitalism'	departing from the past management style, starting again from scratch

Source: Nikkei, 1990; 1995.

First, the post-Bubble recession was the worst recession since the war. Though the Economic Planning Agency declared that the recession reached its bottom in October 1993, the economy has not recovered smoothly. One must question whether the traditional economic system can work well in the future. Secondly, the stable triangle of power between the LDP, the bureaucracy and big business does not exist any more. It has made policy-making unstable. Big businesses can survive by their own efforts, but it is not easy for smaller firms to survive without economic support from the government. Thirdly, a steep decline in stock prices and real-estate prices has diminished *fukumieki* which had enabled the active investment of Japanese banks and firms. In the postwar era, real estate has been the most secure collateral for borrowing money from banks because it had widely been believed that land prices would continue rising for ever. The myth of real estate has died. Fourthly, US manufacturers, who were once believed to have lost their status, have come back. Confident Americans have made the Japanese rethink whether Japanese management can be competitive in the world. However, Japanese managers are not sure that the hire-and-fire policy of US-style employment adjustment is effective or possible in Japan. They are searching for a new Japanese management. The challenge for Japan's managers is further complicated by the new phenomenon of massive outward investments, which the next chapter will address.

SUMMARY

For four decades, from the early 1950s to the early 1990s, Japan enjoyed virtually constant growth, only interrupted by brief spells of recession. The first decade of growth averaged 10%, during the 1970s growth declined, but in the late 1980s it accelerated anew. This Bubble Boom was followed by a period of macroeconomic stagnation in 1992–5. This chapter has detailed some of the reasons for this protracted recession: the simultaneous slump in the financial, real-estate and manufacturing sectors, the lack of new growth products, Japan's international asymmetries, the enormous trade surplus and the surge of the yen, the new *endaka*. The long recession has also displayed some of Japan's fundamental strengths, such as the strong commitment of companies to persevere in spite of hard times, and the robust labour market. Future prospects of low growth could signify real problems of unemployment in Japan. The Asian dynamics provide opportunities for Japanese multinationals, but because of complex economic and political relationships this expansion will not necessarily favour Japan.

The outlook for the domestic economy is further clouded by political turbulence in Japan. The year 1993, the worst of the recession, also marked an end to four decades of remarkable political stability, embodied by LDP's one-party rule. The LDP regime has been followed by short-lived and unstable coalitions. Previously, political incompetence and corruption could be compensated for by the power and prestige of the élite bureaucracies. This time, two key ministries, MITI and the MOF (Ministry of Finance) have both been implicated in economic scandals and political in-fighting. The power triangle between big business, the bureaucracy and the LDP party, which played such an important role during the four growth decades, is breaking down. Japan's export industries have become much less dependent on industrial policies and protection than they were in the 1950s and 1960s, but the instability and the lack of leadership hurt business and consumer confidence in Japan. The declining confidence is addressed in the last section by means of a comparison of mainstream business opinion in 1990 and 1995. This comparison reveals a watershed in attitudes, from the arrogant question in 1990, 'Why are Japanese enterprises no. 1 in the world?' to the assertion in 1995 that 'firms of the twenty-first century should prepare for restarting from zero'. The economic consequences of this lost confidence are not easy to ascertain, but it probably means a weakened support for Japan's particular employment system and more interest in US management practices. As later chapters will show, however, the basic tenets of Japanese personnel management are deeply entrenched and not easily cast aside, even if many personnel managers have lost their belief in their value.

----- 4 -----

HOLLOWING-OUT OR GLOBALISATION

Kudoka or industrial 'hollowing-out' has been a recurrent fear in Japan since the mid-1980s, when the yen started to climb against the US dollar. In 1985 alone the yen–dollar exchange rate shifted from 264 yen to 190 yen. Faced with a still-increasing strength of the yen in the following years, Japanese industries expected to lose competitiveness both on the world and on the domestic market. *Kudoka* was supposed to begin. However, this scenario did not materialise. The Bubble Boom in the late 1980s expanded the domestic market, and supported a broad up-grading of Japanese products to less price-sensitive segments. The fear of *kudoka* disappeared. However, since the burst of the bubble, the spectre of hollowing-out has come back with a vengeance. *Kudoka* means:

1) shrinking domestic production because of declining competitiveness against imports;
2) substitution of production overseas for exports from Japan because of lost competitiveness on the world market;
3) decreasing manufacturing industry in Japan and increasing low-productivity service industry; and as a result
4) deteriorating wages, employment and productivity of the national economy.

By definition *kudoka* is evaluated negatively in Japan. From another, western perspective, *kudoka* is about a logical internationalisation of world-competitive industries, and a long-delayed opening-up of Japan's closed economy. What the Japanese are fearing as 'hollowing-out', western observers view as normal and necessary processes to reduce an enormous trade surplus and to stabilise the yen. As we will see in this chapter, *kudoka* does not imply a trade 'normalisation' as understood in the west, and *kudoka* in the Japanese economy must not be confused with the 'hollowing-out' of Japanese corporations. However, it does mean the transformation of the unique industrial compact which emerged in Japan after the war.

'FULL-SET PRODUCTION' AND THE RISE OF OVERSEAS TRANSPLANTS

The postwar economic structure of Japan has been called full-set production, meaning that all industrial products are produced in Japan. Infant industries such as automobiles and machine tools were protected by tariff barriers, non-tariff barriers or the industrial policies of MITI. Under full-set production, the import of industrial products has been maintained at a minimum.

After the Second World War, Japan rebuilt its economy from the ground. A national consensus was soon formed. Japan has no resources except its own labour. Because Japan has to import all natural resources from abroad, it can only survive when it can export industrial goods. Japan must work hard and export! This was simple, but persuasive. Becoming an export country was a national goal, and it was realised. Germany also restarted from zero after the war and became a prosperous export country. Compared to Germany, however, Japan's export economy has several unique features.

First, when the economy is hit by a recession, Japanese industries come out of the recession by a massive expansion of exports. In the first oil crisis of 1973, for example, Japan's exports nearly doubled from US$28 billion in 1972 to US$55 billion in 1975. Export expansion was repeated in the second oil crisis in 1979, and during the *endaka hukyo* (recession caused by high yen) in 1985. In the post-Bubble recession in the early 1990s, Japanese industries are still seeking a recovery by boosting exports which have increased from US$280 billion in 1990 to US$384 billion in 1994. Usually, economic recessions in Japan coincide with world economic stagnation. Rapidly increasing exports from Japan stand out in a stagnating world economy and have invited sharp criticism from abroad.

Secondly, Japan's exports are concentrated on machinery such as ships, cars, electrical and electronic machines, and general machines. Machinery accounted for only 13.7% of total exports in 1955, but increased to 53.8% in 1975 and 75.6% in 1992. Concentrated export on a limited variety of products negatively affected foreign manufacturers. The market for television sets in the USA and Europe, for example, was nearly monopolised by Japanese manufacturers.

Thirdly, Japan could not develop an intraindustry trade structure. Roughly speaking, Japan imports raw materials, oil and coal from developing countries and exports machinery to the world. Import of raw materials and fuels accounted for 71.5% of total imports in 1984, the year before the Plaza Agreement. This resulted in a huge trade surplus for Japan with industrial countries. Of the USA's trade deficit in 1990, Japan accounted for US$41 billion (40%) out of a total of US$102 billion. This trade structure inevitably led to trade conflicts with the USA and the EU. Such conflicts began as early as the 1960s in textile products and sewing machines. This was followed by conflicts over steel, colour television sets, automobiles, machine tools, videocassette recorders and semiconductors.

The onset of *endaka*

Another result of the Japanese export successes was the increasing strength of the yen. The US occupation authorities established the exchange rate at 1 US$ = 360 yen in 1946. At that time, many Japanese businessmen thought that the exchange rate would negatively affect Japan's economy by increasing imports. However, it soon turned out that the 1 US dollar = 360 yen rate stimulated exports. After 22 years of fixed exchange rates, President Nixon suddenly announced a worldwide reshuffle of exchange rates to the dollar in order to rebuild the US economy damaged by a protracted Vietnam War. Following this Nixon shock, the fixed exchange rate system was abandoned in 1973. The value of the yen began to rise: 1 US dollar was 299.01 yen in 1975 and 217.43 yen in 1980. Irritated by persistent trade deficits with Japan, the US government used the exchange rate as a major tool for improving its own trade position. After the five major industrial countries agreed to a weakening of the dollar at the Plaza Hotel in New York in 1985 (Plaza Agreement), the yen:dollar rate jumped from 264:1 to 190:1 within one year. The exchange rate climbed further to 80 yen to 1 dollar in 1995, and then weakened a bit to 105 yen in the early 1996. It is still uncertain whether the yen will stabilize at this level (Figure 4.1). As intended by the USA, *endaka* is changing the traditional full-set production of Japan in two ways: increasing overseas production and the opening-up of the domestic Japanese market for imports. In this way, the Japanese economy is normalising. However, a major part of this increasing import of manufactured goods is produced by Japanese transplants overseas, above all in Asia. This was certainly not intended by the USA. In this way, Japan remains closed to outsiders, and its trade structure remains different from other OECD countries.

Japan's traditional way of coping with recession, that is increasing exports, has become difficult politically as well as economically. Politically, the export offensives have encountered increasing resistance from the USA and the EU, which has resulted in voluntary restrictions on exports and agreements on local content. Economically, the strong yen makes manufacturing in Japan more expensive. Japanese firms have to expand overseas

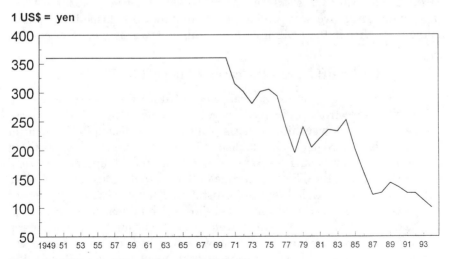

Figure 4.1 The yen:dollar exchange rate, 1949–94
Source: Bank of Japan, *Keizai tokei nenpo*, 1995: 23

million US$

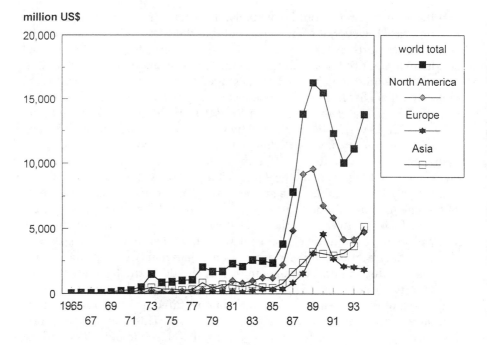

Figure 4.2 Foreign direct investment by Japanese firms (manufacturing industry) 1965–94

production if they want to continue to be global players. For years, Japanese firms were reluctant to move production overseas. The overseas strategy of Japanese firms was almost identical to its export strategy, the establishment of marketing channels and sales outlets. Overseas production began slowly in the 1960s. After the *endaka* in the mid-1980s, however, Japanese firms rapidly increased overseas production. At first they established transplants in the USA, then in the 1990s investment shifted towards Asia (Figure 4.2).

Going offshore – the case of Matsushita Electric

As a typical Japanese multinational, we will trace the history of a giant electrical and electronic industry firm, Matsushita Electric Industrial Corporation. The first Matsushita overseas plant was established in Thailand in 1961. At this time Matsushita established its non-Japanese plants mostly in developing countries such as Taiwan, Malaysia, the Philippines, Mexico, Puerto Rico, Costa Rica, Peru, Tanzania and Venezuela. Most of them were joint ventures, or so-called 'mini-Matsushitas'. They produced a variety of products in small lots (television sets, radios, washing machines and so on) for the domestic market where they were located. The number of employees at these 'mini-Matsushitas' were at most a few hundred. Matsushita expected that they would serve the industrial development of developing countries.

In the early 1970s, Matsushita began production in North America and Europe, while continuing investment in developing countries. Mainly because of trade conflicts, Matsushita decided to establish transplants in Canada in 1972, then in the UK in 1974. In the same year Matsushita bought the television division of Motorola, USA. In the 1980s Matsushita invested further in Europe (the UK and Germany) and in the USA. These transplants also supplied products for domestic markets. In the case of the UK transplant, the domestic market is, of course, the unified EU market.

In the late 1980s, however, Matsushita launched a new strategy, which differed from the 'mini-Matsushitas' of the 1960s in several ways. They concentrated their investment in Malaysia and eight new plants were constructed. The new plants are 100% daughter companies of Matsushita. Secondly, each transplant specialises in mass production of a single product (television sets, compressors, air conditioners, motors, videocassette recorders, colour picture tubes, etc.) using the newest machinery. Thirdly, their products are exclusively for export. Fourthly, an important part of R&D activities is transferred from Japan. Matsushita Television (MTV), for example, began operation in 1988. For television sets, Matsushita established a 'world four-pole strategy', based on Japan, Asia, Europe and the USA. In each pole there is a mass-production centre. MTV is responsible for Asia, particularly the middle east and southeast Asia. MTV produces standard televisions sets, such as 14-inch, 20-inch and 21-inch televisions. All products are exported. However, a mini-Matsushita in Malaysia supplies television sets to the Malaysian domestic television market. MTV introduced the newest test machines that had been used only experimentally in the Japanese mother factory (Tokunaga et al., 1991). In the early 1990s, Matsushita joined the 'don't miss the bus to China' movement and began also to invest in China. As of 1994 Matsushita had 15 joint ventures for production including planned projects (Toyo Keizai, 1994: 302–3). Recent developments of Matsushita and the repercussions of its international strategies in Japan are discussed in Chapter 7.

As Table 4.1 demonstrates, overseas production by Japanese firms is expanding rapidly. In 1994, Japanese makers produced more of their standard products, such as televisions and videocassette recorders, overseas than in Japan.

IMPORTS AND THE FUTURE COMPETITIVENESS OF MADE-IN-JAPAN

Machinery is the most competitive product of Japan. Nearly two thirds of Japan's exports are machinery. *Endaka* is affecting the performance of Japanese machinery makers both on the domestic and world markets. To examine the new trends, we will take two indices. One is the import to export ratio (import:export). This could be viewed as an indicator of international competitiveness: the larger the import to export ratio is, the weaker the competitiveness. That is the usual interpretation in Japan. However, it could

Table 4.1 Ratio of overseas production. (% of total production, in units).

	1985	1990	1994
Colour television sets	38.8	60.1	77.7
Microwave ovens	22.7	45.3	67.8
Videocassette recorders	6.3	18.7	53.3
Refrigerators	18.6	30.9	44.6
Automobiles	5.3	20.0	31.6

Source: *Keizai*, February 1996: 53.

Table 4.2 Japan's machinery trade (in value, %)

	1988		1991		1994	
	Import to export	Imports/ domestic market	Import to export	Imports/ domestic market	Import to export	Imports/ domestic market
Machinery total	14	8.5	19	11.8	21	15.8
General machinery	14	8.6	17	10.6	14	12.6
Machine tools	11	6.2	14	6.4	8	10.1
Electrical machinery	16	8.9	21	12.5	26	18.7
Home appliances	23	3.2	40	4.2	69	5.2
Communications equipment	8	3.6	15	5.7	22	9.1
Consumer electronics	7	12.5	9	22.0	20	43.3
IC	26	9.5	35	12.9	35	22.9
Transport machinery	10	5.7	14	8.4	15	9.6
Passengers cars	8	6.7	12	8.5	12	12.2
Aircraft	673	34.2	599	41.9	581	41.9
Precision machinery	33	93.4	41	108.4	51	195.9

Note: Imports/domestic market = import/(domestic production − export + import).
Import share of precision machinery exceeds 100% because Japan re-exports imported machinery.
Source: Toyo keizai tokei geppo, October 1995: 21–7.

also be conceived as a measure of intraindustry trade. The other index is the share of imports in the domestic market, which we will use to examine competitiveness (or, alternatively, openness) in the domestic market.

As shown in Table 4.2, there has been a general increase in imports relative to exports and to the domestic market from 1988 to 1994. From the Japanese perspective, moulded by the tradition of full-set production, this is a clear sign of eroding competitiveness, and thus a cause for alarm. From a western perspective, this interpretation is close to a mercantilist worldview. Compared to all other industrial countries, the total import share of the Japanese machinery market in 1994 (15.8%), was still uniquely low, in spite of nearly ten years of *endaka*. This could be interpreted as a proof of an overwhelming competitive strength, or as a testimony of the persistence of structural trade impediments (or both). For electrical machinery as a whole, the total import share in 1994, 18.7%, was still low, but for consumer electronics rising imports had become a major trend. The most dramatic case where 'made-in-Japan' has been replaced by offshore production is precision machinery, especially cameras, watches and clocks. (Aircraft is a different story, since Japan never enjoyed any competitive advantage in this area.) Rising imports do not necessarily mean that exports are declining. For consumer electronics (colour televisions, VCRs, CD players, headphone stereos, etc.), the import to export ratio in 1994 remained low, only 20%, which means that Japanese firms continued to enjoy a strong export performance. The data on overseas production of videocassette recorders and television sets presented in Table 4.1 thus give an exaggerated view of the internationalisation of the industry as a whole. Home appliances (microwave ovens, refrigerators, washing machines, vacuum cleaners, etc.) are a different case. Import penetration is very low, only 5% in 1994, whereas the import to export ratio is high. This means that Japanese makers continue to use plants in Japan to supply the domestic market, but are scaling down exports from these plants.

Overall, these figures suggest a gradually increasing openness of the Japanese market. This interpretation is illusory, however. Most Japanese markets have not opened up to industrial products from other industrial countries. Instead, Japanese transplants in Asia are becoming export bases to Japan. Especially in electrical machinery and precision machinery, made-in-Japan products are replaced by products from Asian transplants. In 1993, 51% of the precision machinery and 25% of the electrical machinery manufactured at Japan's Asian plants were re-exported to Japan (Chogin Sogo Kenkyusho, 1996: 52). Automobiles are something of an exception. During the first half of the 1990s, the import share increased to 10% (still the lowest figure of all OECD countries). Only a small part of this rising import originates from Japanese transplants in Asia or the USA.

Exports can be argued to be an important index of competitiveness. Measured in US dollars, Japanese exports increased considerably during the post-Bubble recession, as we pointed out above. However, if measured in yen, exports stagnated starting in 1993, while imports increased during the same period (Figure 4.3). The ratio of manufactured goods to total imports increased from 50.3% in 1990 to 59.1% in 1995. What will be the future of Japan's economy? Will Japan continue to import more from its transplants in Asia? What will happen to the competitiveness of its export industries? A think-tank analysed the future competitiveness of made-in-Japan products (Table 4.3):

1) *Colour television sets and VCRs*: Competition among Japanese firms will continue in Japan and abroad. Exports will decrease and *gyaku yunyu* (import from transplants) will increase further. High value-added products such as wide TVs will gradually be produced in Asia. But imports from foreign companies will remain limited.
2) *Videocameras*: Product technology will progress and high value-added products will remain in Japan. Overseas production will not progress.
3) *Cameras*: Competition among Japanese firms will continue in Japan and abroad. Exports will decrease and *gyaku yunyu* increase further.

Table 4.3 Competitiveness of 'made-in-Japan' products

	Competitiveness on domestic market	Competitiveness on world market	Outward foreign direct investment for importing products from transplant	Outward foreign direct investment for substituting exports	Segregation of products (high value-added products in Japan)	Competition with Asian firms	Competition with US and European firms
Colour televisions	↘	↘	much progress	progress	diminishing	Korea	none
VCRs	↘	↘	much progress	much progress	diminishing	Korea (a little)	none
Videocameras	↑	↑	no progress	a little progress	—	none	none
Cameras	↘	↘	much progress	much progress	yes	none	none
Automobiles	↑	↑	no progress	progress	yes	Korea (a little)	Germany, etc
Automotive parts	↑	↑	a little progress	progress	yes	none	none
Personal computers	↘	—	no progress	no progress	—	Taiwan	USA
Semiconductors	↑	↑	progress	progress	yes	Korea	USA
Machine tools	↑	↑	no progress	progress	—	Taiwan	Europe
Steel	↑	↘	no progress	progress	yes	Korea	almost none

Note: → means maintaining, ↘ declining.
Source: Chogin Sogo Kenkyusho, 1996: 168–9.

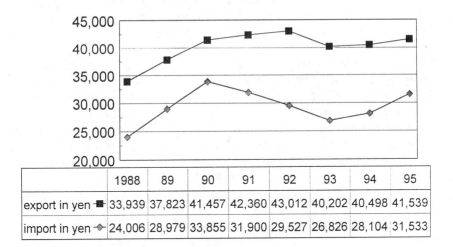

	1988	89	90	91	92	93	94	95
export in yen ■	33,939	37,823	41,457	42,360	43,012	40,202	40,498	41,539
import in yen ◆	24,006	28,979	33,855	31,900	29,527	26,826	28,104	31,533

Figure 4.3 Export and import figures, 1988–95
Source: Ministry of Finance, Gaikoku boeki gaikyo

Production will be transferred abroad. In Japan, only R&D activities for high-value added products will remain.

4) *Automobiles and automotive parts*: Exports to Asia will stagnate because of increasing overseas production. Competition with US and European firms in the Asian market will be severe. No *gyaku yunyu* of automobiles from transplants in Asia are expected, nor are imports of cars from Asian local firms likely. Imports from transplants in North America as well as from US domestic firms will increase. This will also be true of automotive parts.

5) *Personal computers*: Desktop computers will be imported increasingly from Asian firms (Taiwan and Singapore) who are competitive in these products. Neither an increase of overseas production nor export of desktop computers from Japan is expected. Japanese firms are competitive in notebook computers, but Asian demand for these is limited. Export to the USA will be substituted by overseas production.

6) *Semiconductors*: There is a division of labour between mother factories in Japan and transplants. Capital-intensive processes remain in Japan, while labour-intensive processes have been transferred to transplants in Asia. Japanese firms are competitive in DRAM and IC for consumer electronics. Americans specialize in microprocessors and Koreans in DRAMs. Because of this product segregation and division of labour in the production process, both exports and imports will increase.

7) *Machine tools*: Made-in-Japan tools will remain competitive. Overseas production in industrial countries will progress. Demand from Asian countries will be fulfilled by increasing exports from Japan. Imports from Asian countries are not likely, except cheaper models from Taiwan.

A striking feature in Table 4.3 is the total absence of international competitors in a majority of the product areas. Even in the case of machine tools, where Europe is listed as a source of competition, this only applies to high-end segments. For Japan's dominant products in this market, mass-produced CNC-machines, there is virtually no foreign competition (see Chapter 8). In a majority of the cases Japan is competing with itself, 'lost competitiveness' meaning that Japanese production in Japan is replaced by Japanese production elsewhere. Semiconductors is one of the few areas where there is a real trend towards Japanese intraindustry trade. Exports from Japan are increasing but so are imports from other producers, notably Korea (cheap DRAMs) and the USA (microprocessors and specialised control ICs); here 'normalisation of trade' seems to be an appropriate concept.

THE FATE OF TWO INDUSTRIAL DISTRICTS

The fact that leading Japanese manufacturers are maintaining their competitiveness worldwide is a rather cold comfort in the Japanese debate, which is much concerned with the future of the tens of thousands of small firms in the new era. Overall, big firms are better positioned to endure and adapt to the pressures of *endaka*. They have a better chance to develop new products and new businesses than smaller firms. They have the resourses to hoard labour during a recession and can maintain employment by increasing in-house production. Thus *kudoka* will affect smaller firms in Japan more drastically than big firms. Most small firms are incorporated into a pyramidal supply structure. It is expected that orders from big firms will decrease, if new markets are not coming forward. First, with increasing overseas production, exports will decrease. Big firms will purchase materials and parts for offshore transplants from the local market, because of local content policies of governments or because of economic merits. Secondly, the strong yen makes the procurement of parts and components from abroad economically sensible. Thirdly, big firms will increase in-house production in order to ensure the employment of their regular employees.

However, *kudoka* will not appear immediately with increased overseas production. As Japanese foreign investment increases, domestic production of smaller firms may possibly increase, because transplants usually import production facilities and key components from Japan in the initial stage. In the long run, this positive effect will be offset. To examine if *kudoka* has already occurred at the grass roots we will discuss two industrial districts known widely as highly developed areas of smaller firms: Sakaki in Nagano Prefecture and Ohta-ku in the Keihin district of Tokyo-Yokohama.

Sakaki

Sakaki is a small town with a population of 17,000, located 200 km north of Tokyo. Along with Emilia-Romagna in Italy and Baden-Württemberg in Germany, Sakaki has become famous as a successful industrial district of flexible production. Indeed, Sakaki was a symbol of industrialisation in rural districts. In the 1970s, people talked about the 'Sakaki dream'. Small firms were established one after another. The typical career of a founder of such companies runs as follows: born a son of a peasant family, he learned production skills in a small firm, then in the 1960s or 1970s he left this job and set up his own small firm. The ten years from the late 1970s to the mid-1980s were the golden era of Sakaki. The number of firms increased from 266 in 1975 to 365 in 1985, employment rose from 5,000 to 7,000, and total sales jumped from 38 billion yen to 163 billion. In 1985, 85.8% of all firms belonged to the metal and engineering industries. Most firms bought CNC machine tools which strengthened the competitiveness of Sakaki. Smaller firms established a voluntary organisation for mutual help and joint study in technology and management. It was in this golden era that a researcher named David Friedman studied Sakaki and wrote his famous book, *The Misunderstood Miracle. Industrial Development and Political Changes in Japan* (1988), which praised the district of Sakaki highly.

More than ten years has passed since Friedman visited Sakaki. The strong yen since the mid-1980s halted the rapid development of this region. The number of firms has stagnated and sales dropped from 163 billion yen in 1985 to 148 billion in 1993. Employment has fallen from 7,069 to 6,145. Under these severe economic conditions, workforce adjustments were required: voluntary retirement, lowering of compulsory retirement age, reduction of employment status of regular employees to part-timers and so on. Furthermore, some firms began to relocate factories from Sakaki to neighbouring rural areas, due to the higher land prices and wage levels in the former. The decline in Sakaki was brought on by several causes, partly Sakaki specific, partly common to small firms in the metal and engineering industry of Japan:

1) Sakaki firms introduced CNC machine tools very early and thus were able to achieve good quality. With the spread of CNC machine tools all over Japan, Sakaki firms are losing this advantage.
2) Founders of small firms learned machining and production skills by using conventional machines. Nowadays, important machining processes are made 'black box', which makes it more difficult to learn production skills in small firms.
3) Big firms demand high precision. Previously, new small firms could begin with lower-quality machining, then step up into higher quality. Nowadays, this approach is unaffordable.
4) In a shrinking economy, it becomes difficult for small firms to receive enough orders to cover depreciating expensive new machines.

To come out of stagnation, Sakaki firms initiated new policies. First, Sakaki Techno-Centre was established with subsidies from Sakaki Town. This should promote activities for the development of Sakaki: support for R&D, technical support, training in management and technology, schooling for junior and senior high-school students and so on. Secondly, a co-operative

Techno-Heart Sakaki was founded in 1992, which most firms in Sakaki have voluntarily joined. In the planning stage, this co-operative was to deal with the serious labour shortage during the Bubble Boom. At that time, jobs in small and medium-sized firms in the metal and engineering industry were labelled '3K'-work, meaning *kitanai, kitsui, kiken* (dirty, hard, dangerous). Techno-Heart was expected to recruit employees by promoting employment services and improving working conditions and welfare facilities. When it was founded, the labour market had already turned into one of into labour redundancy. The main aim changed to one of promoting the co-operative receiving of orders. Though there are efforts to develop Sakaki as a whole by establishing Techno-Centre and Techno-Heart, Sakaki firms are differentiating. Some are trying to survive as subcontractors by improving their machining technology. Others opt for overseas production. Yet others have tried to develop independent businesses. The stamp of dependent development is imprinted on Sakaki firms. Having developed as subcontractors, it is by no means easy for them to become independent product-producing firms (Seki and Hitokoto, 1996).

Ohta-ku

A similar situation prevails in Ohta-ku, in the metropolitan Keihin district. Quite different from Sakaki, Keihin district is one of the oldest industrial districts located in a big city (Keihin means Tokyo and Yokohama). Both large and small firms locate along the coast of Tokyo Bay. Here there are all kinds of firms specialising in specific products or production processes in the metal and engineering industry. Though most smaller firms are subcontractors, a few of them could become final product producers using their unique technology. There are wide networks among smaller firms for mutual help and co-operation. In a sense, the industrialisation of Sakaki was made possible by Keihin district. During the Second World War, Sakaki Town invited several factories from Keihin district to stimulate the local economy, which was suffering from a declining sericultural industry. There were also firms that moved voluntarily from Keihin district to Sakaki in order to avoid US air strikes. These firms were the pioneers of an industrial Sakaki.

Ohta-ku is the core area of Keihin district. With its many firms that have mastered advanced and unique technologies, Ohta-ku is often called the national heartland of industries. In 1980, there were 8,897 manufacturing firms in Ohta-ku with 95,604 employees. Of these firms, 84.1% were in the metal and engineering industry. Most of them are tiny. Firms with only 1–3 employees account for 43.9% of total employment, and firms with 4–9 employees for 36.5%. It was said that there was nothing that could not be produced in Ohta-ku. Big firms in and around Tokyo utilised small firms in Ohta-ku effectively: particularly when big firms needed trial products, they came here to call upon producers. Any trial product could be swiftly delivered, with the small firms acting co-operatively together.

Table 4.4 From full-set production to kudoka?

1950s–1970s: full-set production	1980s: first *endaka*	1990s: *heisei* recession and second *endaka*
Domestic manufacturing in every industry Large firms supported by pyramids of suppliers and vibrant industrial districts No intraindustry trade	Upgrading and rationalization increase competitiveness; exports are soaring. Trade surplus and trade conflicts Rising value of the yen	Erosion of full-set production: ● relocation of mature consumer products offshore ● conversion of overseas operations into dedicated, high-volume export bases ● Re-exports to domestic market: 'Japan competes with itself' *Large firms* maintain competitiveness by internationalising production *Small firms*, who prospered as suppliers to large clients, face business decline or have to relocate; traditional industrial districts tend to stagnate and lose their vitality.

In Ohta-ku the number of factories decreased from a peak of 9,190 in 1983 to 7,160 in 1993. In 1995, the local government of Ohta-ku published a research report (Ohta-ku, 1995). According to this report, firms with under 9 employees are likely to diminish, partly due to difficulties in finding successors for factory owners who are becoming old and partly due to the high land and rental prices. Firms with over 30 employees display strong entrepreneurship despite the recession. However, it is likely that these firms will try to survive by utilising overseas production or transferring capacity to rural areas. The prospects of firms with 10–29 employees are mixed. New small firms are not expected to increase because of the deteriorating business environment: high land prices, expensive machines, little expectation for receiving orders, as well as hostile feelings against industrial firms among citizens who are suffering from noise and dust. A researcher studying Ohta-ku for over ten years concluded:

> Powerful firms are transferring production capacity to rural areas or abroad. Smaller firms are suffering from labour shortages and a lack of successors. The founding of new firms is stagnating. It seems that an era has ended. In the future, there is no doubt that powerful firms will relocate production capacity and that the number of smaller firms will decrease. Ohta-ku full of vitality will be a thing of the past.
>
> (Seki, 1993: 92)

The decline of Sakaki and Ohta-ku points to the difficulties in sustaining the dynamics of other such industrial districts in Japan: difficulties in maintaining entrepreneurial commitment across generations, changes of relative factor prices within the domestic economy, technological development disadvantaging small firms, etc. However, the firms in Sakaki and Ohta-ku are also affected by *kudoka* and the transfer of production overseas. Their long-term capability for survival and regeneration will be of great importance for the vitality of Japan's manufacturing fabric. Table 4.4 contains an overview of development from the 'full-set production' of the high-growth era to the prospects of *kudoka* in the 1990s.

SUMMARY

In the postwar period Japan developed a uniquely dense export-oriented industrial structure, symbolised by the notion full-set production, meaning that all industrial products were produced in Japan. *Kudoka* represents the Japanese fear that this structure will be hollowed out as a consequence of the regime of high yen, which started in 1985 after the Plaza Agreement. The economic expansion during the Bubble Boom softened these worries, but since the burst of the bubble the fear of hollowing-out has come back. Increasing import penetration (albeit starting from a very low level) in Japan's most competitive industries is interpreted as signs of lost competitiveness within Japan. For western analysts it is a normal and necessary process in order to reduce Japan's huge trade surplus and to stabilise the yen. Overall, the machinery industry has maintained a strong competitiveness: total import penetration in 1994 was still below 16%. However, in specific sectors such as precision machinery and consumer electronics, the import share is growing much more rapidly, whereas exports from Japan are stagnating or falling. This could be interpreted as a sign that Japan is finally doing away with its trade exceptionalism and opening up to normal intraindustry trade.

However, a major part of the new imports originates from Japanese transplants in Asia. In this way, Japan is maintaining a trade profile that differs markedly from other OECD countries. *Kudoka* means that Japanese manufacturers are substituting international growth for growth in Japan. The future of individual companies is becoming increasingly separated from the prospects of Japan. Whereas large companies are maintaining or strengthening their international competitiveness, the domestic economy will grow more slowly. In discussing *kudoka* it is crucial to distinguish between Japan and its large firms. In a number of sectors within the broad machinery industry there are – after several years of *endaka* – virtually no foreign rivals to the Japanese manufacturers. It is also important to differentiate between large and small firms. Smaller firms have fewer buffers. Two famous industrial districts containing smaller firms clearly show the difficulties of the 1990s. Sakaki, once a model case of industrial development in a rural area, has ceased to grow since the mid-1980s. The reasons are complex, but *kudoka* is also believed to play a significant role. In another industrial district, Ohta-ku, the number of factories has decreased in the last ten years. Despite the recession, firms with over 30 employees display strong entrepreneurship, but it is likely that these firms will survive by utilising overseas production or transferring capacity to rural areas. Thus it seems that *kudoka* has begun in the sector of small manufacturing firms in the engineering industry. To avoid an increase in unemployment, new businesses and an expansion of the service sector are regarded as vital.

5

EMPLOYMENT PRACTICES: A CRITICAL ANALYSIS OF THE 'THREE PILLARS'

SECURITY OR SUBORDINATION – THE DIVERGENT WESTERN VIEWS

The particular pattern of industrial relations and personnel policies prevalent in major Japanese firms during the postwar period is often summarised in the concept of the 'three pillars': lifetime employment for male employees; seniority-based pay and promotion; and company-based, 'in-house' unions. Although these employment practices never covered a majority of Japanese workers, they have a status as a general and desired norm in the Japanese public debate. Large companies violating this code are scrutinised and often sharply criticised, especially if they belong to foreign corporations. Two recent cases are Sandoz, a Swiss pharmaceutical company, and SAS, the Scandinavian Airlines System. In 1994 Sandoz, Japan, dismissed 80 workers out of a total of 1,500. This caused widespread agitation and resentment among its employees. In the end the company had to step back, send a new president to Japan and revise its personnel policies (*Nikkei Weekly*, 22 May, 1995). SAS in Japan did a similar cost-cutting move, which cost the company dearly. SAS was brought to court, and the company had to pay very generous compensation to the laid-off workers.

The standard western view of this 'Japanese employment system' has been formulated by Abegglen and Stalk (1987: 199):

> First, the employee is hired directly from school, rather than from an open job market. Second, he is hired for his general characteristics and abilities, rather than for a particular skill or a particular job. Third, he is expected to remain with the company for a life-long career, and in turn expects not to be laid-off or discharged.

A closer look at labour market statistics (see below) provides a much less clear-cut picture of mobility and length of service in Japanese corporations than this simplistic formulation. Nevertheless, large and medium-sized Japanese firms do display major differences to the Anglo-Saxon pattern of recruitment, employment security, pay and promotion. In continental

Europe there is stronger protection of employment security than in the USA, but the basic employment system remains different from the Japanese norm.

The evolution of Japan's employment practices after the Second World War is closely linked to the development and diffusion of its system of 'alliance capitalism' and the rise to power of career employees within corporations, at the expense of shareholders and outside directors. The two aspects of Japan's postwar system, the paramount importance of internal labour markets and the co-operative group structure of firms, both serve to stabilise firms and employment during economic downturns. This was apparent during the oil crisis of 1974–5, when growth suddenly fell from 9% to negative figures, without the sharp rise in unemployment which occurred in Europe at the same time, and later proved to be irreversible. The distinctiveness of Japan's employment system has triggered a long-standing western debate. A part of this debate has concentrated on its merits and demerits, another part is concerned with its prospects for the future.

A recent summary of the merits of the Japanese system is provided by Fingleton (1995b). According to Fingleton, there are so many advantages in Japan's 'jobs for life' system that companies will not give it up: employers can invest in extensive training without risk of job-hopping. The long-term accountability built into the lifetime employment system provides for good managers. Companies are encouraged to invest in R&D, since they know that their proprietary knowledge will not leak to competitors via the job market. A 'tight lid' is kept on top salaries and thus Japan avoids the excesses of the US system of executive compensation and the tensions and conflicts it generates. There are also disadvantages in the Japanese system, of course. Companies cannot easily adjust to downturns in business, and a 'turnaround' of a bleeding company takes a long time to implement. The problems of the Mazda Corporation in the 1990s are a stark illustration of this predicament. Consolidation and mergers in declining industries are extremely difficult to accomplish. Further, the system is predicated on growth. When companies cease to hire new employees, the average age and thus the wage costs will increase swiftly. On the other hand, this is a powerful incentive to invest in new products and technologies in order to find growth in new fields.

For employees, the system provides security but restricts opportunity and mobility. In critical accounts, for example Eberts and Eberts (1995: 254), this lack of freedom is presented as a main feature of the system:

> . . . the employee must do whatever is demanded by the company. The employee accepts the salaries given to him; his market value can never be tested . . . lifetime employment was associated with power, control and authority rather than loyalty or motivation. The practice of lifetime employment fits well with management's need to reduce uncertainty and to exercise power.

The conclusion is that the Japanese system is a one-way street, with no real employee benefits. The best way to test such a critical position is to examine management practices during a protracted recession: is permanent employment also a real commitment in bad times? The four industry studies (Chapters 6–9) provide ample illustrations that this really is the case: Japanese companies do restructure and adjust their labour force, but as a last resort after applying a spectrum of other measures. By demonstrating these very real employment obligations, however, the industry studies also illustrate the difficulties of Japanese firms to adjust to slow growth, especially when it is combined with strong pressure for internationalisation of production.

These difficulties take us to another aspect of the western debate on Japan's employment practices: will they survive? Do they form a stable and sustainable system, or will Japan gradually converge to the 'western' (US) pattern of market-mediated employment relations and wage determination? This theme has been a favourite one for more than two decades. In his famous study *Japanese Blue Collar* in the 1960s, Robert Cole had already discussed pressures for change in the seniority-based promotion and pay systems. According to Cole (ibid.: 82), the ageing of the 'vast numbers' of young workers recruited during the period of high growth was perceived as a potential threat, since it would result in a serious cost problem for companies. Hence he observed a 'recent willingness of Japanese management to reappraise their wage-rate structures and look for alternatives or modifications of the nenko wage system'. More than ten years later Abegglen and Stalk argued that with slower overall economic growth 'the system is under real and continuing economic pressure' (1987: 210) and posed the question: "When will the employment system change?' Their answer was cautious. The authors perceived employment security and the union structure as basically stable components, whereas the system of compensation would probably be reformulated to reduce the impact of seniority and age. This change was only expected to take place gradually, however.

In 1990, after another half a decade of Japanese competitive successes, Lincoln and Kalleberg (1990: 248) turned the convergence thesis upside down by advancing the 'welfare corporatist hypothesis', which 'holds that the Japanese employment system has become the beacon of economic rationality and modernity, and it is the industrial countries of the West who are now faced with the necessity of sloughing off the shackles of tradition and other sunk costs in the older, market-based modes of organizing'. The final sentence in their book ends with the prophecy: 'We suspect that in the years to come we will see still further shifts in the US patterns of work organization and employment which . . . will impel US industry further toward the model of Japan' (ibid.: 258).

In the mid-1990s, after five further years of corporate restructuring and downsizing in the USA and a decline of Japanese competitiveness, few would subscribe to this bold claim, which could be seen as another product of the 'Japan as no. 1' atmosphere of the late 1980s. In Japan itself there has been a revival of interest in US management and personnel policies and self-critical reassessments of its own practices, as we have shown in Chapter 3. Does that mean that now, at last, the traditional version of the convergence concept will be relevant? Have three years of economic standstill and the adjustment to the prospects of low growth within, for example, the auto-mobile industry resulted in a situation where postwar practices are pro-foundly questioned, and new policies are emerging? What is the current debate in Japan, and to what extent is it reflected in real changes within companies?

In the following sections, we first provide some qualifications to the stand-ard western image of Japan's 'three pillars'. This is followed by a detailed account of recent reform proposals from employers and unions. A separate subsection deals with the role of Japanese women on the labour market, a field where very few reform proposals are presented. The final section re-turns to an overall assessment of the resilience of the Japanese employment system. Robert Cole's account of the debate in Japan in the 1960s is a re-minder of an important aspect of this system: reforms and changes have been proposed for decades, but there is a huge gap between intentions and ideas and real change.

THE LIMITATIONS OF LIFETIME EMPLOYMENT

In its most simplified form, 'lifetime employment' is defined as follows: regular employees, both white-collar and blue-collar workers, are recruited immediately after they leave school. As school ends at the end of March, they are employed from April by companies. Employees stay in the same firm until the compulsory retirement age (60 years in big firms, previously 55). This means that employees do not quit the firm until this retirement age, and the firm guarantees their employment. Only regular employees enjoy 'lifetime employment,' while all peripheral employees (temporary workers, seasonal workers, subcontract workers, part-timers, dispatched workers known as *haken* and so on) are excluded from this privilege. Does the life-time employment system defined above really exist in Japan? Do Japanese employees stay in the same firm for nearly 40 years? Do Japanese firms guarantee employment to these workers?

The reality of *shushin koyo*

The Japanese words for 'lifetime employment' are *shushin koyo*. These words did not exist until 1958. In that year a US researcher published a small book entitled *The Japanese Factory* (Abegglen, 1958). This book was immediately translated into Japanese, entitled *Nihon no Keiei (Japanese Management)*. Abegglen writes (ibid.: 11):

> At whatever level of organization in the Japanese factories, the worker commits himself on entrance to the company for the remainder of his working career. The company will not discharge him even temporarily except in the most extreme circumstances. He will not quit the company for industrial employment elsewhere.

He labels this 'lifetime commitment' or 'permanent employment', which was translated as *shushin koyo*. This is the first time that the words *shushin koyo* appeared in Japanese. The words *shushin koyo* spread through the mass media very rapidly. Since then, the idea that Japanese employers practise *shushin koyo* has been widely shared. However, the fact that the words *shushin koyo* came from a translation suggests their ambiguity.

Employment in smaller firms differs from practices in big firms. In small and medium-sized firms employment is fluid. Workers often quit the firm to establish their own small firms or to find a job in another firm. Small and medium-sized companies are strongly affected by business cycles and tend to dismiss employees relatively frequently. It is only in big firms that we can see lifetime employment, if any. To obtain a detailed view the statistics on employment practices in big firms published by the Ministry of Labour are of great value (Table 5.1). These statistics show whether employees stay in the same firm where they are first employed.

Table 5.1 'Standard employees' in firms with over 1,000 employees in different age groups (%)

Age	School career		
	Junior high school	Senior high school	University
20–4	13.1	53.4	88.9
25–9	13.1	50.3	59.5
30–4	27.9	42.9	57.1
35–9	32.5	52.6	49.9
40–4	25.6	41.4	58.9
45–9	17.1	39.1	53.4
50–4	8.4	24.3	53.2
55–9	6.2	14.3	31.7

Note: 'Standard employees' are those who stay with the same firm in which they were employed immediately after they left school.
Source: Ministry of Labour, *Koyo Doko Chosa (Employment Trend)*, 1991.

Junior high-school education ends at the age of 15, senior high school at the age of 18 and university at the age of 22. Though junior high-chool graduates are surveyed, they are not relevant because of the limited sample size. Nowadays about 95% of junior high-school graduates enter senior high school. The official statistics reveal that in 1991 even in big firms with over 1,000 employees, half of senior high-school graduates quit their first firm within a few years. Among 50–4-year-old employees only a quarter can be classified as 'lifetime employees'. University graduates more commonly accept lifetime employment, but even among them only half do so. The reality is far from the perceived image of lifetime employment in Japan.

The low ratio of workers under lifetime employment comes from two simple facts: voluntary turnover and employment adjustment. When the economy grows rapidly, it is easy for workers to find a job in another firm. They are more likely to quit a firm when they are dissatisfied. Taking the automobile industry as an example, 20–30% of newly recruited young production workers left within a year after being recruited in the late 1960s and early 1970s. A similar situation reappeared in the Bubble Boom of the late

1980s. While an MIT group appraised the 'lean production system' of Japanese automobile companies as humanised work, workers under this system left companies because they thought that the work was dirty, difficult and dangerous. The turnover rate in the late 1980s was nearly the same as in the late 1960s and the early 1970s.

The four postwar waves of employment adjustment

Big firms do not guarantee employment. In difficult times they have dismissed employees or offered so-called 'voluntary retirement'. There have been four periods of major employment adjustment in postwar Japan. In the first two periods, massive dismissals were used; in later periods, much more indirect and subtle measures were applied. It is significant that the four periods coincided with structural changes to the Japanese economy.

The first period was immediately after the end of the war. The munitions industries that had grown enormously during the war now had to dismiss employees. Hitachi, for example, reduced its employees from 117,579 in March 1945 to 44,753 in March 1946 (Hitachi, 1960: Appendix). The massive dismissals were an unavoidable consequence of the transition from a war economy to a peace economy.

The second period was during 1949–50, when a US banker named J. M. Dodge, an adviser to the occupation authorities, recommended drastic policies to stop inflation. The 'Dodge line' brought a wave of dismissals. Altogether, 700,425 employees in private firms were made redundant. NEC reduced the number of its employees by 35%, Hitachi by 17%, Mitsubishi Electric by 10%, Nissan by 23%, Toyota by 21% and so on. In addition to the massive labour-shedding in the private sector, the public sector also fired 120,000 employees.

From 1955, the Japanese economy began to grow at a high pace. Though there were some declining sectors like the coal-mining industry, Japanese industries as a whole expanded rapidly. There was no fear of unemployment. But in 1973 the third period of employment adjustment was suddenly triggered by developments in the middle east. The first oil crisis in 1973–4 caused a deep but short recession in the entire economy. For most companies, however, growth and prosperity soon returned. During the recession, they preferred labour-hoarding instead of trying to adjust their workforce. For several sectors, however, the oil shock resulted in a structural depression. In such sectors, even big firms used employment adjustment measures, particularly workforce reduction. But during this crisis they introduced a new method that seemed less drastic than dismissals. This was 'voluntary retirement' (kibo taishoku). Kibo taishoku literally means 'quitting a company of one's own free will'. However, it is often said that kibo taishoku is 'quitting a company by the company's will'. Kibo taishoku is, in fact, quitting a company voluntarily and/or compulsorily. The recession hit the shipbuilding industry most seriously. In the late 1970s seven of the biggest shipbuilding companies reduced their workforce by nearly 10% using 'voluntary retirement'. The eight shipbuilding companies next to the seven biggest companies cut employment by 31%. The gentler method of 'voluntary retirement' had its intended effect. In contrast to the massive dismissals of 1949–50 voluntary retirement caused almost no serious labour disputes. This was the first experience for Japanese industries of carrying out workforce reductions without any major labour conflicts.

The fourth period came in the early 1990s after the burst of the bubble economy. This time, industries introduced another new method of employment adjustment, the 'early retirement scheme' (*soki taishoku*). Incidentally, there is an early retirement scheme in Europe, whereby employees are targeted for early retirement when over 55 years of age. In Japan, the target is either 40 or 45 years old. We should call the Japanese early retirement scheme the 'too early retirement scheme'. The words *soki taishoku* sound softer than *kibo taishoku*, which is the main reason why firms prefer this term.

Japanese big firms use dismissal practices like *kibo taishoku* and *soki taishoku*. However, there are differences in employment practices between Japan and the 'hire-and-fire' Anglo-Saxon countries. Japanese firms use *kibo taishoku* or dismissals as a last option. Before taking these measures, big firms use other soft methods of employment adjustment such as eliminating overtime, not renewing employee contracts, dismissing temporary workers and part-timers, reducing or stopping recruitment, temporarily releasing employees from work as defined by governmental subsidies for employment adjustment, and *shukko*. When management offers *kibo taishoku* or dismissals, in many cases several top managers retire from their posts to take responsibility for the hard employment adjustment. *Kibo taishoku* or dismissals are interpreted as one of the biggest failures of management. Corporate image deteriorates significantly when *kibo taishoku* plans are reported in the press. This is especially true for makers of consumer goods. Once a firm announces *kibo taishoku*, it will lose the consumers' trust. Consumers will assume that the firm is dying, that it will not offer good after-sales service, that the quality of the firm's products will worsen and so on. (In the last section, we return to the difference between Anglo-Saxon and Japanese post-Bubble practices.)

Kibo taishoku is a mixture of programmed workforce reduction and true voluntary retirement. The most important task of personnel managers in *kibo taishoku* is to make a list of employees who should quit the firm. Managers press these employees to apply for *kibo taishoku* (*katatataki*), while blocking other 'good' employees from leaving voluntarily. This process is so confidential that no evidence is available, but in unofficial interviews it is clear that such practices are extensively used. Because Japanese firms carry out employment adjustment including dismissals, voluntary retirement and early retirement, the Japan Productivity Centre proposes that the term 'long-term employment' or 'stable employment' should be used instead of *shushin koyo* (Japan Productivity Centre, 1994: 78–9). This suggestion is widely shared in Japan.

Japanese firms target middle-aged and older employees when they plan *kibo taishoku* or early retirement. A paradox in Japanese personnel practices is that pay and promotion are mainly based on age or length of service, whereas employment security is much less related to the length of service than in unionised western firms. Therefore, the term 'voluntary retirement' carries a negative image in Japan. When management announces a voluntary retirement scheme, it also singles out what categories of employees should volunteer. In the case of Sumitomo Heavy Industries, one of the top seven shipbuilding firms, management asked all the following employees to quit voluntarily in 1977:

(a) those who were born before 1923. (b) if both a husband and his wife are working in the company, one of them should quit. (c) those who were imposed penalty of pay cut or suspension in the recent five years. (d) those who were absent over three days in a year or over six days in the recent three years. (e) those who did not accept suggestion of transfer to another workshop, job change, shukko or relocation by the firm without acceptable reasons and those who claimed new job unsuitable without good arguments. (f) those who are working at workplace to be outsourced. (g) those who cannot perform job sufficiently. (h) those whose work morale is low and those whose work performance is not good.

(Kamata, 1993: 110–12)

For the application of similar schemes in the machine tool industry in the 1990s, see Chapter 8.

According to a research by the Japan Productivity Centre (1998: 219), 68.5% of manufacturing companies decisively denied introducing a seniority system as a means of securing employment for middle-aged and older employees. Only 4.4% think that such a seniority system is worth examining.

The new idea of the Japanese Employers' Federation

All recent research shows that there is no consensus on the future of *shushin koyo* among Japanese firms. According to studies by the Ministry of Labour (1995a: 88), for example, 51% of manufacturers hoped to 'maintain *shushin koyo* in principle', but 43.3% believed that 'minor changes in the *shushin koyo* system are inevitable'. However, what are minor changes? A new document put out by Nikkeiren, the Japan Federation of Employers' Associations, suggests a future system of Japanese employment.

Nikkeiren started a project on a 'New Japanese-style management system' in December 1993. The first interim report was published in August 1994. The final report of May 1995 is a revision of the interim report under the title *Japanese Management in a New Era – Direction and Concrete Policies*. The two reports evoked big discussion among employers as well as among labour unions. The Nikkeiren's documents propose to distinguish three categories of employees in the future:

- *Group 1*. Employees with long-term employment. These are managers or their candidates and core production workers. Their working conditions are similar to those of present regular employees: wage increases every year, bonuses, good welfare benefits.

- *Group 2.* Employees whose professional ability is valued for immediate use, but without the expectation of long-term employment. Wages are strictly based on results within the firm and are paid in the form of an annual salary. No retirement pay is paid.
- *Group 3.* Rotating employees (e.g. part-timers) who perform simple tasks. Pay is an hourly wage. No retirement pay is paid.

Nikkeiren recommends building up the 'employment portfolio' of individual firms for the effective utilisation of human resources. Needless to say, the number of employees in Group 1 will be minimised and employees in Groups 2 and 3 will increase. Groups 1 and 3 already exist. For these groups, Nikkeiren's proposal is only to reduce the size of Group 1, something that is already practised in many companies. The most notable idea of Nikkeiren's report is to create and utilise Group 2. The major jobs of Group 2 are chief researchers, project leaders, chief analysts and other highly specialised jobs. The initial wage is determined mainly by the market price. The second-year wage is based on individual performance the previous year. This type of employee will move from one company to another seeking work, or job-hopping in a Japanese style. This idea is combined with a recent management policy to make the employment of middle-aged and older employees more flexible.

Some companies have already begun to go in this direction. In January 1994 Toyota, for example, announced the recruitment of some designers under the following conditions:

Job – car designer. Qualification – experiences with cars or industrial design, regardless of academic career, job career, nationality, sex and age. Number to be employed – several. Salary – 10 million yen for the first year. Pay will increase in the following years based on performance. Working hours – required to come to the firm once every working day. No definite working hours. Holidays – Saturdays and Sundays. Working place – headquarters.

Some 150 designers applied for this position, but in the end only two were employed. One was a 29-year-old Italian, the other a 42-year-old Japanese. Their salary may increase up to 15 million yen if they perform exceptionally. Their employment contract can be prolonged every year up to five years. If the company evaluates their performance negatively, their contract will not be prolonged (*Rosei Jiho*, 3 February 1995: 35–7).

In the Japanese industry as a whole, Group 2 is still negligible. Whether it will increase rapidly in the near future depends on the labour market and the personnel policies of firms. Under the post-Bubble recession, many firms feel that they are overmanned. They cannot afford to employ additional specialists. If they succeed in slimming employment and business conditions recover, then it is likely that the number of Group 2 employees will increase, as Nikkeiren expects.

However, there is another consideration. The main categories of Group 2 are chief researchers, project leaders, chief analysts and other highly trained specialists. Until recently, Japanese firms used only regular employees for these jobs. Firms believe that project leaders or chief researchers require information and knowledge on firm-specific conditions like corporate culture, human relations, job procedure, etc., that are accumulated during a long length of service with the same firm. Can new temporary specialists work well without this same knowledge? There is another concern. A manager of Kanto Auto works, a group company of Toyota, told us: 'We had negative experiences employing temporary production workers during the Bubble Boom. They had to be paid higher wages, but were less responsible and created a lot of friction among regular workers.' So far, company response to Nikkeiren's ideas has been rather reluctant, and it remains for each firm to consider its merits and demerits.

THE EROSION OF SENIORITY: FROM *NENKO* TO PERFORMANCE

Nenko and *nenko*-based pay

We could fill many pages trying to explain the Japanese wage system in detail. From a broad point of view, however, the Japanese wage system is not so complicated. It consists of two main parts: basic pay and allowances, such as family allowance, overtime allowance, shift allowance, midnight allowance, etc. The peculiarity of the Japanese wage system is found in the basic pay, which is often called *nenko*-based pay, or 'seniority-based pay'. However, this is not a good translation and might lead to misunderstandings. Seniority is based only on the length of service. *Nenko* is more ambiguous. *Nenko* means age, length of service and/or length of job experience. Another factor affecting individual basic pay is an individual assessment conducted by management every year.

To explain the principles behind *nenko*-based pay, we take two senior high-school graduates who are working as production workers. Both of them were employed as regular employees, that is, they are employed by a firm immediately after leaving senior high school. In the first year they received the same amount of basic pay. At the end of the first year management evaluated each employee on performance, ability, attitude, cooperation, leadership and so on. Though the basic pay of the two workers increased in the second year, each individual's increase is different depending on the result of the assessment. The higher the assessment, the more the worker gets in his or her wage increase. Thus, differences in the amount of basic pay between the two workers escalates every year, because it is very likely that a highly valued worker will continue to perform well over the years and be assessed highly by management. In short, under *nenko*-based pay, individual pay increases every year but not equally among employees.

Needless to say, each firm has its own wage system. For example, Toyota has productivity pay for production workers. But productivity pay is not common in Japan. Among 11 car makers, only Toyota has productivity pay.

There are several unique aspects in *nenko*-based pay. First, basic pay for university graduates is determined in the same way as that for high-school graduates. The same wage system is applied both to blue-collar and white-collar workers. Secondly, mid-career entrants (*chuto saiyosha*) are ranked lower than regular employees in basic pay. This practice has a negative effect on labour mobility. Thirdly, under *nenko*-based pay there is no difference in individual basic pay among skilled, semi-skilled and unskilled production workers if age, length of service and individual assessment results are the same. Differences in skill level is not reflected in basic pay. We have asked many personnel managers why skill is not a factor in determining pay, but they could not give us persuasive answers simply because they had never thought about this question. For them, equal pay between skilled and semi-skilled workers is a matter of course and is never questioned. *Nenko*-based pay is deeply established in Japanese management. A personnel manager from Toyota said that from the viewpoint of management, all production workers, regardless of their skill level, work for the company and thus there should be no difference in pay (interview in August 1984). This answer is very illustrative of the history of the wage system in Japan.

Historical background of *nenko*-based pay

Nenko-based pay for production workers began in big companies in the 1920s. During the Second World War, the government compelled all firms to adopt a living-wage system. The basic idea was that all Japanese people should work for the fatherland as hard as possible. Though the performances of individual workers differ, this was not considered important. One's wage should provide for living costs that were thought to increase proportionally with age. That is the reason why the only criterion for wage was age. This living-wage system is different from the *nenko*-based pay in that no individual assessment is conducted.

Immediately after the war, labour unions exerted a strong influence on the management of big companies. The powerful Workers' Union of the Electric Power Industry (Densan) created a wage system and succeeded in implementing it in 1946. This is the famous Densan wage system, and it has become a model for many companies. The essence of the Densan system lies in its individual assessment and a wage curve proportional to the age of workers. In a word, the Densan wage system is a typical *nenko*-based wage system, combining a living wage and individual assessment.

It is interesting that individual assessments were demanded by the labour unions. In the Densan system, basic pay consists of living pay, seniority pay and ability pay (*noryoku kyu*). Living pay is determined by two factors: age and the number of family members. Seniority pay is based on length of service in a company. Ability pay should be determined by individual assessments. However, Densan did not specify what should be evaluated in the individual assessment. Densan only states that ability pay is 'pay corresponding to skill, ability, experiences, knowledge and so on', which should be determined by an individual assessment. Ability pay should account for nearly one third of basic pay. Furthermore, Densan did not suggest who should conduct the individual assessments and how. Densan left almost all the details about the individual assessments to management (Endo, 1995). In the labour movement immediately after the war, egalitarianism prevailed. But it did not exclude individual pay differences based on individual assessments conducted by management. This idea was shared by employees in many of the big firms.

Nenko-based pay was demanded by the labour unions. This fact explains some features of *nenko*-based pay. Strongly inspired by egalitarianism, the labour unions demanded the abolition of 'class societies within the company' and equal treatment of white-collar and blue-collar workers. In other words, the same wage system should apply to both categories. There should not be a distinction in pay between skilled workers and unskilled workers. The difference between the highest and the lowest paid employees should not be large. Egalitarianism, however, prevailed only among the regular employees within a company. Enterprise unions did not demand equal treatment of peripheral workers like temporary workers or part-timers, nor were they concerned with the working conditions of suppliers and subcontract companies.

The performance of individual employees is not directly reflected in basic pay. In the individual assessments conducted once a year to determine basic pay increases, individual performance is only one of the evaluation items. But in the individual assessments conducted twice a year (summer and winter) for the determination of bonuses, individual performance is the most important evaluation item. Bonus accounts for nearly 30% of the total yearly income. Still, the difference between the highest and the lowest bonus is not large. It is because of this that Japanese firms complain: they say that neither *nenko*-based basic pay nor bonus pay provide incentives for higher performance.

Any time a recession hits the economy, companies try to change the pay system to reward higher performance. There is a call to change 'from a *nenko*-based pay system to an ability-based pay system (*noryoku shugi chingin*)'. This ideology is continually promoted by Nikkeiren. But this campaign has not resulted in a fundamental reorganisation of the wage system but only in minor changes in *nenko*-based pay by exaggerating the differences between the highest and lowest levels.

New developments after the Bubble Boom

In the post-Bubble recession, a new type of wage system emerged in big companies like Honda, Fujitsu and Sony. It is called 'annual salary' (*nenpo sei*). In its ideal form, annual salary would be determined once a year depending on the results of individual assessments. Annual salary would fluctuate up and down according to annual individual performance evaluations. However this ideal form has not come into being. Nikkeiren and some famous consultants recommend introducing a 'Japanese-style annual salary'. Annual salary would be divided into two parts: basic pay and bonus. Basic pay would be more or less oriented towards a living wage. It would be stable and proportional to living costs. Bonuses should be determined by individual assessments.

What are the major differences between a *nenko*-based pay and a Japanese-style annual salary? The first difference is that an annual salary is applied only to managers or white-collar workers. It is difficult to apply an annual salary system to production workers because production workers' performance is thought to depend more on collectivism than on individualism. Further, since a manager's salary is higher than that of production workers, living costs might be covered by basic pay. Ups and downs in bonuses would not endanger the stability of managers. The second difference from the *nenko*-system is that the results of individual assessments and company performance affect the total amounts of bonus more than previously. The third difference is that the proportion of bonus pay in one's total salary will be larger than previously. Nikkeiren is recommending increasing its proportion from 30 to 40% (Nikkeiren, 1995: 85).

Basic pay in a new 'Japanese style annual salary' is still inspired by the living-wage idea. Does this mean that *nenko*-based pay is sustainable despite the fanfare for ability or performance-based pay? We do not think so. First, regular employees of big firms will decline in number as Nikkeiren suggests. Even if *nenko*-based pay is sustainable, its scope will be limited. Secondly, some leading companies have introduced performance-based pay systems. Fujitsu, for example, introduced an annual salary for about 7,000 managers in 1994. This is composed of basic pay and performance pay (bonus). Basic pay does not decrease even if an individual's performance is the worst among managers, but bonus strongly fluctuates in accordance with individual performance. As the weight of the bonus is much higher than previously, total annual salary will decrease below the previous year's if one's performance is evaluated poorly (*Rosei Jiho*, 7 September 1995: 23–7). Once new systems such as that of Fujitsu show a better performance, then other companies will follow suit. Japanese companies are seeking for a new system. However, we do not think that the change will be dramatic. The idea of a living wage is deeply rooted in Japanese business. This is evident from the fact that the Japanese wage system has not changed radically for many years, despite Nikkeiren's slogan 'from *nenko*-based pay to ability-based pay'.

THE ROLE OF WOMEN: STABILITY AND CHANGE

The feminist movement was late in arriving in Japan. In the late 1960s and early 1970s there was a weak 'women's liberation' movement. Together with

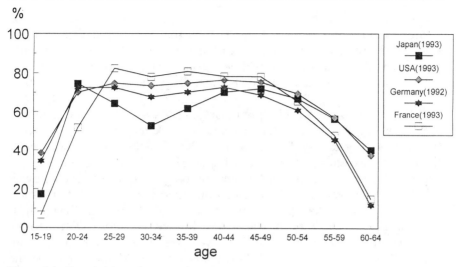

Figure 5.1   Female labour force participation

other social movements, the women's movement died away with the first oil crisis. Since the mid-1980s feminists have increased in influence, but not yet as deeply as in Europe and the USA. We can still talk about the traditionalism of the woman's role at home and in the workplace.

Stability . . .

Many standard texts on the Japanese employment system focus squarely on male employees. During recent years, researchers, inspired by feminist theories, have started to fill this gap. Studies in the 1980s came to a common understanding on Japanese female employment (Takenaka and Kuba, 1994):

1) Quantitatively, female labour force participation is surprisingly stable: 49.9% in 1970 and 50.7% in 1991. In the post-Bubble recession, it had slightly decreased to 50.2% in 1994. There has been no feminisation of employment in terms of numbers. Qualitatively, however, the number of employed females increased rapidly from 54.7% in 1970 to 74.0% in 1991, while self-employed and family-employed women decreased.

2) Though employed women are increasing (26.1 million women in 1994), self-employment and family employment are still high. About 665,000 women are working as home piecework workers. These workers are at the bottom of the pyramidal subcontracting system.

3) Female labour participation still forms an *M*-curve, that is, a high ratio of young women work, then quit in their late 20s and early 30s and work again in their 40s. Among industrial countries, Japan is an exception in that female labour force participation is still an *M*-curve (Figure 5.1). The typical life cycle for female employees in big companies is that they get a full-time job immediately after leaving school. Upon marrying or having a baby they quit the company and devote themselves to the care of their

children. The unofficial 'rule' for married women to quit work is still strong in big companies. In their 30s after their children have grown up, they seek employment once more but this time as part-timers. Most firms, however, do not like to hire middle-aged and older women as full-timers but many women want to tackle both family work and a part-time job.

The *M*-curve is backed up by public opinion. As recently as 1990, 56% of women were of the opinion that men should work and women stay at home to take care of the family. This is claimed to be the highest percentage among the industrial countries (Inoue and Ehara, 1995: 45). Male employees are expected to work for many years in one company. To utilise male employees effectively, management trains and educates them for advanced jobs. If male employees were to take repetitive and simple work, it would not be productive from the point of view of wages, which increase every year due to the *nenko*-based pay system. Female employees are expected to quit the company while young and when their wage is still low. Management sees no need to educate or train female employees for higher jobs. This treatment demoralises female employees and encourages retirement. In production, it results in a Taylorist division of labour between the genders, as typically implemented in the electronics and the machine tool industries (Nomura, 1993a; see also Chapter 8).

Part-timers are predominantly married middle-aged and older women. Japanese part-timers have several idiosyncracies. First, based on the usual definition of a part-timer, working hours should be shorter than that for full-timers. However, it is extremely difficult to distinguish between part-timers and full-timers by working hours. Nearly 20% of part-timers work as long as full-timers and do overtime as well. Secondly, there are many part-timers who work for one company for more than ten years. Nevertheless, their employment contracts are not guaranteed. They have to renew their contracts periodically while regular employees have indefinite employment contracts. Thirdly, despite similar working hours and long service records, pay for part-timers is definitely lower than that for full-timers. The hourly wage for female part-timers is only 59% of that for full-timers (including bonuses), while in other industrial countries it is nearly equal. An economist reached the conclusion that productivity differences cannot explain this large pay difference. The real reason is found in the separate pay systems for part-timers and regular employees (Osawa, 1993a: Chap. 6).

Fourthly, Japanese manufacturing industry employs many part-timers, while in other industrial countries part-timers are hired mostly in the service sector. About a quarter of all part-timers in Japan work in manufacturing industry. Needless to say, they do simple and repetitive jobs. Some Japanese feminists insist that being a part-timer is a 'status'. Part-timers cannot be distinguished from regular employees by working hours or length of service – they are paid less simply because they are labelled as part-timers. There is no rational economic reason for the large pay difference between part-timers and full-timers (Osawa, 1993b: Chap. 2).

Unemployment is distributed unequally between the genders. In 1994, the unemployment rate for women was 3.4% while that for men was 2.3%. However, the definition of unemployment is different among countries. The US Bureau of Labor Statistics publishes seven indices of unemployment from U1 to U7 in order to measure unemployment correctly. U5 is the total unemployed as a percentage of the civilian labour force. This U5 is identical to the Japanese official unemployment rate. In 1994, U5 was 2.7% in Japan and 6.5% in the USA. The Japanese government only publishes U5. Another unemployment rate, U7, includes discouraged workers who are jobless, want work and are presumably available for work, but who abandon seeking a job. It is calculated that U7 is 8.9% in Japan and 8.8% in the USA. The difference between the genders in U7 is much larger than in U5. In Japan, U7 is 5.0% for men and 14.7% for women (this corresponds to a 6% lower level of labour force participation among Japanese women compared to the USA). It means that latent unemployment is much higher in Japan than in the USA and that women tend to be unemployed though officially they are not registered as unemployed.

. . . and change?

Ten years has passed since the Equal Opportunity Law was enacted. The law obliges employers to give women equal opportunity for recruitment, promotion, training, welfare and retirement. However, the positive effects of the law have been very limited. First, there is no punishment for employers who ignore the law. The law only says that 'employers have to make efforts' towards equal opportunity.

The law has had no effect on female production workers. When a firm recruits production workers, usually it simply advertises as 'hiring production workers'. There is no inequality at this point. Inequality begins after they are employed. Female production workers are not given an equal opportunity for training and therefore for promotion. This practice is not questioned because many regular female workers are expected to retire when young. Even female workers who have worked for many years in one company are regarded as less able than men due to socially shared prejudices. The law does nothing about part-timers, of course.

The law has possibly helped female university graduates. Before the law, almost all female white-collar workers were treated as an auxiliary workforce in the office, while almost all men with university diplomas were expected to become managers. After the law was enacted, many big firms introduced a two-track system. When a woman or a man applies for an office job, he or she is given a chance to choose either *sogoshoku*, candidate for manager, or *ippanshoku*, an auxiliary job. But there is still segregation between men and women. Male university graduates are almost exclusively hired as *sogoshoku*, while only a limited number of female university graduates are employed as *sogoshoku*. Women *sogoshoku* feel uncomfortable in the office. On the one hand, male managers do not know how to deal with *sogoshoku* women. They are a kind of alien in a man's world. On the other hand, they are segregated from *ippanshoku* women, whose pay is clearly lower. The resulting stress causes the mass retirement of *sogoshoku* women, which invites criticism from men that women are irresponsible and useless.

The situation of working women is highlighted by recent cases where women have sued companies: Tokai Radio (1990), Nippon Life Insurance (1991), Sumitomo Life Insurance (1992; 1994), Kanematsu Trading (1992; 1995), Sumitomo Metal (1994), Sumitomo Chemicals (1994), Sumitomo Electric Industries (1994), Sumitomo Life Insurance (1994), Central Bank of Commercial and Industrial Co-operatives (1994), Nankai Broadcasting (1995). There have also been lawsuits by part-timers (Hayashi, 1995). Traditionally, the Japanese do not like lawsuits. Only when they cannot endure a situation any more do they go to court. Therefore, lawsuits from women are interpreted as wide discontent among women and have become a topic of discussion in the mass media.

In the case of Sumitomo Metal, one of the five biggest steelmakers in Japan, a plaintiff reported on the details (Kitagawa, 1995). Ms Kitagawa entered the firm as a white-collar worker in 1961. For many years she was not promoted and therefore her wage remained low. Fortunately, the firm set up a grievance procedure for employees, which is exceptional in Japan. The firm is obliged to answer to charges when employees formally submit a grievance. Until recently, she had not used this procedure. She feared that her bosses would feel criticised if she appealed through this procedure. After 31 years of employment, she asked the personnel department about the individual assessment system and her assessment results. The assessment system evaluates employees as OA, A, B+, B, C+, C and OC, the last being the lowest. She had been almost always evaluated as C since her marriage in 1965, while before marriage she was given B, the average. Since the worst grade of OC is given only to exceptionally bad employees, the C grade is in fact the worst. A personnel manager consoled her: 'Ms Kitagawa, you are not the only one being discriminated against. Almost all women are evaluated as C.' She remembered that no job was allocated to her for one and half years after marriage in an attempt to encourage her to retire. At that time, there was an informal rule in the firm for women to quit when they married. She ignored this rule and became the only married woman in the firm. After she gave birth to a baby in 1968, her boss insulted her openly: 'Even cats and dogs are taken care of by their mother. You bring your baby to a nursery. You are worse than an animal. Are you a machine producing babies?' In 1994, with six other female employees, she appealed to the arbitration committee set up by the Equal Opportunity Law. This was the first case in ten years. The arbitration committee has been called the 'never opened door'. After hearings, the committee presented an arbitration proposal in February 1995. It suggested that the firm should give women equal opportunity for promotion and training. That was all – no judgement determining if discrimination had existed, no relief to the plaintiffs. The disappointed woman sued the firm at the local court in August 1995.

Table 5.2 Three models of employment practices

	Anglo-Saxon (UK, USA)	Standard Japanese, large firms	New Japanese
Recruitment	Direct from external market when needed	Core: annual hiring from universities and high schools; periphery: temporaries and *paatos* from external market	Reduced core is complemented by professionals on limited contracts; increased use of peripheral workers
Promotion/management selection	Mixture of internal and external; fast track for high potentials.	Internal, based on systematic rotation between departments and plants. Slow promotion linked to length of service	Dual career tracks. Somewhat lower-status specialist tracks are added to traditional hierarchical careers
Main pay determinants	Performance and position in hierarchy; traditional separation of WC and BC partly replaced by stress on individual assessment	*Nenko* (length of service), living costs, plus personal assessment of attitude and ability; unified system for white and blue-collar workers	End of unitary treatment WC/BC; annual salary for managers and white-collar workers: stable basic pay plus large and variable bonus based on performance and individual assessment.
Employment security	Increasingly a short-term variable; profit declines prompt workforce adjustment; layoff decisions raise stock value and executive compensation	Implicit, far-reaching corporate obligations; dismissals a last recourse for companies fighting for survival; redundancies often prompt president to resign	Reduced staffing levels, mainly by soft and slow measures; increased use of limited contracts; position of middle managers (not union members) expected to become less secure.
Role of women	Women increasingly enter professional and managerial positions (except top slots); Strong correlation between education and professional career	Jobs rigidly segregated by gender; female employees quit after marriage; later rehired as *paatos*; many family or self-employed; no correlation between education and career	Companies are forced to offer career track to women, but hard to combine with family duties; reduced core hiring affects women negatively
Shareholder vs. managers	Footloose capital focus; maxi-misation of shareholder value in downturns, strong pressure on CEO to reduce workforce to protect share price	Management-controlled cross-ownership mitigates stock market pressure; market share, growth and stable employment are key concerns	Financial institutions more profit-oriented but do not change basic stability of 'alliance capitalism'

During this process, the woman asked the enterprise union to present wage data to prove discrimination. The union rejected the request, saying that difference in pay is a result of differing ability. They claimed that there was no discrimination against women. Furthermore, the union said that wage data are confidential. After the woman appealed to the court, the union employed a lawyer to keep the wage data confidential. The case of Sumitomo Metal reveals the problems of the Equal Opportunity Law: the 'never opened door' of the arbitration committee, powerless arbitration and a lack of support from the enterprise union. The road to real equal opportunity is still long.

Nothing remains the same as time goes by. Neither do Japanese women. The average marrying age of women was 24.2 years in 1970 and 26.1 years in 1993. Women who do not marry are increasing. Among women between 25 and 29 years, 40.2% were not married in 1990, while the number was 20.9% in 1975. Between the ages of 30 and 34 years, 7.7% were unmarried in 1975 and 13.9% in 1990. Apparently, women who prefer a single life are increasing. Women now enjoy higher education: 21% of female graduates from senior high school entered four-year universities courses in 1994, while the number was 12.5% in 1975. Higher academic performance will strengthen women's consciousness for equal treatment in the long run. However, it is not thought that Japanese women are now hurrying in the same direction as US and European women. The female labour participation of university graduates, for example, is lower than that of senior high-school graduates in middle age. Of mothers, 65% expect their boy to be a university student, but only 35% their daughter (Inoue and Ehara, 1995: 135). The traditional opinion on the division of labour between the two genders is still shared by many women. Japan is in many ways a conservative and slow-changing society.

The situation of women illustrates the basic stability or 'perseverance' of many aspects of employment and labour market practices in Japan. Table 5.2 shows the 'standard' (postwar) Japanese pattern and assesses recent changes against a stereotyped version of current Anglo-Saxon practices. Of course there are variations and dynamics within the Anglo-Saxon type. In the 1950s and 1960s (the age of 'Organisation man') this type certainly contained many more 'Japanese elements', such as life-long male employment in huge corporations. Table 5.2 focuses on Japan and attempts to summarise the above discussion of changes in, for example, wage systems and what impact they have on the postwar system. It must be noted that, as usual, we concentrate on the employment and career pattern within large private corporations. In the concluding section we return to a discussion of forces of divergence and convergence in assessing the future strength of Japanese employment practices.

UNIONS – CREATIVE POLICY, INEFFECTIVE IMPLEMENTATION

Traditionally, Japanese 'industrial unions' have been eager to implement industrial policies which should benefit both firms and employees. However, until recently society ignored the industrial policies of industrial unions. As expected, when the economy and industry are working well, few show interest in the union's industrial policies. When the first oil shock resulted in a severe recession in 1973–4, unions too lost their cool judgement and could not suggest alternative industrial policies. In the post-Bubble recession, however, the industrial policies of the two most influential 'industrial unions' attracted the attention of the mass media with their innovative ideas. These two unions are the Confederation of Japan Automobile Workers' Unions (JAW) and the Japanese Federation of Electrical Machine Workers' Unions (Denki Rengo).

JAW – Japan Automobile Workers' Union

The industrial policy of JAW became a hot topic in the early 1990s. JAW insisted that it had been a partner of the automobile companies since its foundation in 1972. But in 1992 JAW suddenly published a very critical review of the Japanese automobile industry. The report, entitled *The Japanese Automobile Industry in the Future* (1992), asserts that the Japanese automobile industry is damaged by the 'triple sufferings': labour shortage, low profitability and criticism from both abroad and from within Japan (see also Chapter 6).

JAW proposed a new concept for the automobile industry: 'coexistence'. The Japanese automobile industry should change towards coexistence with the world, consumers and employees. The surplus in exports should be corrected by 'coexisting' with the world. The car industry should provide accurate information on waiting periods for delivery and reduce sales negotiation efforts in order to 'coexist' with consumers. The workplace and working conditions should be humanised in order to secure 'coexistence' with employees.

This radical industrial policy was, however, short lived. It was formulated during the Bubble Boom and a period of serious labour shortages. The burst of the bubble turned the labour market from one of serious labour shortage to one of serious labour redundancy. In the Bubble Boom, JAW thought that the Japanese automobile industry would decline, with low profitability and labour shortages. Now JAW faces overcapacity and overmanning which might threaten future employment severely. How to revive the industry and how to avoid unemployment have become the hottest issues for JAW. JAW enlisted the Mitsubishi Research Institute to simulate future employment trends of the Japanese automobile industry. The ups and downs of domestic production largely depend on exports, which are strongly affected by foreign exchange rates. According to the estimates of the Mitsubishi Research Institute, a yen:dollar rate of 85:1 in the year 2000 will result in an employment loss of 160,000 in the automobile industry, whereas an exchange rate of 100:1 will result in only 25,000 lost jobs (JAW, 1995).

Thus the most important policy is to keep foreign exchange rates stable. But this is far beyond the influence of JAW. JAW is examining whether the following measures will stabilise employment:

1) Work-sharing by reducing working hours.
2) *Shukko* and *ohen* (short-term transfer) within the automobile industry and with other companies.

3) The creation of new businesses by developing new technology.
4) The creation of high value-added products.
5) The creation of new business by deregulation.
6) An increase in domestic demand by reforming the tax system related to automobiles.
7) The systematic use of natural attrition with unfilled vacancies caused by the retirement of employees who have reached the compulsory retirement age.

JAW is moving to formulate concrete policies to implement these ideas.

Denki Rengo

Denki Rengo, equally as influential in the labour movement as JAW, is discussing the effects of rapidly increasing production overseas. It is the electronics and electric industry that faces the hollowing-out problem most seriously. To counter the looming unemployment problem Denki Rengo proposes the following measures:

1) An appropriate foreign exchange rate.
2) The vertical and horizontal division of labour between domestic and overseas production. High value-added production should remain in Japan.
3) The collection of fair profits (dividends, royalties) from overseas plants.
4) Avoiding more excessive competition. Securing appropriate profits. An early start in the multimedia business.

Denki Rengo acknowledges that a restructuring of the industry is unavoidable. It will be accompanied by reforms of the employment system resulting in flexible employment. Firms will transfer their employees within a company more flexibly and utilise *shukko* more often. Flexible employment will inevitably change the *nenko*-based wage system which was founded under the precondition of long-term employment. In the future, according to Denki Rengo, there will be several categories of employment even among regular employees in a single company. A group of employees will work during scheduled working hours as before. Another group of employees will not be bound to scheduled working hours. Mid-career entrants will increase. With such a variety of employees, the pay system cannot remain the same. Annual salary, ability-oriented pay and other pay systems will coexist in one company. Unions will have to accept plural pay systems within one company. *Nenko*-based pay will be reformed to resemble performance-based or ability-based pay. Denki Rengo recommends that enterprise unions negotiate with management on three points. First, minimum standard pay for living necessities should be negotiated. Secondly, ability-based pay or performance-based pay should be founded on a fair individual assessment system. For this purpose, management should give sufficient training to evaluators. Assessment criteria should be objective and should be explained to each employee. Thirdly, with plural wage systems coexisting in one company, employees should be given the choice as to which pay system they prefer to work under (Denki Rengo, 1995a). Denki Rengo's call for a new individual assessment system indicates that present assessment criteria are not objective and are not explained to employees, and nor are the results given to employees.

Difficult policy implementation

As seen in the industrial policies of JAW and Denki Rengo, industrial unions have clear goals. The weakness of the union movement is not in policy-making but in policy-implementing. Industrial unions in Japan are not industrial federations in the sense of Europe or the USA. Japanese industrial unions are federations of independent enterprise unions. Enterprise unions have full autonomy. They can elect their union officers, determine union fees, and negotiate with management. Industrial unions have neither the right to negotiate with companies nor the power to intervene in the election of officers of enterprise unions. Industrial unions can only recommend their policies to enterprise unions. This system generates a huge gap between policy-making and policy implementation.

For example, when an industrial union decides on a target for working hour reduction, each enterprise union negotiates with its management. Management will argue the following: 'We cannot reduce working hours simply because it will lower our competitiveness in the market. What would be the result if only our company reduces working hours and other companies do not? Can you guarantee that other companies will also reduce working hours?' It is difficult for enterprise unions to answer these questions, because no enterprise union knows if the other enterprise unions are intent on realising the same goals or if they are negotiating only as a gesture. This is not an imaginary story. In the early 1980s, Nissan Union succeeded in reducing the working hours of workers at Nissan dealers, while other enterprise unions did not. Nissan dealers had to close their shops earlier than the other dealers. A top manager of Nissan told us: 'Do you think this is reasonable? It has contributed to our deteriorating market share. We will never accept such a stupid demand from the union again' (interview, July 1987).

In the extreme case, when an enterprise union strikes, the enterprise union of the rival company supports it by lending money or organising campaigns for the strike. Nominally, this is a solidarity action between enterprise unions. However, it might be motivated by a wish to defeat the rival company hit by the strike. It is said that such cases happened in the early 1950s and resulted in the mutual distrust of enterprise unions, though it is difficult to find evidence on this matter. In any case, there is a strong tendency towards mutual trust between an enterprise union and its management, on the one hand, and mutual distrust between different enterprise unions on the other.

A widening representation gap

It is often said that Japanese enterprise unions have a say on management policy through collective negotiations or joint consultations. Recently, Rengo asked officers of enterprise unions if they negotiate or consult with management on workforce reduction. Astonishingly, only 38% of enterprise unions in the manufacturing industry in 1994 negotiated or consulted on workforce reduction schemes (Rengo, 1995).

An opinion survey conducted by Denki Rengo in September 1994 confirms this image. Union members in electronics and electric companies with over 10,000 employees evaluate the activities of enterprise unions as a whole negatively. Only 1.2% answered that they were 'very satisfied with union activities', 31.3% 'satisfied to some extent', while 4.4% answered 'totally unsatisfied' and 15.9% 'rather unsatisfied'. Some 46.6% answered 'don't know'. Notably, union members have a strong mistrust of union activities on employment problems. Asked if their union defends union members in cases of workforce reduction, only 29.4% answered 'yes' while 53.6% answered 'no'. Also asked if the union can be relied upon to protect its members in cases of unfavourable transfer to another workplace, or *shukko*, 27.4% answered 'yes' and 55.8% 'no'. These are the opinions of union members when employment problems are most serious (Denki Rengo, 1995b: 135, 143).

Nikkeiren wants to keep the enterprise unions as they are, though it proposes to reform the pay system and employment practices:

> Enterprise unions have contributed to the development of firms and stable employment by reacting flexibly to job reorganization caused by technological changes through in-company communication. In the future, fundamental functions of enterprise unions should be maintained for the survival of firms and stable employment in the changing external environments.
>
> (Nikkeiren, 1995: 58)

Enterprise unions are faced with low trust from union members and high trust from employers' associations. In severe recessions, enterprise unions have alternatives: looking at rapidly changing management practices passively or implementing the industrial policies of industrial unions. If they remain passive, they will have no influence over this process, where fundamental aspects of the Japanese management and employment system are redefined. If on the other hand they try to implement industrial policies, they will face structural difficulties in setting up solidarity between them. The initiatives of industrial unions need to be strengthened. Through joint consultations between the industrial union and its counterpart association, rather than through negotiations at the firm level, the chances of implementing their industrial policies will be enhanced.

NO CONVERGENCE – JAPAN'S DIFFERENT WAY OF RESTRUCTURING

In preceding sections we have emphasised that the Japanese employment system does not mean any guarantee for lifetime employment. Significant workforce adjustments have taken place during several periods in the postwar period, including the post-Bubble recession. However, compared to developments in western countries, and especially Europe, where workers traditionally enjoyed more job security than in the USA, Japan's corporate system of maintaining high employment has been remarkably robust. This stands out in a comparison with the fragility of, for example, the Swedish system. Here full employment was a politically central goal for more than half a century, and was achieved successfully during the postwar period. When Sweden experienced a combination of international recession and domestic austerity policies in the early 1990s, however, unemployment suddenly soared beyond control from 1.5 to 12%. Economists as well as politicians seem to have abandoned the belief in ever returning to a state of full employment. In Japan, too, official unemployment has risen markedly, but is still below 4%. The problem with this resilience, however, is hidden unemployment within companies. According to estimates by MITI officers in 1993, this amounted to 3% of the labour force. In previous downturns, most Japanese companies were able to weather the storm. They accepted the costs of excess employment in the expectation of a new strong upturn. This practice is also an important part of Japanese labour market policy, where the government subsidises overstaffed companies with so-called employment adjustment subsidies on the precondition that they do not fire any employees. In 1994, 4.7 million workers in 224 industries were covered by such subsidies (Shinmura and Ishizawa, 1994).

The business community was not very happy with this state of affairs. Leading management magazines such as *Shukan Daiyamondo (Diamond Weekly)* published meticulous calculations of overmanning in all major firms. The invitation to a more ruthless, 'western-style' labour-shedding was obvious. Few large companies were prepared to follow this path, however. In particularly hard-hit industries, such as machine tools, programmes for 'voluntary' or 'early retirement' were introduced. However, the majority of Japanese companies resorted to their traditional adjustment instruments. The most widespread response to the decline in production has been to reduce overtime, from very high levels in 1990–1 to virtually zero at the bottom of the recession in 1993–4. In some sectors, such as the machine tool industry, the reduction was very substantial. In 1990, this industry's employees often worked 15–20 hours or more overtime *per week* but in 1993 overtime had been reduced to zero. This Japanese pattern of keeping employees, but reducing overtime, contrasts with the Swedish pattern during the recession of 1991–3. While companies were laying off workers on a massive scale, overtime in Sweden actually increased to a record level.

Companies in Japan have also tried to reduce bonuses, but since employees have lost so much of their overtime pay resistance has been considerable. In 1993, Toyota attempted to cut the winter bonus but had to withdraw its proposal. Nissan, suffering from losses for a second consecutive year, managed to negotiate a reduction, albeit a very insignificant one. The Japanese pay system does not seem to be as flexible as is believed by western observers. More symbolically, many companies also reduced bonuses for board members and eliminated benefits for managers. NEC, the big electronics company, implemented an innovative scheme according to which part of the bonuses for management from mid-level *kacho* and up was converted to vouchers for company products (*Rosei Jiho*, 1993: 89). More specific measures to deal with overmanning include various forms of transfers, from headquarters to subsidiaries or from manufacturing to sales outlets. In some cases this is a disguised dismissal, since employees will find it very difficult to cope with the new tasks. All these measures are strikingly similar to those adopted in mainstream industries in the recessions of the 1970s (Dore, 1986).

The difference between Japanese and western practices is illustrated by the automobile industry. In 1993, Nissan announced its decision to shut down the Zama plant, close to Tokyo. In Europe and the USA, plant closures in the automobile industry have been frequent during the last decade. In Japan, this had never happened before. Still there is an important difference between Japan and the west. When, for example, Volvo decided to close its Swedish Uddevalla plant in 1992, the decision was implemented in six months. Less than 5% of the plant's highly skilled workers were re-employed at other Volvo sites (18 months later the plant was reopened again, which illustrates the short-termism of the company's planning and employment policies). At Nissan, the closure of Zama was a slow and painstaking process, and the company was obliged to make comprehensive efforts to offer new jobs to the redundant workers (Yahata, 1993). The reason was not only the poorly developed labour market for mid-career workers but also their difficulties in finding jobs with equivalent pay outside the company. The Japanese reluctance to fire regular, male workers is deeply embedded in the personnel and promotion systems, and is linked to the public perception of firms. In the fiscal year 1993 which ended at 31 March 1994, Mazda posted its worst losses since the company was established in 1920 (Sumiya, 1994a). The losses continued during 1994 and 1995. Yet the company has not resorted to layoffs and redundancies. Personnel and plant capacity are only to be contracted slowly. A major reason for this prudence is the necessity of preserving the company's public image. If Mazda started to dismiss employees, Japanese consumers would lose all confidence in the company and boycott its products *en mass*.

In the short term, the recession in the 1990s has largely resulted in a return to Japanese (not western) normalcy, after the detours of the Bubble Boom. In spite of various programmes for early retirement, the overwhelming majority of Japanese companies have resorted to established measures to adjust employment. They have ceased to recruit mid-career entrants and do not re-employ temporary or foreign workers. The hiring of peripheral workers has been drastically reduced, although this is probably only a temporary phenomenon since an upturn in the economy is expected to favour recruitment on a temporary and part-time basis. The traditional emphasis on regular male workers is reinforced, which means that the prospects for female university graduates to find jobs commensurate with their skills are further diminished. This return to normalcy also includes employee attitudes. In the

1980s, the changing attitudes of young and affluent Japanese were supposed to be a major factor driving change towards more mobility and a more flexible labour market. In the deep recession, a conservative shift has apparently taken place. In its annual survey of new recruits conducted each spring, the Japan Productivity Centre found that a clear majority of 1,900 polled in 1995 aimed to stay in their companies for as long as possible. In 1990, 66% had said they would quit a job they didn't like. Five years later only 41% shared this opinion. A *Nikkei Weekly* journalist commented: 'New employees lack the hell-or-high-water commitment to their companies that their predecessors showed, but they are not job-hopping. Instead they opt for security' (Sato, 1995a). The strength of traditional values is also reflected in a recent study of executive promotion. A survey of 334 new company presidents by Nikkei's *Who's Who* found that

> when it comes picking the boss, the top organizations remain solidly loyal to their traditions of seniority-based advancement, educational elitism and sexism [only one of the 334 was female, replacing her husband] . . . The overall statistics fly in the face of reports claiming that the seniority system is on its lasts legs. The survey results also question the notion that companies are placing more emphasis on employee's abilities and track records than on their educational background . . . '
>
> (*Nikkei Weekly*, 24 July 1995)

SUMMARY

This chapter started with a summary of the standard western view of the Japanese employment system: employees are hired directly from school on the basis of general abilities not particular skills. Salaries are based on seniority rather than on performance. Employees remain with the company for a life-long career, and in exchange for hard work they expect not to be laid off in difficult times. The link between employment practices and the system of 'alliance capitalism', where shareholder interest and the financial community have little leverage, was emphasised. Paradoxically, the Japanese words for 'lifetime employment' are a translation from a US study. It has always been restricted to large and, to some extent, medium-sized firms. Also in large firms many workers do not correspond to the standard image of lifetime employees. The reason is voluntary turnover as well as involuntary retirement – that is, employment adjustment. The chapter highlights four major periods of workforce adjustment. Redundancies are often disguised behind euphemisms such as 'voluntary' or 'early retirement'. However, the workforce reduction that does take place differs from Anglo-Saxon practices in several ways. It is the last resort, when a company is bleeding and the repertoire of 'soft measures' has been exhausted, 'voluntary retirement programmes' are seen as a major failure for management, and leading company executives normally have to resign. They imply a serious loss of public image, especially in consumer-oriented industries. During the long post-Bubble recession the future of the concept 'lifetime' has been at issue in Japan. In this debate there is no consensus. The employers' federation has suggested a system of several categories, including professionals hired on limited contracts and paid for performance. The response from companies has been cautious.

Another part of Japan's employment system is *nenko* pay, which is based on length of service and on individual assessment. Performance only plays a minor role. The same system applies to all regular employees, blue-collar as well as white-collar workers. There is no difference between skilled and unskilled workers. Historically this system was inspired by union demands. In times of recession, the employer's federation has repeatedly voiced demands for reforms. In the post-Bubble recession, more performance-related salaries have been introduced for managers and white-collar workers in several companies. Despite the demands from Nikkeiren, no dramatic change in the *nenko* system is expected.

For Japanese unions, the most important target is to safeguard employment. This is particularly true in sectors where hollowing-out is a real danger. Denki Rengo, the Japanese electrical, electronic and information union, has proposed several reforms to increase flexibility and to safeguard employment in Japan. The industrial unions can only recommend their policies to the enterprise unions, however. Japanese unions face a serious risk of marginalisation if they cannot find new ways of effective co-ordination.

Typically, the Japanese employment system has been restricted to male employees. During the last two decades important demographic changes have taken place, including an increasing marrying age and a decreasing marriage frequency. These trends have not changed the basic pattern of female work, however. Female labour force participation still displays an *M*-curve, with the first peak among young women, before marriage, and the second peak when women are in their 40s. Average labour force participation has remained constant for 20 years. Higher education does not result in more rewarding work. After the introduction of the Equal Opportunity Law, companies have formally opened career tracks for women, but very few are given real opportunities. In this aspect, too, Japanese personnel practices seem to be very resilient. The long post-Bubble recession has reinforced traditional attitudes, among employers as well as parents.

A great deal of debate concerning personnel practices is happening within Japan, but the majority of companies have utilised very conventional Japanese means to deal with overmanning and cost problems. The short-term pattern is a return to *Japanese* normalcy. In the long term more diversity is envisaged, and a strong tendency to minimise the core of standard employees. This tendency is evident in several of the industry studies which follow.

Figure 5.2 seeks to summarise the main forces of convergence and divergence affecting the future of the Japanese pattern. The upper half of the figure spells out the domestic and international factors that are building up a convergence pressure (these factors have been discussed in Chapters 2–4). These convergence forces, however, must be viewed in relation to the shock-

Forces driving convergence

Pressure from **financial markets** because of eroding *fukumieki* and increased profit demands from low-performing banks and insuring companies	Long recession and **low growth** in Japan force companies to reduce permanent employment	**Kudoka**: transfer of manufacturing because of *endaka* and trade friction	New **information technology** and networking reduce the need for administration and 'human relations'-oriented management	Reborn **US competitiveness** fuels employer interest in flexible employment and downsizing	**International pressure** on Japan to open up and deregulate protected sectors; **declining domestic power** of industrial policies and élite bureaucracies

Forces potentially sustaining diversity

No change in basic corporate governance	Stable ownership permits **piecemeal adjustment**		Human **networks remain crucial**	**Society expects** firms to honour their obligations	**Dogged resistance** to foreign pressure

Figure 5.2   Japanese capitalism versus Anglo-Saxon forces of convergence and divergence

absorbing, countervailing factors of the Japanese economic and social fabric which are listed in the lower half of the figure. Here these factors are only sketched very briefly – Chapters 6–9 will analyse them in more detail. In Chapter 10 we return to a more complete version of this 'force field'-analysis, and try to ascertain the net result against the backdrop of the four industry studies in Chapters 6–9. Here it suffices to say that in spite of the many initiatives to modify the postwar Japanese compensation and employment system, at company level as well as the level of employer and union organisation, it is difficult to identify any broad trend towards convergence with western (Anglo-Saxon) practices. Japan's particular employment pattern prevails in key sectors. This does not mean that Japan is an unchanging society; rather that it is holding on to its tradition of dynamic conservatism and gradual change. Possibly there is also a trend towards increasing diversity within these manufacturing sectors, as the industry studies below demonstrate. Some maintain their traditional employment structures, but tend to make them more closed when the hiring of new employees is reduced to a fraction of the previous level. Other companies devise new production and employment structures to cope with increasing unpredictability and variation. In Chapter 10 we return to the overall significance of these developments.

PART 2

FOUR INDUSTRY STUDIES

6

AUTOMOBILES: GLOBAL EXPANSION AND DOMESTIC CONTRACTION

Starting in the early 1950s, the automobile industry was Japan's premier growth machine for nearly 40 years. In 1990, the automotive industry (including the parts sector) accounted for 13% of total manufacturing output in Japan, 22% of capital investment and 23% of Japan's manufacturing export. The first decade after the Korean War growth was almost completely driven by domestic demand, but in the 1960s exports started to increase rapidly. In 1970, Japan exported 1 million vehicles; ten years later exports totalled 6 million, and in 1985 exports peaked at 6.7 million cars and trucks, which was about half of the total Japanese production: 12.3 million. The growth of the automobile industry was of major importance for the development of related and supporting industries, such as steel and other materials producers, die and mould-makers, and the machinery industry. More than half the output of the machine tool industry, for example, was supplied to the automobile industry. Of all competitive Japanese industries, the automobile sector has been the most influential in the west, as a provider of new paradigms for manufacturing organisation, product development and supplier relationships. In the late 1980s, a number of international studies extolled the virtues of Japan's car industry, and the Toyota's manufacturing principles in particular: small-lot production, short set-up-times ('single-minute exchange of dies'), quality assurance at the point of production and a relentless drive to eliminate all stocks and buffers.

An important part of the Toyota production system was the emphasis on continuous, incremental improvement, *kaizen*. The *kaizen* activities seemed to imply a broad involvement of rank-and-file workers; work was standardised but, at the same time, the standards were the subject of constant improvement, and thus Toyota embodied a new type of organisation, 'the learning bureaucracy' (Adler, 1992). Product development was another case of rapid organisational learning and a broad international study revealed a productivity gap in product development similar to the gap in manufacturing efficiency: Japan developed new models in 3.5 years compared to 5 years for Europe's mass producers, and 6 years for its luxury car makers. Japanese makers need 1.7 million engineering hours per average model project, compared to the European average of three million hours (Clark and Fujimoto,

1991). Moreover, the best Japanese makers were able to combine this frugality in resource consumption with an impressive level of product integrity and design quality. Thus, in the late 1980s, a movement to implement the Toyota system wholesale in order to catch up with Japan gained momentum in the west. In Japan, however, there was no jubilation.

COLLAPSE FROM WITHIN: THE CONCERNS OF JAPAN'S AUTOWORKERS

While the MIT book on 'Lean production' (Womack et al., 1990)' was translated into different languages, the Japanese debated the problems of their automobile industry. In 1991, JAW, the Confederation of Japan Automobile Workers' Union, under the leadership of a new chairman from the Toyota Union, published a highly critical study. As a highly unusual measure, this report was also translated into English. JAW argued that the industry needed fundamental reorientation in order to avoid a serious risk of 'collapsing from within': 'The automobile industry is bogged down in triple sufferings – the employees are exhausted, the companies make only a little profit, and the automobile industry is always bashed from abroad' (JAW, 1992: 1–2).

When the yen was sharply appreciated in 1985 (see Chapter 3), there had been a short recession in Japan. But increasing export difficulties were soon compensated by a domestic boom and in 1987–90 car registrations in Japan increased from 3.3 million to 5.1 million. Production volumes and sales revenues increased year by year, but there was one problem. As JAW pointed out, the industry earned very little money, in spite of the boom time. This problem also applied to the industry leader, Toyota. In the peak year 1990, total sales increased from 4.0 to 4.2 million, but the profit margin decreased from 7 to 4% and the decline continued in 1991. Earnings suffered from the ever-expanding number of models, the increasing development expenses and the production of many models in small numbers. Contrary to MIT assertions, flexibility was not free even at Toyota. The problems in the manufacturing system surfaced in administrative and engineering departments. From 1982 to 1991, Toyota's unit volume in Japan increased by 20% and the average product value by much more. This was matched by an increase of the blue-collar count by 18%; the number of white collars, however, increased by as much as 45% (Lillrank, 1994: 17–18). (The figures probably do not take account of Toyota Motor Corporation's sourcing policy. Only 60% of all Toyota cars in Japan are assembled by TMC, the rest by various subsidiaries and affiliated companies such as Kanto Auto Works, Hino Motors and Toyota Auto Body. The extent of outsourcing is not disclosed in Toyota's annual reports.) During the 1970s, physical labour productivity (vehicle/worker) in Japan's motor industry had increased a robust 6.3% per year, but in the 1980s, annual productivity growth slowed down to a meagre 0.3%. Because of the move to more complex models and the proliferation of model variations, labour input per unit tended to increase, and that tendency was particularly strong during the Bubble Boom years of 1987–91 (Fujimoto and Takeishi, 1994: 56, 265). Profits were also squeezed at the other end of the value chain because of a costly sales and distribution system that was heavily dependent on door-sales. In order to survive in a fiercely competitive marketplace, dealers had to carry huge inventories. This exacerbated the problems of widespread discounting. For JAW, the increasing profitability problem during a period of record sales was a serious warning, and a symptom of excessive competition within the industry.

The most publicly debated problem in the industry, however, was the overworked and exhausted workforce. With reference to 'The machine that changed the world', the union report enquired: 'We wonder if the Japanese automobile industry is competitive in the true sense of the word. We need to take into consideration the fact that we work about 2,200 hours each year in order to maintain competitiveness in terms of quality and prices' (JAW, 1992: 17). In a unique survey of a large sample of employees, the union had documented widespread discontent. In response to the question 'Would you recommend your children to get jobs in the automobile industry?', 43% of all respondents answered no, 43% found the question difficult to answer, and only 4% gave a positive response. The pattern was basically the same for all employee categories with sales and service staff actually being most dissatisfied. The main reasons among production workers for a reluctance to recommend the automobile industry were a too intensive work pace, too low wages, too much overtime and holiday work and too much shift and night work (JAW, 1989: 29). As a result of the discontent, the automobile industry faced increasing difficulties in recruiting and keeping young workers, and had to resort more and more to temporary workers. That only aggravated the problems for the regular workers. In 1990–1, turnover during the first year among new hirees soared to 30–40%. Were conditions at automobile plants worse than at plants in, for example, the consumer electronics sector? It is difficult to know. The problems of the automobile firms were highly publicised because they were so entirely dependent on young male workers. In contrast, if female workers at, for example, Matsushita quit, this was not noticed in the media since labour turnover among women has never been an issue in Japan. Another problem of the automobile industry was the heavy burden placed on product development engineers. On average, employees in Japan's major car and component manufacturers worked 2,250 hours per year in 1989–90. The worst case was Hino, a producer of commercial vehicles within the Toyota Group. Here overtime exceeded 500 hours annually.

The third 'suffering' discussed in the JAW report was the increasing trade surplus and trade friction, the fact that 'the automobile industry is always bashed from abroad'. The report concluded:

> If the Japanese automobile industry continues on its present course of production and sales, then the following three outcomes will result: (1) the industry will collapse from the inside, due to the labour shortage and low profits; (2) as a result of the above, the industry will be

reshuffled and reorganized in an unsatisfactory manner; (3) the industry will be isolated not only from the international economic community but also from the Japanese economic community.

(JAW 1992: 17)

The need for reforms within Japan's automobile industry was repeated in the public debate by two sharply critical books written by the management critic Kajiwara and the car reviewer Tokudaiji, the approximate translations being *The Auto Industry Destroys the Country – the 'Justice' of Toyota and Nissan is the Sin of Japan* (1992) and *Reforms of the Short-Term Profit Orientation – Japanese Enterprises Depart from Ugliness* (1993).

AMBITIOUS REFORMS: THE NEW PLANTS OF NISSAN AND TOYOTA

The automobile makers viewed the situation seriously. At a time when the European producers tried to adopt the Japanese methods of the 1980s and abandoned many of the previous efforts to humanise factory work, partly because of the fierce Japanese competition, the Japanese themselves embarked on a process of change. In 1992, Volvo decided to close its innovative Uddevalla and Kalmar plants. The very same year Toyota inaugurated its new Kyushu facility with an assembly shop strikingly similar to original Kalmar ideas. The key themes espoused by the plants constructed by Toyota, Mazda and Nissan during this time were increased automation and a 'worker-friendly' redesign of the production system. Based on plant visits in 1993, we will give some highlights of this important new departure.

'Welcome to Nissan Human Land'

Nissan's operation on the southern island Kyushu started as an engine manufacturing facility in 1975. In 1993 it comprised two complete car factories, two engine 'pavilions' and several component plants, all in all employing 5,500 workers. Total capacity of 600,000 cars per year made Kyushu Nissan's main assembly complex. The 'assembly pavilion no. 2' came on stream in 1992 and is officially called 'The Factory of Dreams'. In the planning of the plant there were three major guiding principles:

1) High flexibility.
2) Good work environment and high safety standards.
3) Friendly to the natural environment.

Advanced equipment was introduced to raise productivity and eliminate heavy tasks. The plant boasted 720 robots, and a 20% degree of automation in final assembly. According to the plant brochure the intent was to raise this level to 'as high as 50% in the future'.

'Farewell to the factory of despair?'

Toyota Tahara is a huge manufacturing complex close to the sea and at a psychologically important distance from Toyota City. In 1993, the site included one moulding shop, two aluminum casting and two machining shops, two body and stamping shops, and four assembly plants. During our visit, a general manager described Toyota's traditional automobile plants as 'three K' plants (the 'three K' symbolising demanding, dangerous and dirty work), and even referred to them as 'factories of despair', using the title of Kamata's famous book of 1973. The proclaimed philosophy of the new body and assembly plants in Tahara was to build high-quality vehicles in modern facilities in a way friendly both to humans beings and the environment. The assembly plant, 'Tahara no. 4', started up in October 1991 and employed 460 workers per shift. The design was different from other Toyota plants, both with respect to technology and layout. Compared to the crammed lean production plants, Tahara no. 4 is unusually spacious. Instead of one long line, the assembly line is divided into eight mini-lines, with a several-minute buffer at the end of each section. The insertion of buffers is a deviation, tantamount to heresy, from the principles of Taichi Ohno, the famous founder of the Toyota Production System. For Ohno stocks and buffers were the most evil kind of *muda* (waste). Management at Tahara motivated the buffers by stressing their importance for effective online quality control and for the goal of making each section self-completing in terms of quality. According to the textbooks on lean production, online quality control is a characteristic of the *traditional* Toyota lines! Obviously, Toyota's experience differed from the textbooks. In fact, the introduction of buffers facilitated the operation of important principles of the system, for example, the right and obligation of workers to stop the line by pulling the red Andon chord if quality problems cannot be solved. At the traditional one-kilometre-long lines, there were strong psychological inhibitions to really using the red Andon. At the plants with short and buffered lines, workers seemed to be using the Andon much more frequently.

Tahara also departed from traditional Toyota policies in its technological strategy. Ohno was an ardent proponent of incremental, low-cost improvements. Tahara took another route by its large-scale investments in automation. Further, Tahara put much more effort into improving ergonomics than traditional Toyota plants, where ergonomics were never an important consideration. At critical sections in Tahara, the car body is mounted on dollies with elevators to ensure comfortable positions. Much of the new equipment has been expensive, especially the automated sections. Management justified the investments on the basis of the plant's high quality and personnel stability. In 1992, none of the employees hired during the year left the plant. In 1993, 10% of the annual intake quit – still much lower than Toyota's average that year: 25%.

Toyota Kyushu – a fresh start

Toyota Kyushu is located deep in the countryside of this southern island. The company has taken great care to integrate the plant into its beautiful natural surroundings, choosing a colour, for example, that harmonises with the usually cloudy sky. Opened in December 1992, the plant added a second shift in August 1993. In November, 2,000 employees produced the up-market model Mark II at an annual rate of 150,000 cars. The facilities comprise a full car plant – stamping, body, paint and assembly – as well as two component plants. Kyushu is not a branch plant of Toyota Motor Corporation but incorporated as a separate subsidiary. This provides leeway for testing new solutions. The plant is more automated than a traditional 'Ohno' plant, but less advanced than Tahara, which reduced the construction costs by 20% compared to Tahara. The main innovations at the plant are not in technology but in areas such as working hours, the pay system, suggestion schemes and management style. Several of these changes were later introduced at other Toyota plants, especially the new shift system, but the Kyushu operation was the most articulated exponent of a new way within Toyota in the early 1990s. Hence we will analyse its features in some detail.

The plant operates on two shifts. They work in a so-called 'continuous shift system', the first shift 06.00–14.50, the second 15.05–23.55. In the traditional system in Japanese automobile plants, there is one day and one night shift, with several hours between the end of one shift and the start of the next. These hours are used for overtime, often assigned at very short notice. This has constituted a very important buffer in the lean production system. In the continuous shift system, this time buffer does not exist, which means that production pressure has to be alleviated. In 1993, 49 people, or 3% of Kyushu's production workers were women. With the previous shift system it was not possible to employ women, since Japanese law forbids female employees to work night shifts. The recruitment of female workers was important from the perspective of public relations. After years of criticism for greediness and arrogance, Toyota wanted to portray itself as a friendly company, where even women can work on the line.

Traditionally, Toyota placed a very strong emphasis on productivity incentives. Pay was calculated on the basis of cars in relation to the standard time in a *kumi* (a section headed by a shopfloor supervisor, *kumicho*). Thus the pay could be boosted if *kumicho* worked on the line, and so they did. In the mid-1980s, this became a growing problem, since *kumicho* tended to neglect their supervisory tasks (Nomura, 1993b). At Toyota, Kyushu abolished productivity pay completely in favour of an a individualised evaluation system. The suggestion scheme was also revamped. At Toyota's traditional plants, there are usually high targets for employee suggestions. Each year these targets are revised and new ones calculated, based on the previous year's number plus a certain percentage. At Kyushu, management was not interested in numbers of suggestions and accordingly there were no targets at all. Workers should demonstrate that their suggestions will result in a real rationalisation before submitting them.

Kyushu has taken the redesign of the assembly process further than Tahara. The assembly line is divided into 11 mini-lines, each constituting a *kumi*. Breaking with the Ohno doctrine, there is a five-car buffer at the end of each mini-line. The idea was to make each line responsible for one complete function of the car, for example engine dress-up and mounting, or the assembly of the electrical system ('functional assembly' in Swedish parlance, and one of the original ideas of the Volvo Kalmar plant). The purpose was to give the *kumi* a clear sense of purpose, a possibility that, according to Kyushu managers, did not exist elsewhere at Toyota. Management tried to locate heavy machinery and equipment at the outer ends of the mini-lines, and concentrate workers in the centre of the line. In that way it is easier for supervisors to exercise control and contact, and encourage assemblers to work hard: '*Gambare!*' At each mini-line there is an inspection station staffed by a specially trained operator. Each team (*kumi*) is responsible for its own line. As a result, there is less reworking at the end of the assembly process. On the traditional long Toyota lines, assembly workers who discover an error mark it on the car, and subsequent workers do not continue the assembly of that particular component, which is often perceived as frustrating. Only at the end of the line is it possible to complete the car. Like Nissan, Toyota Kyushu also emphasises its ergonomic innovations, such as the height-adjustable car platforms and the tilting of the bodies which takes place on some mini-lines.

A central idea of Toyota's traditional personnel policies was that the alienation originating from the repetitive mass-production work should be compensated for by human relation activities *after* work (Nohara, 1991). These policies were developed in the 1960s, when Toyota expanded rapidly and recruited thousands of young workers from rural areas who found it difficult to adapt to the hard and monotonous work. One interviewed *kacho* elaborated on the different management style at Kyushu:

> Kyushu will not adopt the human relation activities of the traditional Toyota type. There are many problems connected with these activities which consume nearly all the free time there is. People always see the same faces, and they all tend to think and behave in the same way. It is such a closed society. When Monday comes, you have to say to yourself, 'now it is work', otherwise you would not notice it. Here, at Kyushu, we want to have more of a separation between working hours and 'free hours'. We think that the work itself should be more humane. In Aichi [Toyota City] there was always less manning than needed. That made work very painful for the employees. For Kyushu, automation is not a goal in itself. Attractive work is the important thing. In Aichi there is always pressure from management to participate in 'voluntary activities'. This has resulted in problems, and the attendance rate at these activities is falling. Here we don't have that pressure. Yet, when the company organised a sports event recently, 100% of the employees

attended. At Toyota, Aichi, there is always the manual. People grow conservative, and are afraid of failures. Here there is freshness, and that is a big motivation.

DIFFICULT TRANSITION TO ZERO GROWTH

Nissan Kyushu and Toyota Tahara and Kyushu represented ambitious attempts to reform and improve assembly work in the Japanese automobile industry. The same was true for Mazda's second Hofu plant which started operation in 1992. Unfortunately, the high-tech approach of these plants turned out to be very expensive. Nissan's new 'assembly pavilion' in Kyushu was estimated to be 2.5 times more expensive than a conventional plant, and the extra cost of Tahara was of the same magnitude. To recover the high fixed costs the new plants were heavily dependent on full-capacity utilisation. In the overoptimistic atmosphere of the Bubble Boom this was taken for granted. During their first year of operation, however, business conditions turned out be completely different from the situation at the time of their inception. This prompted a major reassessment of the automation strategy. In the 1980s, the degree of factory automation increased for each new model launch – in Japan as well as in Europe. After the burst of the Bubble Boom this trend had been reversed. When Toyota launched its new recreational vehicle RAV4 at the renovated Motomachi plant in 1994, the level of automation was significantly lower than at Tahara. The degree of automation in the body shop, for example, is only 70%, compared to 98% at Tahara. One reason is that robots did not save as many workers as expected. Another is that it is easier to adapt to volume changes in plants with lower automation, and that less advanced equipment means a much lower break-even level.

No more expansion in Japan

The new Nissan and Toyota facilities in Kyushu and Tahara and Mazda's second Hofu plant will probably be the last new plants constructed by any Japanese automobile maker for a long time. The era of domestic expansion has come to an end. As early as 1985, exports from Japan started to decline. Five years later, exports had fallen by more than a million vehicles. Initially, the slide in exports was compensated for by the brisk domestic demand. Total production in Japan actually increased from 12. 4 million in the fiscal year 1985 to 13.6 million in 1990. That was the peak year. Because of the surging yen, exports continued to decline, and in 1991 domestic demand also started to fall. In contrast to previous downturns the automobile makers could find no new growth market of significance. In the four years 1991–5, production fell by more three million units. Table 6.1 summarises production and export data, 1985–95.

Table 6.1 Vehicle production (cars, trucks and buses) in Japan, 1985–95 (millions)

Year	Exports	Domestic registration	Total production
1985	6.7	5.6	12.3
1986	6.6	5.7	12.3
1987	6.3	6.0	12.2
1988	6.1	6.7	12.7
1989	5.9	7.3	13.0
1990	5.8	7.8	13.5
1991	5.8	7.5	13.2
1992	5.7	7.0	12.5
1993	5.0	6.5	11.3
1994	4.5	6.1	10.6
1995	3.8	6.4	10.2

Source: *Jidosha Sangyo Handobuku*, 1993. (*Handbook of the Japanese Automobile Industry* (in Japanese)); *Jidosha Shinbunsha Tokyo*, various years; *Automotive News*, 29 January 1996.

More serious than the sharp decline during the recession is that an upturn is not predicted – even in the long term. According to the Industrial Bank of Japan, domestic production will not exceed 11 million by the year 2000 (Kato, 1993a). This zero-growth situation is completely new for Japanese automobile makers, who experienced 40 years of almost uninterrupted expansion. In the Bubble Boom, virtually all manufacturers expanded their plants. After the burst of the bubble overcapacity has become an endemic problem. In 1993–4, the operating ratio at Nissan's new 'assembly pavilion' in Kyushu hovered around 50%, far below break-even level. The highly automated body shop at Toyota Tahara operated at 30% of full capacity, the assembly shop at 50%, rendering both of them unprofitable. Also Toyota Kyushu was operating below economic optimum and, in 1994, workers had to be sent on *shukko* to other Toyota facilities. Mazda's Hofu plant no. 2 needs 90% capacity utilisation to break even; in 1995 the operating ratio was less than 30%, on good days! (Kinutani, 1993; Toga, 1995). In the Japanese market, new niche vehicles, such as Toyota's and Mitsubishi Motors' recreational cars, sold very well, but overall domestic sales were recovering slowly. The situation was aggravated by the new *endaka* in the mid-1990s and the accelerated decline in exports. In 1995, Nissan closed its Zama plant, the first plant closing ever in Japan's motor industry. Several analysts argued that there was an excess capacity for at least three million units, and that more plants must be laid idle; some of them, for example Lehman Brothers, were very pessimistic: 'Zama plant is only the first one . . . They have to scrap 10 plants at least' (Sumiya, 1995a).

Other observers were more optimistic and pointed to the fact that when production was at its peak in 1990, the industry was operating far above its normal capacity with overtime requirements that were not sustainable. A shortening of labour hours from 2,300 per year to 2,000 (the US standard) means a reduction of production by almost 2 million vehicles compared to the level in 1990, without laying off any workers. As we will see later, this is in part how the Japanese makers have reacted to the recession. Further, if no new plants will be constructed in Japan, old factories have to be renovated and then some extra plants are needed in order to meet production schedules. This perspective points to the long-term adjustment capability of the Japanese industry. The problem in 1993–5 was the coincidence of several adverse factors – domestic stagnation, declining exports because of a soaring yen and a reborn western competitiveness.

THE WESTERN CATCH-UP

Whereas productivity growth in the Japanese automobile industry stagnated in the late 1980s and early 1990s, western manufacturers made determined efforts to close the performance gap by systematising and implementing Japanese methods. This 'reverse catch-up' is reflected in MIT's second international assembly plant study covering productivity and quality performance at 88 plants worldwide in 1993–4 and comparing the data with a corresponding survey in 1989 (MacDuffie and Pil, 1996). According to this study, there had been a significant closing of the gap: on average, European plants had improved from 36.9 to 25.3 assembly hours per vehicle, a productivity increase of 30%; US-owned plants in the USA had improved by 13% whereas plants in Japan had only improved by 4%, from 16.8 to 16.2 hours per vehicle. In terms of quality, measured as the number of assembly-related customer complaints per 100 cars sold in the USA, European makers had improved from 91 to 61 defects, US makers from 86 to 63 and Japanese makers from 63 to 55 defects per 100 cars. Again Europe had improved the most (33% defect reduction), and Japan the least (13%). Overall, Japanese companies remained leaders in quality, productivity and in their capability in handling model mix variety; however, the differences between companies within countries tended to be much larger than average differences between countries.

Another follow-up study traces the western catch-up efforts in product development performance (Ellison et al., 1995). The previous study by Clark and Fujimoto (1991), which was referred to above, compared projects where the models were introduced in the period 1980–7. The follow-up study covers the development of models introduced in 1991–3 in Japan and in 1990–5 in Europe. Overall, the new study found a strong pattern of convergence, both in performance and in organisational pattern (see Table 6.2).

Table 6.2 The western catch-up

| | Engineering time per project* | | | Total lead-time in months* | | |
	Japan	USA	Europe	Japan	USA	Europe
1980s	1.7	3.4	2.9	45	61	59
1990–5	2.1	2.3	2.8	55	52	56

Note: *adjusted for project complexity.
Source: Ellison et al., 1995.

The US catch-up is remarkable. From a 2:1 gap in engineering productivity in the 1980s, performance in the early 1990s has become basically equal. The Europeans have been moving more slowly. One reason is probably that their catch-up effort started later – North America was exposed earlier to the Japanese onslaught. Another reason might be that the European sample consisted of significantly more complex projects than the American, which was not entirely compensated for by the statistical adjustments. In total product quality the European producers were fairly close to the Japanese average, but there was still a considerable gap between Japan and the USA. The USA–Japan gap is reflected in J. D. Power's ranking of car models according to customer satisfaction in the USA. Here Japanese models consistently occupy the leading positions. In 1993 and 1994, Lexus, Toyota and Infiniti commanded the three top positions in Power's survey of initial customer satisfaction; in 1995, Infiniti, Lexus, Acura, Honda and Toyota occupied all the five first ranks (Rechtin, 1994; Wernle, 1995).

The remarkable reduction of total lead-time in the US industry was a result of shorter planning cycles (time spent in product planning and concept development) and a successful adoption of simultaneous engineering, resulting in much more overlap between the planning and engineering stages. This was mainly an organisational feat. Chrysler's way of bringing together all major organisational functions in integrated platform teams is an example (Scott, 1994). The engineering lead-time as such (product development, process engineering, pilot production and ramp-up) was not changed in any radical way. In terms of manufacturing capability and effective supplier co-operation the Japanese industry also remained superior in Clark and Fujimoto's follow-up study. Thus the Japanese retained a strong lead in lead-time for prototypes (6 months versus 9–12 months in Europe and the USA) and dies (15 months compared to 23 months in Europe and 20 in the USA). However, Japanese makers spent more time in concept development than they did in the 1980s, and there was less overlap between the planning and engineering stages. Consequently total product development time increased considerably. How is this decline in performance to be explained?

In the late 1980s, Japanese firms had gone too far in their strive for ever-increasing product quality and had fallen into the trap of overengineering, or 'fat design'. In Japan this was called the 'Lexus-syndrome'. Following the initial success of Acura, Lexus and Infiniti, R&D engineers at all divisions wanted to upgrade their models. Obviously, this affected development productivity adversely, and as Ellison et al. (1995: 19) observed, it created 'a tension between the development of excellent individual projects and the ability to co-ordinate and share costs across a coherent portfolio of projects'. The sudden end of the Bubble Boom, and the necessity to refocus on product cost and price initially resulted in a state of confusion within many manufacturers. The product development process had to be reassessed and the independence of individual projects curbed in favour of product platform management. This painful process was reflected in increased planning and concept development lead-times. While they were closing the gap in product lead-time, western producers also strengthened their traditional advantage in important product areas, such as safety features. The surge in demand for airbags and side-impact protection in the mid-1990s left the Japanese producers behind. One reason was the lack of rigorous standards and testing procedures in Japan, and the weakness of organised consumer opinion and, in general, product-liability legislation. In this area the producerist orientation of Japanese industrialism resulted in a lack of powerful drivers for advanced product development.

RESPONSE IN THE RECESSION: RETOOLING THE LEAN MACHINE!

Was the stagnating productivity in manufacturing and development in the early 1990s a sign that the Japanese automobile makers 'had hit the development frontier'? The trend after the burst of the Bubble points to another explanation: after a period of distraction the Japanese industry is back in the productivity race, and the western catch-up might be temporary. The recession and *endaka* have unleashed sweeping rationalisation programmes among the Japanese automobile makers, from plants to R&D departments. Operations are streamlined. Indirect activities are especially singled out for cost-down efforts. At Daihatsu, a small car specialist in the Toyota Group, for example, total employment stood at 12,000 in 1995. Half of them were direct production workers, half white-collar employees or indirect production workers employed in maintenance, trial production, etc. As part of the company's three-year cost-down programme, these 'indirect employees' will be reduced by 1,000. The target for manufacturing productivity is a 6% increase per year, in spite of stagnating or falling volumes. At the same time, products are scrutinised by means of value engineering in order to reduce component costs and eliminate unnecessary variation. The same approach is applied to machines and facilities.

Most important however, are the efforts to 're-lean' the product development in order to reduce product costs, compress the development cycle and start the manufacturing of new models even more efficiently than before. As we have seen above, the Japanese industry also remained superior in engineering lead-time after the US catch-up in the early 1990s. In this new round, Japan's automobile makers are trying to make product and process engineering even more effective by cutting out as much as six months of the engineering lead-time. Comprehensive computerisation has become an important tool to reduce cost and time in product development. By using computer-aided engineering, crashes can be simulated and the number of trial cars reduced. Previously, the CAD database of the R&D department could not be used directly for die-making. Because of improved data accuracy Toyota, for example, now utilises an integrated product database. Dies can be produced directly from the design database, which significantly reduces engineering lead-time. The drive for shorter lead-time is also profiting from the business slump. During the Bubble all resources were scarce, workers as well as die-making capacity. In the recession the waiting time for dies has fallen markedly.

At Daihatsu, a new Move model was introduced in 1995. This car was developed in 20 months from the freezing of the styling to mass production. For the next model with the same high ratio of carry-over (60%) the target is 15 months. For a completely new car the target is 20 months. Toyota has set the same target. According to estimates by Fujimoto (personal communication, 12 September 1995), the total development lead-time in Japan was likely to range from 25 to 35 months in 1996. The time from model freeze to production was only 15–25 months, a significant improvement since 1991–93 (the period of the latest international comparison). New ways are devised for organising the planning process in order to shorten concept development; one approach is to run several concept development teams in parallel. At the other end of the process, production ramp-up is streamlined to an almost incredible extent. Toyota's results are especially impressive. In the mid-1970s, at the time of the first oil crisis, the plants had to be shut down for one month to install new equipment when a new Corolla was introduced. The shutdown time was subsequently reduced to one week, and in 1995 equipment was installed in only two to three days. The set-up was prepared outside the production line by maintenance workers and production engineers who spend much time (especially during weekends) on this. When mass production actually starts, there is normally a loss of output during the first week. For several years, production during the first week was 70% of the normal output. With the introduction of the new Corolla in 1995, the production rate during the first week was as high as 90%! The goal is 100% – a vertical production ramp-up. Honda has set the same target, both in Japan and for its US factories. Other companies have not been equally effective in standardising model change; one month still seems to be the norm for reaching normal output and quality after the launch of a new model. There is a downside to vertical production ramp-up, which was explained by managers at one company in the Toyota Group:

> Now the launch of a new model has become so boring for the plant. Previously, the introduction of a new model was a festival. There were so many things that did not work, parts that did not arrive; many people had no time to sleep, but it was fascinating and they enjoyed it. Now it is nothing special at all, just like ordinary production.

The most important goal for the new product development processes is not shorter lead-time, however, but reduced product costs. To achieve this, the role of the previously so powerful *shusa* (the chief engineer of a project) is de-emphasised, and synergies across models are stressed. From expertise in single-project management, Japanese automobile makers are now devising structures for multiproject management. Toyota, for example, has divided its huge development organisation, which used to employ 10,000 engineers, into four different centres comprising 2,000 people each (three vehicle centres and one components centre). In this way, the company has installed a multimatrix organisation similar to Ford's international development system. Across the industry, parts commonality has top priority. Honda, for example, has created so-called large project leaders to oversee the chief engineers: 'We spent more money on the 1990 Accord than we had ever spent in the past . . . We learned a lesson from that' (Johnson, 1994a). As a result, the Accord introduced in 1994 has 50% commonality compared to 10% for the 1990 model. The year 1994 was the first year when the savings of the reoriented product development came into effect. According to calculations by Fujimoto (1995), Toyota incurred a 160 billion yen cost increase this year because of the surging yen, but was able to offset 150 billion because of more frugal product design. With a four-year product cycle, the full impact of this first wave of cost-saving designs will have materialised in 1997, when all major models will have been redesigned. This is not the end of the cost-reduction programmes, however. Reversing the up-grading trend of the 1980s, Japanese makers seem to have embarked on a long-term journey of 'decontenting', eliminating low-volume options, taking out technological gadgetry, and replacing and simplifying expensive components. Honda, for example, has eliminated four-wheel steering for some models and replaced four-wheel disc brakes by disc–drum combinations, Nissan has taken away independent rear suspension, Mitsubishi has shelved plans of expensive engine options and so forth (Rechtin, 1996a). 'Decontenting' was implemented as a defensive strategy during the height of the *endaka*, when the yen:dollar exchange rate was approaching 80:1. In 1996, when the yen was diving below the 100:1 mark, the cost reduction achieved by these measures was used as a basis for a renewed offensive in the market. In the USA, Japanese makers announced significant price cuts for their new models, amounting to several thousand dollars per model (Rechtin, 1996b).

The challenge for the car makers is to maintain a balance between cost and content reduction and consumer appeal. In 1995, Toyota failed in this respect. During the Bubble Boom, the company suffered from the Lexus syndrome and overengineered its models. In the recession, the company went to the other extreme, and single-mindedly focused on cost savings. In this the company remained true to its reputation of being an efficient, but conformist machine. The new cars introduced in 1995, especially the bread-and-butter Corolla model, were perceived as unimaginative and uninspiring by Japanese consumers. Sales declined and Toyota's market share fell below 40% for the first time in ten years. The virtue of the compressed development time, however, is the possibility to redesign a product rapidly which has not reached its sales target and to catch up in neglected areas, such as safety.

Another challenge is the changing consumer behaviour in Japan, which to some extent is a consequence of market saturation. A manager at Daihatsu, interviewed in September 1995, explained the new situation in the following way:

Previously it was easy to sell new cars, you just had to upgrade the next model. Now consumers are much more selective. You have to add real value and be distinctive. Some new models are best-sellers overnight, others fail miserably. It is very difficult to predict. The new Move, for example, has become an instant best-seller. Within one month after the launch, orders for 40,000 cars had been booked. Production for more than six months had been sold out, because our initial production capacity was only 6,000 per month. We, as all other makers in Japan, have become very cautious in our capacity planning because of the recession. Now we had to do everything to increase capacity. Within one month, the company succeeded in increasing production by 60% still far short of demand.

Toyota has experienced a similar demand surge for its RAV4 vehicle, whereas several other models have failed. This unpredictability means that volume flexibility and ability to change production mix rapidly are of crucial importance in order to exploit unforeseen market opportunities. Compared to western rivals, Japan's automobile makers were already well ahead in flexible manufacturing. The current challenge will take their capacity for flexible adjustment to a new level.

ACCELERATED INTERNATIONALISATION

In the competitive see-saw game of the global automobile industry, the Japanese had lost much of their lead in productivity, quality and development lead-time by the early 1990s. With the burst of the Bubble Boom and the new *endaka* their competitive position was seriously challenged. The decline is temporary. In the recession, Japanese makers have become more competitive in virtually all aspects: in operating efficiency, development lead-time and product costs, and on top of that flexibility! However, because of exchange rate factors and problems of trade friction this will not translate into a new export boom, which could safeguard domestic Japanese production. Instead, Japanese makers will accelerate their internationalisation. From 1985 to 1994, Japanese production in North America increased from 360,000 vehicles to 2.5 million, and the trend is set to continue. In mid-1995, Toyota unveiled plans to raise production in the USA by 50% to 1.1 million by 1998. Honda announced that its US production will increase from 610,000 to 720,000 in 1994–7, plus a 50% increase in automobile engine production. In Europe the level of penetration is much lower. In the UK, the major Japanese production base, output totalled 330,000 cars in 1994. Further expansion was planned, but Japanese makers seem to be more focused on the new growth markets in Asia. Several of them, for example Thailand and Indonesia, are practically owned by the Japanese industry. In Thailand alone, total sales were predicted to pass 500,000 vehicles in 1995, and to double by the year 2000. Japanese models enjoy a 70% market share, and for Toyota, Thailand is its third most important market (*Asahi Evening News*, 30 September 1995). The annual demand for vehicles in Thailand, Indonesia, Malaysia and the Philippines is expected to reach 1.9 million by the year 2000. The Japanese makers will mainly serve these markets by local production. Toyota will double its production in southeast Asia from 220,000 in 1994 to 410,000 in 1998. By this year both Toyota and Honda will offer specially designed, low-cost Asian cars to the new-growth markets (Sumiya, 1995b). The Japanese makers will be able to take advantage of a comprehensive regional supplier network, developed over a long period by Japanese parts makers. Apart from Korea, the only exception to Japanese predominance in Asia is China. Here firms from France and Germany have gained a strong foothold, but Japanese makers are making inroads here too, and Toyota has announced plans to build local manufacturing bases in the other remaining big markets, such as India and Brazil (Isaka, 1996). In 1995, Japanese vehicle production abroad exceeded exports for the first time, and this relocation trend is set to continue. At the same time, however, operations in Japan remain a crucial concern and automobile makers strive hard to maintain domestic production volumes in spite of falling exports. In 1996 all major manufacturers announced efforts to strengthen domestic sales by increasing their investments in new-product development and in dealer networks. In the absence of any large-scale consolidation within the industry, these programmes will reinforce the historic pattern of intensive competition and rapid performance improvement in the Japanese automobile industry.

A DIFFERENT FORM OF PERSONNEL ADJUSTMENT

For 40 years, the Japanese industry and its system of employment relations, internal labour market and career systems had been dependent on constant growth, more so than any of its counterparts. Suddenly growth disappeared, but the regained competitiveness of the Japanese industry is small comfort for its Japanese employees, since the long-term outlook for domestic production is so bleak. According to officers at JAW's industrial policy unit interviewed in September 1995, this is quite a new situation: 'We sounded the alarm already in 1991, but never thought that it could be so serious.' For the Japanese automobile industry, the post-Bubble crisis is not just a long recession but also signifies the end of an era. However, in spite of the difficult situation caused by several years of output decline and domestic zero-growth prospects, the employment situation in the Japanese companies has remained remarkably stable. During the crises of the 1980s in Europe and the USA, tens of thousands of workers were laid off, and dozens of plants closed. By contrast, more than three years of recession in Japan only resulted in one assembly plant closure and in no outright lay-off measure. In 1994, the industry as a whole employed 850,000 people, of them 300,000 at the 11 vehicle assemblers and engine manufacturers (including Yamaha and Nissan Diesel). Since the peak, employment at the assembly companies had decreased slightly, but the main supplier companies actually increased their employment from 1992 to 1994. During the Bubble Boom, the labour market was so tight, that supplier firms could not recruit all the workers they needed, so they also continued recruiting after the onset of the recession.

Further, supplier makers were not affected adversely by overseas production in the same way as the assemblers. Export to overseas transplants is still a good business for Japanese suppliers – which is reflected in the trade friction with the USA. For the assembly companies, however, the question remains: how could they absorb a drop in output from 13.5 to 10.5 million?

In 1990, Gerhard Bosch, a German expert on working time, tried to calculate the effectiveness of various buffers. One important buffer would be variation in overtime. According to Bosch, the extreme level of overtime in the boom year of 1990 would enable firms to reduce output by 20% in a subsequent downturn:

> Moreover, firms can allow the employment contracts of temporary workers to expire, which . . . represents a potential reduction in capacity of a further 10 per cent. An additional source of capacity reduction is [to urge workers to use] unclaimed holiday entitlement . . . All in all, Japanese manufacturers are able to reduce output by up to 30 percent in recessionary times.
>
> (Bosch, 1995: 350)

The disadvantages for employees in this system, according to Bosch, was that there would neither be any permanent reduction in working time nor any decoupling of operating hours and individual working time. These calculations have turned out to be fairly accurate, although somewhat optimistic, since they assumed that overtime would be reduced to zero during the business trough. This has not been the case, because of uneven demand for different models and big differences between manufacturers (Bosch assumed that all manufacturers would be hit by the recession to the same extent) (see Table 6.3).

Table 6.3 Overtime in the Japanese automobile industry 1990 and 1994

	Total working time (hours)	Average	Overtime Highest	Lowest
1990	2,246	352	529 (Hino)	210 (Honda)
1994	2,006	168	305 (Hino)	111 (Honda)

Source: JAW (1994).

The average reduction in total working time was 240 hours, corresponding to an 11% decrease in output. In 1990, Toyota, Nissan, Mazda and Mitsubishi all had more than 400 hours overtime. In 1994, Toyota and Nissan were down to 120 hours, whereas Mitsubishi, whose recreational vehicles were selling very well, reported 220 hours of overtime. Honda has always been an exception, by utilising much less overtime than the other car makers.

Another important buffer has been to reduce the number of temporary workers. In 1990, 8% of the total workforce of Japan's vehicle assemblers were temporary workers. In 1994, this proportion had dropped to 3%. Figure 6.1 demonstrates how Daihatsu has utilised this mechanism to preserve

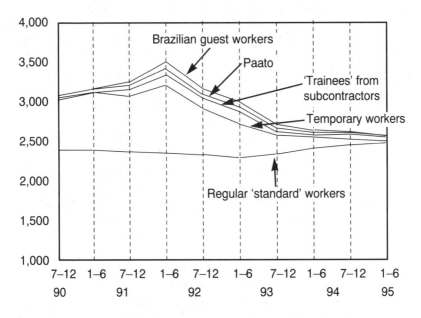

Figure 6.1   Stability of core employment at Daihatsu, Ikeda plant 1990–95

the level of regular workers intact, in spite of an output decline from 900,000 vehicles in 1990 to 670,000 in 1994. It must be remembered, however, that the use of temporaries as an employment buffer was no planned personnel policy measure. During the peak time, the industry could simply not recruit as many regular workers as it needed, because of the tight labour market in general and the low reputation of factory work in particular. The companies were more or less forced to recruit temporary workers, which caused considerable problems for shopfloor relations, especially the *kaizen* and quality-control activities (see below). All in all, less overtime and fewer temporary contracts reduced labour input by 16% in 1991–4, an important contribution to adjustment, but not enough. Another traditional adjustment mechanism has been to send employees, both white collar and blue collar, on *shukko* to sales companies. These *shukko* periods are normally three years. According to industry sources, the productivity of these dispatched employees is generally not so high as professional salesmen, but at least they bring some contributions to revenues and the cost for their wages is there anyway. Further, when they return (if they do), these employees have valuable experience of direct contacts with customers, and a new attitude to their old workplaces. From 1990 to 1994 the number of employees on *shukko* increased by 6,000, thus contributing to another 2% adjustment. It is often said that the large Japanese companies use their suppliers as a buffer during recessions, by sending excess employees to them. The evolving pattern is more complex, however. During our fieldwork in the Japanese automobile industry in September 1995, we did not come across such transfers; on the contrary, several vehicle assemblers had had to take on excess employees from their suppliers, who could not support them any more.

In sum, the measures analysed by Bosch have been important but not sufficient to avoid 'underemployment' of regular employees in several sectors of the industry. The difference between the Japanese industry and its western counterparts is that in Japan there is no recourse to rapid 'downsizing' measures. Natural attrition and reduced hiring are important measures at almost all companies. At Daihatsu, for example, total recruitment fell from 1,080 in 1990 to 120 in 1995. For the first time since the company was listed on the Tokyo Stock Exchange in 1951, Nissan did not hire any university graduates for clerical posts during the annual spring recruitment in 1994 (Sumiya, 1994b). At Toyota, 800 new university graduates entered the company in 1992. For 1996, the company only planned to recruit 140, the lowest level since 1982. This kind of mechanism is typical of the slow and gradual adjustment taking place among Japanese core companies. To some extent, the two loss-making companies Mazda and Nissan have encouraged 'early retirement' among their older employees, sweetening their offers with generous retirement allowances. But even when, in February 1993, Nissan announced its decision to shut down the Zama plant, it stuck to its gradualist approach. During a period of widening corporate losses Nissan worked hard to find jobs for each of its Zama employees in its facilities in Kyushu, Oppama, Murayama, Yokohama, at Nissan Shatai, etc.: 'We consulted with each employee three times or more', according to a Nissan spokesman (Lashinsky, 1995). The position of Toyota is much more robust than Nissan's or Mazda's. However, because of sliding sales and market share in Japan, there was considerable pain at the periphery of the Toyota Group in 1994–5, in companies such as Kanto Auto Works or Daihatsu. Kanto produced 470,000 vehicles in 1990; four years later output was down to 310,000. Typical of the slow and careful adjustment process, however, was the fact that employment had remained essentially stable – 6,200 regular employees in 1990; 6,600 in 1995. Kanto Auto Works was trying to endure the crisis, betting on an upturn in sales. Meanwhile the pressure for personnel adjustment was mounting. In September 1995, all the measures discussed above had been taken, but the company had to go further. The second shift was reduced from eight to six hours, but in order to avoid a corresponding reduction in pay, management introduced a two-hour overlap between the first and the second shifts. These two hours were spent on education and 'morale-up'.

One of the problems of using natural attrition as an adjustment mechanism is that this will increase the average age of the employees. In the traditional Japanese wage structure, where the *nenko* or seniority component is very important, higher average age means an automatic increase in labour costs. This was one of the reasons for a renewed interest in wage reform in the automobile industry in the mid-1990s, with merit pay being a popular catchword in the business press (see Chapter 5). JAW acknowledged the need for changes, the problem being how to change the old system. One way might be for companies to introduce a 'two-line system', where already-employed workers continue to enjoy the *nenko* system, whereas new recruits will be paid by performance. Feeling the pressure of the *endaka* in 1995, JAW for the first time put forward the idea of work-sharing, a popular proposal with the German trade union movement in the 1980s, but previously always rejected by the Japanese. Interestingly enough, this idea gained support from the chairman of the Japan Automobile Manufacturers' Association, incidentally also a vice chairman at Toyota: 'One choice may be work-sharing. Negotiations have not taken place on this issue yet. But sooner or later, employees and employers – together – will have seriously to tackle this question' (Mori, 1995). Another way of stabilizing employment was to send workers from depressed to prosperous companies, from Kanto Auto to Hino within the Toyota Group for example. An idea publicly discussed in 1995 was to expand this 'worker swapping' on a larger scale to include also exchange across the group boundaries.

REVIVING TRADITIONAL OHNOISM?

In spite of the severe recession and the prospects of zero growth, the majority of the adopted personnel adjustment measures have been traditional – the partial change in the *nenko* wage system is the only major exception. At the same time, the pressure for workplace reforms of the kind JAW championed in the late 1980s has abated. The changing priorities are spelled out by an industry policy strategist at JAW interviewed in September 1995: 'To my knowledge, the work intensity in Japan's auto industry is still the highest in the world, but now the problem of employment security overrides all other issues. To create an attractive workplace is still important, but speaking frankly, management has neither the time, nor the money.' Recruitment problems are no longer an imminent concern. Will the recession and the new financial conservatism result in a retreat to traditional 'Ohnoism', with its emphasis on constant shopfloor rationalisation and production without any material or human buffers? Certainly, the reassessment of the automation strategy and the adoption of low-cost solutions of the type employed by Toyota's renovated Motomachi plant are in line with the Ohno tradition. A return full scale to the traditional Toyota style of line design, management and labour deployment is difficult to accomplish, however. Paradoxically, the most orthodox representative of Ohnoism now seems to be the Kentucky complex of Toyota Motor Manufacturing USA (see Mishina, 1994: 11). The traditional Toyota philosophy depended on standardised production and work. This was combined with human relation activities and quality circles after work in order to keep up the motivation of production workers. The backbone of the Toyota-style shopfloor rationalisation, *kaizen*, was not this circle activity, however, but the constant efforts of the *kumicho*, the first-line foremen, and *hancho*, the subforemen or 'team leaders' to devise more effective methods and tools. This process seemed to work very effectively until the late 1980s, but thereafter it has encountered increasing difficulties. This was borne out by production and personnel managers in a Toyota Group company on a plant visit in 1995:

> Previously, *kumicho* and *hancho* always gathered together for *kaizen* after work. They had a very good knowledge of the production system, so they could often discover improvements, for example hand-made automation of such good quality that they could apply for a patent. In the Bubble Boom, the demand on output was increasing all the time. We had to recruit many temporary workers and pay them much higher wages than regular workers. This destroyed morale on the shopfloor. The turnover of new recruits was 40%, and *kumicho* and *hancho* were occupied by problems in personnel management instead of doing *kaizen*. Now, there are no temporaries at all, but *kaizen* has not recovered. Theoretically, it is possible to restart *kaizen*, but in reality it is difficult, both for technical and social reasons. Electronics and robots have become black boxes for *kumicho* and *hancho*, they are only open for production engineers. The attitude of production engineers *vis-à-vis* the *kumicho* and *hancho* is 'don't touch it'. Another reason for the problems of *kaizen* is the change in social values. Many production workers are not interested in the Quality Control Circles, they want to go home directly after work. These attitudes persist in spite of the recession, and there is no sign of a return of traditional values. Young workers have formed their attitudes before entering the company. They come here only to earn money.

At this company, the ideal was that *kumicho* should spend 80% of their time on *kaizen* and 20% on direct management. *Hancho* should spend 20% on *kaizen* and 80% on running the organisation. A survey in 1993 revealed a different picture: *kumicho* only spent a third of their time on *kaizen*, and *hancho* only a tenth. The main activity for both of them was production administration. At highly automated lines, this tendency was most pronounced; the function of *kumicho* and *hancho* was just to collect and administer data. The attitude survey of 1993 was a shock for management, because it revealed that the morale of *kumicho* was so low. Another problem was the increasing age of *kumicho*. From 1990 to 1995 their average age increased from 40 to 45 years. To halt the increasing age gap between *kumicho/hancho* and rank-and-file-workers, the company planned to introduce a new system. Older *kumichos* will be transferred to a new category of 'specialists' for administrative and support work. This will make it possible to promote younger workers and, it is hoped, raise their morale. At this company, *kumicho* normally lose their positions at the age of 50, and should then return to ordinary production work, which in reality is very difficult. The proposed change would only reduce ages when *kumicho* and *hancho* lose their titles and functions.

As we have seen, the Japanese automobile industry has been remarkably successful in preserving employment security for its regular workers in spite of the long recession. Other consequences of the end of expansion and growth are more difficult to overcome. The changing values of the young generation, its lack of interest in quality circles and similar activities seem to be general phenomena. And the problem of an ageing workforce, and especially of ageing foremen, has no easy solution. In the 'classical' period of the Toyota/Ohno system, steady expansion made the internal labour market dynamic and also opened up careers for blue-collar employees. After 10 or 15 years of hard and repetitive work on the line they could be promoted to *hancho* and then *kumicho*. In the 1990s career opportunities on the shopfloor are rapidly diminishing. At one of the smaller assembly plants in the Toyota Group, the number of new *kumichos* decreased from 80 in 1990 to 18 in 1995. This had serious repercussions on the morale of shopfloor workers. To create the semblance of career opportunities, the company planned to use the in-company rank system more flexibly. According to this plan workers would be able to advance in ranks to '*kumicho*' level and above, without actually having a *kumicho* position. Instead they would be called 'experts'. Such transfers and relabelling of *kumicho* will not conceal their loss of status and responsibility, however, and could result in a further loss of motivation.

For several reasons there seems to be a shift in the Toyota system away from the '*gemba*'-philosophy, the strong focus on shopfloor rationalisation, and also a tendency towards an increased division of labour. Production ramp-up of new models is more efficient than ever, but this process is mainly taken care of by engineers and maintenance workers. The *gemba* focus is being replaced by an emphasis on streamlining the entire system, from the very beginning of new car development.

INCREASING INTERFIRM DIVERSITY

Two other consequences of the crisis are growing divergence between the prospects of Japan and the prospects of its companies and an increasing diversity between firms. Previously, the strength of Japan and Japanese automobile companies tended to be treated as a single entity. This is no longer a very helpful perspective, especially not in the automobile industry. From 1980 to 1993, Japan was the largest producer of automobiles in the world. In 1994, the USA recaptured this position – with the help of Japanese transplant production in North America. Given the prospect of domestic zero growth in automobile production, Japan will never again be no. 1. The majority of the Japanese automobile makers will continue to expand sales and operations, but in other countries. Japan as a high-cost production base will still play a very important role for developing new cost-down strategies. Applying these strategies in offshore plants will challenge the notion of a successful western catch-up. The combination of substantial operations in Japan, which are committed to preserving employment security and thus have no other option than to regain competitiveness, and an expanding global plant network will render the competitiveness of the Japanese companies even more formidable. This was one of the major conclusions in a Ford study of Japan's automobile industry after the *endaka* (Johnson, 1994a).

Similar to the situation in the machine tool industry, there has been no shake-out in the industry. The firms have persevered, determined to endure. In the view of widespread western expectations of a consolidation of the excessively competitive Japanese industry structure, this perseverance is a remarkable feat. The companies cannot be treated as a uniform bloc, however. An important consequence of the post-Bubble crisis is the increasing diversity between firms (this is also documented by the international assembly plant study referred to above). Of Japan's nine car makers, only Isuzu has withdrawn from passenger car production to specialise in commercial and recreational vehicles as well as diesel engines. This has been complemented by an OEM deal with Honda, whereby Isuzu supplies RVs to Honda and Honda cars to Isuzu, so the company has remained a player in the marketplace. The small manufacturers Suzuki and Subaru have been able to survive and prosper as niche producers of small cars and wagons respectively, taking advantage of the increasing fragmentation of the market. Toyota has raised its stakes in Daihatsu, and is expected to integrate the smaller company's product line more closely with its own in order to avoid competition in the marketplace. The most hard-hit companies during the recession have been Nissan and Mazda, who used to rank two and four respectively in the Japanese market. Sales volume or scale of production have obviously not been the decisive factors.

In 1993 Nissan announced a plan to trim 5,000 jobs to a level of 48,000 by 1996. Two years later, the company acknowledged a need to eliminate an additional 6,000–7,000 positions, but only through a combination of retirements and reduced recruitment. The annual intake of new employees would be reduced to less than 100 compared with the usual figure of 2,000. For several years, the company had lost domestic market share. Capacity utilisation in Japan fell from 95% in 1991 to 58% in 1995, before the closure of the Zama assembly plant. This was followed by the closing of a new engine plant in Kyushu. Nissan has also incurred losses in its global operations, especially in Spain and Mexico (Lashinsky and Sumiya, 1995). The company was an early mover in developing offshore production, but much less successful than the late-coming arch-rival Toyota. In the USA, Toyota surpassed Nissan in the late 1980s. In Australia in 1992, Nissan had to lay its plant idle, whereas Toyota expanded capacity, and in south-east Asia Nissan had no strong presence at all. Only in Britain did Nissan still enjoy an advantage. Reflecting its problems in its overseas operations, the Nissan Group continued to report losses on a consolidated basis in 1995. In Japan, however, the company was back in the black, the major reasons being its programmes for employment adjustment and cost reduction, combined with strong domestic sales. A new, more interactive and flexible method of developing new products helped the company launch a series of successful new products. Nissan took the lead in Japan in introducing safety features, for example airbags, as standard equipment. Whereas Toyota suffered from flat or declining sales, Nissan expanded its domestic market share markedly and thus compensated for declining business overseas (Isaka, 1995b).

The company most seriously affected by the long recession was Mazda. During the Bubble Boom the company embarked upon an ambitious growth strategy. The Hiroshima company added plant capacity, expanded the dealer system to a total number of five separate channels in Japan (the equal of the much bigger Toyota) and released a stream of new products – 20 new models involving 16 new platforms in only four years. When the recession became severe, the company was financially exhausted. It was the Japanese automobile maker most vulnerable to exchange rate moves, but could not afford the overseas plants it needed. In Japan, the Hiroshima company suffered from a severe market, taking home market sales from 600,000 in 1991 to 350,000 in 1995. To survive, Mazda had to request Ford, who owns 25% of Mazda, for assistance. Ford Motor Co. assigned three senior executives to Mazda in order to overhaul its product programme and increase co-ordination with Ford's model strategy. This co-ordination effort turned out to be a very difficult mission, however, and Mazda's role in Ford's global strategies remained uncertain. The North American Escort had previously been based on Mazda engineering, but in Ford's new world-car strategy, Europe was designated as Ford's small-car centre, which included the design of all Escort versions. The European centres would probably take on more Ford vehicles previously developed by Mazda (Johnson, 1995). In Japan, from the early 1990s, Mazda's Hofu plant was an outright disaster. The automated facility had been dedicated to building luxury cars, which Mazda could no longer sell. When the company finally had a hit on a product in Japan, the camper van Bongo Friendee, it was not possible to build it at the expensive plant because its equipment was too specialised. To survive, analysts urged the company to scale back, reduce the workforce further and prune the model programme (Toga, 1995). In April 1996, Ford took effective management control by raising its stake to 33.4% of Mazda's shares, which gave the US company veto power over Mazda's board of directors. A Ford executive was appointed Mazda's new president, and Ford moved to introduce more rigorous financial control and market discipline to the once so-proud engineering culture at Hiroshima (Nakamoto, 1996).

Frugal Toyota had also been carried away by the buoyant mood of the Bubble Boom. The enormous success of the luxury Lexus model made engineers and designers lose their traditional cost-consciousness. The marketing slogan of Lexus, 'the relentless pursuit of perfection', was an engineer's dream. In the boom time, all divisions of the company wanted to upgrade their products and design 'mini-Lexuses'. The organisation of design and engineering departments around 'product champions', a feature strongly recommended as key to high-product integrity and short development lead-times by Clark and Fujimoto (1991), resulted in excessive internal competition and a proliferation of designs requiring unique components. In 1992, Toyota started a comprehensive cost-cutting programme, centred around value engineering and value analysis in order to simplify designs, improve manufacturability and increase the proportion of common parts. Product development was consolidated in four centres based on model types – front-wheel drive, rear-wheel drive, four-wheel drive and common components, respectively. To rekindle demand, Toyota announced an aggressive model and market programme. From 1994 to 1997, the company planned to introduce 31 new models, either full replacements of current products or completely new vehicles, such as the new small sport-utility RAV4. Despite all the criticism in Japan of overworked engineering and manufacturing departments, the company will keep the four-year product cycle intact for all volume models, and has restated its goal of achieving 10% of the global automobile market (Johnson, 1994b). Its global operations are surging ahead, but in Japan its position is less comfortable. Export volumes are rapidly declining because of increasing offshore production and US trade pressure and, at the same time, the company has lost domestic market share. In mid-1995 the company announced that without a recovery of its Japanese sales, employment stability would be in jeopardy. The financial resources of Toyota are enormous, however, so the company would have no problems in implementing a cautious and long-term adjustment programme.

Japan's automobile makers have long been presented as a role model not only for western car makers but also for all manufacturing. This section has discussed the problems the Japanese makers faced in the Bubble Boom: declining profit margins and severe difficulties in recruiting workers. As a result, the leading firms started to reform management systems and plant design. Most spectacular were the new plants of Toyota, which signalled a significant departure from the orthodoxy of Ohno, the founder of the Toyota Production System. The recession and *endaka* 1992–5 spelled out the end of an era of uninterrupted expansion in Japan. No more growth of domestic car production is expected, and employment security rather than 'attractive workplaces' has become the first priority. After the end of the Bubble Boom there is a serious overcapacity problem and the automation strategy has been reassessed. The cost pressure has forced the automobile makers to devise new ways to improve operations, reduce product cost, compress development lead-time and streamline production ramp-up of new cars. Their rationalisation efforts were targeted to bring down the cost base in order to break even at a yen:dollar exchange rate of 80–5:1. When the yen was considerably weakened in 1996, approaching the 105–10:1 rate, the Japanese automobile makers could improve their earnings and competitiveness rapidly. After a period of western catch-up, the Japanese makers seem to be widening the gap once more. The performance is uneven however, and diversity within the industry has increased. For Japanese car makers, a rapid downsizing of the workforce is no option. Their cautious and long-term personnel policies are designed to implement adjustment in a piece-meal way. Worldwide the leading Japanese makers are continuing their expansion, and US industry observers are expecting a third wave of Japanese automobile competition (Updike et al., 1996). In contrast to the previous periods of Japanese competition, this third one will not be marked by any easy market share gains, and western makers are determined to respond. The Japanese are competing from a much broader base than before, however, in terms of international manufacturing, product range and product price. The approach to Europe is still cautious, but in the North American market the Japanese have a stronger manufacturing presence than ever. Their aggressive price cuts in 1996 were only the first signal of a new round of competition for Detroit.

SUMMARY

For most of the postwar period, the automobile sector played a central role in Japan's industrial growth. In the 1980s, its manufacturing productivity and product development efficiency were widely admired in the western world. At the same time, the automobile makers faced several problems in Japan: a labour shortage, declining profitability in spite of increasing volumes and public criticism. The companies responded by constructing new more automated plants, and investing in 'human-friendly' equipment and work environments. The new factories had barely started operating when the Bubble Boom came to an abrupt halt. Domestic demand declined and exports were severely hurt by the surging yen. For the first time ever, the Japanese industry faced a serious problem of overcapacity. At the same time, western competitors were aggressively catching up in productivity and development lead-time. After some initial confusion, the Japanese makers responded by comprehensive programmes for regaining their competitive edge, which consisted of three main components: accelerated internationalisation, continued investments in North America and rapid increases in southeast Asia; reorganisation of the product development process in order to reduce costs of new products and compress the lead-time even more; and streamlining of manufacturing in Japan, including a reduced degree of automation and increased volume flexibility to adapt to unpredictable market volatility.

In spite of a fall in production from 13.5 to 10.5 million vehicles in Japan between 1990 and 1994, the level of regular employment has been remarkably stable. The industry has adjusted in a very gradual way, reducing overtime and the use of temporary workers, sending workers on *shukko* to sales outlets and increasing training rather than laying off employees. The deliberately slow closing of Nissan's Zama plant illustrates the peculiar Japanese way of employment adjustment, as contrasted to the Anglo-Saxon pattern of rapid downsizing. As a consequence of the drastically reduced hiring of new employees, the average age will increase and career opportunities diminish. This drives an industry interest in wage reform away from the *nenko* system and in new forms of personnel management. The traditional *gemba* (shopfloor) focus of Toyota and other companies tends to be replaced by an increased emphasis on process engineering and total development optimisation; vertical production ramp-up of new models rather than incremental improvement. The internationalisation of the major Japanese companies will guarantee their future as major players in the industry; at the same time Japan will remain as a very important manufacturing base, and a hot-house for cost-saving innovations. Within the industry there is an increasing divergence: whereas the weakest players will hardly remain as independent manufacturers, companies such as Toyota are stronger than ever, determined to build a truly global manufacturing presence and increase overall market share.

7

CONSUMER ELECTRONICS: IN SEARCH OF NEW PRODUCTS AND NEW PRODUCTION STRUCTURES?

The transportation sector and the electrical and electronics sector have been the major manufacturing industries sustaining Japan's postwar growth. In terms of intensive competition, rapid volume increase, manufacturing and product development skills there are many similarities between the sectors. In other aspects, differences are more conspicuous:

- The automobile industry is a monoculture. The Japanese electrical and electronics sector comprises a broad variety of end-products at different stages in their product life-cycles. Furthermore, it has a world leadership in several key component technologies, which are relatively insensitive to shifts in currency exchange rates.

- In the automobile industry, the basic product technology is stable, and technological change incremental. The engines, for example, are still built on the basic concepts developed by the Germans in the 1880s. The electrical and electronics sector is rapidly evolving technologically, often in qualitative leaps. There is a constant stream of new products and devices; some fail, others are produced in tens of millions. Traditional products are incrementally refined over long periods of time, as in the automobile industry. Then there is a technological breakthrough and they are completely reinvented. Such a mature, mass-produced item as cathode-ray tubes, for example, will probably be replaced by plasma or LCD screens in the next 5–10 years. This will reinvigorate the entire TV industry.

- The supplier structures and suppliers relationships are very different. The automobile companies have developed intimate and long-term relationships with carefully selected and groomed component specialists. They have created tightly linked production chains operating on JIT principles. By contrast, the supplier structure of the electronics industry is much more volatile. Because of rapid technological change long-term relationships are not the general norm. The overwhelming majority of components are small in size and the price per unit is low. Therefore JIT supplies have never been of any real relevance. Vital components, such as semiconductors, are frequently short in supply, and strategic buffers rather than minimal stocks are a business necessity.

- Companies in the electronics sector started production overseas earlier than the automobile makers. The consumer electronics industry, in particular, has internationalised at a much faster pace than the automobile industry, expanding manufacturing in southeast Asia, while converting production lines in Japan. Rapid transfer is facilitated by the more flexible and less closely knit supplier structure. However, for a long period overseas expansion was combined with inward investment. Because of constant technological innovation and the crucial role of key components, firms continued to invest heavily in Japan and contributed to domestic growth.

The electrical and electronics industry is difficult to delineate. The major corporations, such as Matsushita, Hitachi or Toshiba, are conglomerates, whose products range from household appliances and audio-visual products to electronic components and machinery; in the case of Hitachi, also computers and telecommunications equipment. Sony and Sharp are more focused, but Sharp too has a broad range: white goods, audio-visual products, electronic components and small computers ('personal digital assistants'). In this chapter we will not discuss household appliances. With the exception of microwave ovens and air conditioners, this is a stable and domestically oriented business, with a low level of exports, offshore production and reimports. In 1994, only 14% of the washing machines assembled in Japan were exported. Imports accounted for a meagre 7% of Japanese domestic demand (Wada, 1994).

We will focus here on consumer electronics, and in particular the production of colour television sets, CTVs. This product played a vital role in the development of the industry, and together with VCRs it is still the most important mass-produced item. When we discuss different corporate strategies to cope with the employment situation in Japan in the wake of internationalisation, we will also touch on LCD production, which is now an increasingly important part of the computer components industry. Chapter 9 will return to computers and components in more detail. Of the total production of Japan's electronics industry in 1994, consumer electronics accounted for 2,800 billion yen; industrial electronic equipment for 10,100 billion yen; and electronics components for 8,600 billion yen (EIAJ, 1995: 11). Industrial electronic equipment comprise computers and peripherals, communications equipment, medical and measuring instruments. Although the major corporations in the industry also manufacture household appliances, this product category is not included in industry statistics. The chapter is organised around four broad themes:

(1) The accelerated internationalization of mature products.
2) The different strategies for stabilizing employment in Japan.
3) The search for new growth products and reinvigorated 'kaisha dynamics'.
4) The evolution of new personnel and production structures in Japan.

Specifically, three different companies will be discussed: Matsushita, the cautious industry leader, Sharp, the bold innovator, and Hitachi, the pioneer of new production structures. For Matsushita and Hitachi the 'perseverance mood' of 1993, at the bottom of the recession, is compared to the evolving new strategies of 1995.

EARLY MOVERS IN OFFSHORE PRODUCTION

In the mid-1970s, Japan accounted for half the worldwide production of TVs and 75% of total exports (Fransman, 1995). At this time, Japanese manufacturers started large-scale production of CTVs overseas, and in the mid-1980s, at the time of a new *endaka*, production of VCRs followed suit. During the 1990s this relocation has accelerated (see Table 7.1).

Table 7.1 Production of CTVs and VCRs in Japan and overseas. (million units; peak volumes in bold)

	CTVs			VCRs		
	Production in Japan	Exports	Overseas production	Production in Japan	Exports	Overseas production
1980	10.9	4.0	5.7	4.4	3.4	—
1982	11.4	4.4	7.3 (est.)	13.1	10.6	—
1984	**14.5**	**6.0**	10.8	27.1	22.1	0.8
1986	13.0	4.6	12.4	**31.3**	**27.7**	2.7
1988	13.2	3.7	15.9	28.2	21.9	5.3
1990	13.2	3.7	20.0	27.9	25.8	7.3
1992	12.0	4.1	23.2	19.7	17.7	10.7
1994	9.3	3.5	33.0	15.4	15.2	21.9

Source: EIAJ, 1995: 18–19.

Domestic production and exports of CTVs peaked in 1984. By that time Japan produced 15 million units, and offshore production amounted to 6 million. In 1994, Japan produced 9 million units domestically and 33 million overseas. The relocation of VCR production has been more drastic. In 1986, the domestic output totalled 33 million units, while overseas production was less than 3 million. In 1994, domestic production had been cut by half, whereas overseas output had increased eight-fold, to 22 million units. According to estimates for the fiscal year 1995, Sony planned to produce 3.8 million VCRs overseas compared to 0.6 million in Japan; Sharp 3.7 million overseas and 1.7 million in Japan; and Hitachi 1.2 million overseas and 0.8 million in Japan. Only Matsushita, in Japan viewed as a cautious and conservative company, planned to keep most of its production in Japan: 6 million units compared to 2.4 million overseas (Fushimi, 1995).

Despite this reputation of being conservative, Matsushita has been expanding internationally since the mid-1970s. In 1993, overseas markets accounted for 49% of the group's sales. With 101,000 overseas employees of a total workforce of 252,000, Matsushita has probably the largest non-Japanese workforce of all Japanese companies. In Malaysia it has 20,000 employees, in Singapore 15,000 and in Thailand 10,000. In Malaysia there is a growing labour shortage and so like other Japanese companies, Matsushita has started to focus on Indonesia, with its low wages and abundant supply of relatively highly educated workers. The southeast Asian countries are export bases, not only to western markets but also back to Japan. Matsushita has found it much easier to transplant its highly disciplined Panasonic manufacturing system to southeast Asia than to the USA and Europe. According to managers at its overseas planning department in Osaka, interviewed in October 1993, the Japanese feel they are welcome and respected in southeast Asia. Malaysians are much more eager to learn and adopt Japanese practices than westerners. In contrast to Matsushita's UK and US operation, the Malaysian TV company, MTV, is profitable and expanding.

In the Japanese TV market, Matsushita is ranked no. 1 and Sharp no. 2. Compared to the larger Matsushita, it is a more international company, with half of its 100,000 employees outside Japan. Basically all TV production has been transferred overseas. In Malaysia, Sharp produces 3 million TV sets per year, at the largest plant in the country, much bigger than Matsushita's MTV.

Similar to other companies, Hitachi first moved production of small-screen TVs overseas. In 1995, the company decided to discontinue domestic production of large TV sets, and import all conventional CTVs from its southeast Asian plants. Worldwide, Hitachi produced more than 200,000 TV sets per month. Of this volume, less than a quarter was manufactured at the Japanese main plant in Gifu (more about this plant below). The company had developed a global production network, comprising plants in Mexico (for the NAFTA market), Wales (for the European market), Brazil, Thailand, China and Indonesia (for domestic markets) and Singapore (for exports to the Japanese market). In the future the company plans to expand in Indonesia, both to serve the local market and to develop a low-cost export base, which could partly replace assembly in Singapore. Basically, all plants use the same methods and production technology. According to Hitachi managers, there is no need for skilled workers in modern TV production. Testing, for example, has been automated. The low-cost sites are using more manual labour for handling operations, and other simple tasks, but critical operations are done automatically in all plants. As a result, quality performance is standardised worldwide.

THE PROBLEMS OF PRESERVING EMPLOYMENT IN JAPAN

In the 1980s, this internationalisation proceeded smoothly. Matsushita and Hitachi, like other Japanese firms, moved mature production offshore but did not reduce capacity in Japan. Instead, the domestic factories were upgraded. The *endaka* of the mid-1980s was offset by the Bubble Boom's strong domestic demand. In spite of the rapid expansion of overseas plants, total production of consumer electronics in Japan in 1991 was basically the same as in 1985. From 1991 to 1994, however, a slump in domestic demand coincided with a sharp fall in exports. In three years Japan's production of consumer electronic equipment declined by more than 40%, from 4,700 to 2,800 billion yen. Suddenly, manufacturers became riddled with huge over-capacity and a severe pressure on employment. The pressure was also felt in several of the related industries. According to Denki Rengo, the Japanese electrical, electronic and information union, total employment in this broad sector stood at 2.5 million in 1993. It was reduced by 80,000 in 1993–4 and a further 120,000 in 1994–5. How to preserve employment in Japan, both during the recession and in the long term, became a major issue for the industry's leading corporations. The three companies in our study, Mat-sushita, Hitachi and Sharp, responded differently to this challenge.

Matsushita – no drastic change

Matsushita with brand names such as National and Panasonic, has been moving slowly in relocating its mature products overseas. In 1993, the total Japanese TV market was 'balanced': 3 million sets were imported, 3 million were exported. Panasonic, however exported 1.6 million sets, and imported only 350,000. In an interview a manager at the company's overseas planning office in Osaka remarked that the exchange rate made it quite clear what they had to do, but how, and at what speed, was a difficult question. He stressed emphatically that restructuring and voluntary retirements were the last thing they wanted to do. In 1992, the company's profit margin was a poor 0.5%. According to the Matsushita managers, it was impossible to solve the problems by increased exports, but commitment to maintaining Jap-anese employment prevented them from accelerating the relocation process as much as would be economically rational. The problem is illustrated by the situation of the TV plants. Matsushita's main Japanese plants are located in Utsunomiya and Ibaraki. The following account is based on interviews at the Ibaraki plant in October 1993. At its peak, the Ibaraki plant produced 100,000 sets per month. In 1993, the monthly output was only 57,000 sets. The TV plant had 970 workers, 400 of whom were women. In spite of the decline in output, no workers had been laid off. Instead, the Ibaraki plant had increased the rate of in-house production and reduced the workforce in the packing and service sections, which were staffed by workers from out-side companies. Employees were also transferred internally from conven-tional TV production to high-definition TVs. The HDTV volume was small, but the work content much higher since a HDTV required ten times more assembly time per unit compared to a conventional TV set. In addition, 100 employees at Ibaraki, mostly white-collar workers, were sent on *shukko* to sales departments for three-month periods. Managers at the plant stressed that employment adjustment without layoffs was a constant worry for mid-dle and top management.

In 1995, after another two years of recession, there had been surprisingly little change. Matsushita maintained a production volume of 3 million TV sets in Japan, and planned to export 1.7 million sets, the same number as in 1993, although managers in charge of overseas planning acknowledged that these plans would be very difficult to achieve. China had been the major market for Panasonic TV sets, but the Chinese government had recently adopted a very strict policy on imports. Matsushita opened a cathode-ray tube plant in Beijing in 1989, and the new regulation would force the company to start local assembly in China as well, at the expense of Japanese exports. Several other Japanese makers, including Hitachi and Sanyo, are already active in China, so Matsushita is a late entrant. The crucial problem after three years of recession is how to safeguard Japanese employment. The company had not announced any employment adjustment and according to its management, will never do so officially. The basic idea is to persevere until the new generation of technologies in consumer electronics takes off. For a company such as Matsushita with it strong brand name and corporate reputation, it is not possible to dismiss workers as long as the Japanese operations as a whole are profitable. It does not matter if a division is losing money as long as the corporation is in the black – it has to take care of its employees. In this situation the company pursues several complementing strategies.

First, Matsushita continues its international expansion, with a particular focus on Asia. According to MITI statistics for all Japanese manufacturing in Europe, the USA and southeast Asia, Asia is by far the most profitable region. This conclusion is supported by Matsushita's experience. Further, the rate of saturation for household appliances and audio-visual products is low, which means good business opportunities for conventional technologies. China, for example, is the largest market for television sets in the world, with annual sales of 12 million sets, compared to 8 million in Japan. By developing its business in Asia, Matsushita attempts to save the time needed for the development of new products to be launched in Japan. In addition to China, India is also changing, and Matsushita is planning the local manufacture of television sets as well as audio equipment. The profits from operations in Asia will be used to bolster R&D in Japan, and thus help the company to endure hard times.

A second, and complementary strategy is to develop the company's business in the non-consumer areas. Of Matsushita's total business in 1994, consumer electronics comprised 38% and was declining. Communications, industrial equipment and computer peripherals comprised 24% and its share was growing; components and electronics, such as semiconductors and LCDs, comprised another 23% and was also growing. Learning a lesson from Sharp, Matsushita has organised a 'key device division' as part of the drive to bolster production of advanced components and equipment and to reduce its dependence on the consumer electronics business.

Mean while, a policy of cost containment and gradual adjustment is being implemented in Japan. There is a strict control on salary increases, which is communicated to all employees. The hiring of new graduates has been reduced by 75% compared to the peak in 1990–1. Apart from the R&D department, overtime has been reduced to virtually zero. International procurement is actively promoted. From 1990 to 1995 the share of imported materials and components increased from 10.8 to 18.9% – still very low from a European perspective! In 1994–5 in an effort to streamline a 'bloated' management structure, the company shifted 6,000 of its 20,000 administrative personnel throughout the entire group to production and sales (Matsuzaka, 1994).

The fourth element of Matsushita's strategy for preserving its Japanese base is to develop new advanced consumer products, from HDTVs to digital camcorders, digital video-disks, etc. Matsushita managers interviewed in September 1995 were convinced that new technologies will generate new growth products; the question is how long it will take – and what position Matsushita will command in the new markets. On the face of it, Matsushita's strategy is surprisingly conservative: no drastic personnel reduction, no change in its expensive distribution system, no capacity reduction in Japan. The company has the resources needed to endure, however – a broadly diversified structure, a strong international operation, especially in Asia, and a huge war chest. Matsushita commands, as does Toyota, enormous financial assets, estimated to be at least US $22 billion in cash and short-term instruments, in addition to the revenues from the sale of MCA Inc. (Bremner and Updike, 1995).

Hitachi – a difficult balancing act

The structure of Hitachi is much more diversified than Matsushita, with major businesses in heavy electric machinery, components, computers and software. The consumer electronics division only accounts for 10% of total sales. The corporation has formidable resources to absorb problems in this business. On the other hand, its share of the Japanese consumer electronic market is much smaller than Matsushita's, and its brand name is weaker than Panasonic or Sony. The very diversity of the company's activities makes it difficult to identify a cohesive strategic response. This problem is exasperated by the corporate structure of Hitachi. Hitachi is famous in Japan for its factory-centred approach to organisation and management, and the weak role of the divisional level. This has allowed for broad diversification, but makes restructuring and concentration very hard to accomplish (cf. Fruin, 1992). We will focus on the image systems operation, TV production in particular, in order to provide a more detailed account of its adjustment agonies. Hitachi's production of television sets in Japan is concentrated on the Gifu plant. During the plant's busiest time in the 1980s, Gifu produced nearly 200,000 units per month, the majority being shipped to China. Then Hitachi started a rapidly expanding joint venture in China. In 1993, the volume at the Gifu plant was only 80,000 television sets per month. At the time of our visit in October 1993, the Gifu plant had 540 Hitachi employees, the majority of them in final assembly. There were also 500 workers from 'affiliated' companies, taking care of subassemblies, materials handling and logistics. Of the workforce, 25% was female. During the peak production years in the 1980s, the plant employed a large pool of temporary workers. Managers went all over Japan, to Hokkaido in the north and Kyushu in the south, to recruit them. In 1993 there were practically no temporaries at all. For production workers overtime had been reduced from 30–40 hours per month to only two. Several employees had been sent on *shukko*, both to subsidiaries and to non-Hitachi affiliates. When selecting workers for transfer, management considered the conditions of their personal lives. For the long-distance transfers, bachelors were selected first. As another form of *shukko*, managers were transferred to sales. This was an unusual step within Hitachi. According to a manager in the production engineering department, it was a difficult process since many white-collar workers are not good salespeople. He struck a very pessimistic note: 'We have never had such a bad domestic demand, and it is very difficult to see any upturn in the market.'

Two years later, output had fallen further, to 46,000 units per month, and exports had ceased completely. For three years Hitachi's TV operation had been in the red. In spite of this, there had been no further employment adjustment. The plant still had 500 regular employees, the same number as in 1993. There had been no overtime to reduce since 1993, and no expansion of the *shukko* programme. The only significant adjustment had taken place outside the plant. Two years ago, Gifu had utilised 400 workers as subcontractors for PCB assembly. In 1995, this figure was down to 180 and in 1996 it was only 70–80. There had also been an up-grading of the product mix. In 1993, the plant mainly produced conventional TVs, plus a minor volume of projection TVs. In 1995, 75% of the output consisted of widescreens. These sets have a rectangular format, mimicking the panoramic look of cinema films. Because of a wider screen angle the picture tube is heavier and requires more power, which makes it more complicated and labour intensive to manufacture. Whereas the standard assembly time at Gifu for a 29-inch conventional set was 60 minutes, the time for a corresponding widescreen was 110–20 minutes. This up-grading had been very important for the plant, but not enough to secure its future. Part of the TV production lines had been scrapped, and the automatic PCB assembly was only operating at 60% of its capacity. To regain profitability, the plant would have to reduce its workforce by at least one third but, obviously, management was hesitant about how to implement this reduction. At Takayama, a branch plant to Gifu, Hitachi had already tried to realise a radical restructuring plan. The Takayama plant used to produce tuners for TV sets. When this production was transferred abroad, the company first planned to close the plant and lay off those workers who could not be relocated to other Hitachi facilities. These workers were mainly married women, but being regular workers Hitachi had an employment responsibility. Takayama is a small town with a dearth of manufacturing jobs, so the local government intervened. Hitachi reversed its plans and decided to continue in Takayama, replacing tuners with CD-ROM players.

Before Hitachi moved new production to Takayama, all transferable employees, mostly men, were relocated. The plant was taken over by a Hitachi subsidiary. Then the remaining, mainly female, workers were dismissed and rehired by another daughter company. This involved a significant wage cut, especially for the middle-aged and older employees. If they had still belonged to the Gifu organisation, it would have been impossible to introduce different wages and conditions. The Takayama case illustrates how difficult it is for a blue-chip Japanese company to close plants, and also how complicated it is to change employment conditions, in spite of the alleged flexibility of the personnel system. The Takayama plant survived, but in a production structure which is very different from Hitachi's previous ways of operating. We will return to this below.

Sharp – the bold innovator.

Compared to Hitachi, the Osaka-based Sharp corporation is much more focused on electronic products and components. For a long time it was thought of as another Sanyo, a second-tier producer of low-end consumer products distributed through mass retailers. In the mid-1990s, the company's image was completely different, and it was referred to as the inheritor of Sony, which had lost much of its innovative ability. Sharp's turnaround started in the previous *endaka*, in the mid-1980s. With its low-margin products, the company was particularly hard hit by this recession. A new strategy was worked out comprising three main elements: increase overseas production; reduce the dependence on end-products and expand sales of components and devices; and strengthen domestic sales, which are insensitive to currency fluctuations (Normile, 1995).

The first policy meant that Sharp rapidly moved production of conventional CTVs and VCRs offshore. Wide screens, in 1995 still regarded as a more sophisticated product, were manufactured in Japan, however. The second policy implied a major increase in R&D, from 6.2% of sales in 1985 to 10% of sales in 1994. During the 'calculator wars' of the early 1970s, when Sharp was Casio's main contender, the Osaka-based company pioneered the use of LCDs for the first palm-top calculator. At that time LCDs were a low-margin item, based on passive matrix technology which offered a rather dim picture. In the late 1980s, Sharp became a leader in second-generation, active matrix displays, where each picture element is switched on and off by its own miniature transistor. This coincided with the worldwide boom in laptop computers and an almost insatiable demand for the new pin-sharp colour screens. In 1992, the global LCD market was estimated at US$3.8 billion, in 1995 it had doubled to US$8.4 billion and analysts estimated a further doubling to US$15.2 billion in the year 2000 (Gross and Carey, 1994). Japan owns 95% of this market, and Sharp alone enjoys 40% of the world market. In the three years 1992–4, its LCD business grew by more than 30% per year. This vibrant market attracted a number of Japanese rivals, of course, in a rehearsal of the famous '*kaisha* dynamics' of the 1960s and 1970s, so aptly described by Abegglen and Stalk (1987): intensive competition;

rapid capacity expansion; repeated output doubling when competitors strive to maintain and expand their share on the booming market; constant lowering of costs; widening of markets; and a search for new applications. The following account from *Nikkei Weekly* illustrates this capacity race in the LCD business in 1995 (Mitsusada, 1995a): Sharp opens a new plant in Taki, Mie Prefecture, capable of producing 150,000 units per month. At the same time it expands production at its key plant in Tenri, Nara Prefecture, from 180,000 to 310,000 units per month. NEC opens a second plant in northern Japan, multiplying the firm's capacity from 60,000 to 150,000 LCDs per month. Toshiba–IBM increase capacity by 200,000 a month with a new plant in Shiga Prefecture. Mitsubishi Electric builds a plant with a monthly capacity of 60,000 units per month, Kyocera plans an expansion to 70,000 per month. All in all, Japan's total LCD output per month is estimated to leap 60%, from 550,000 in 1994 to 900,000 by the end of 1995. Close behind the Japanese, Korean and Taiwanese companies are entering the battle. Intensified competition implies rapidly falling prices. Sharp was determined to maintain its leading market share by massive investments, mostly in Japan. A dominant position in a growth market means superior economies of scale and depreciation schedules, which will probably allow Sharp to remain the industry's low-cost producer.

Sharp's business in components and devices is not restricted to LCDs. The company has 35% of the world market for mask ROMs, an important component in video-game machines and microwave ovens. It holds a dominant share for laser diodes, the source of light in compact-disc players. Instead of diversifying or trying to 'integrate hardware and software' by investing in Hollywood, Sharp has used its manufacturing skills to create strategic alliances (Morris, 1994). In a partnership with Intel, it produces flash memory chips – in Japan. In another partnership, Apple Computers consigned production of its Newton palmtop computers to Japan. Sharp used this alliance to develop the Zaurus, a similar product for the Japanese market. This digital assistant is capable of recognising hand-written *kanji* (the Chinese characters forming the bulk of the Japanese language) – and has been much more successful than Newton in the USA. The Zaurus thus contributed to Sharp's third strategic goal: to expand domestic Japanese sales. The basic idea is to use Sharp's key devices and competences to build innovative products. The most well-known implementation is the ViewCam camcorder, where the conventional viewfinder is replaced with a 4-inch LCD screen, making it possible to watch the video while it is taken. Introduced in 1992, the ViewCam became an instant best-seller, and increased Sharp's share of the camcorder market from 2 to 20%.

The first policy, to transfer mature products overseas, would by itself cause difficult adjustment problems in Japan and create no long-term competitive advantage. Complemented by the second and third policies, Sharp has instead been able to expand in Japan and let high-tech divisions absorb potential redundancies in its mature businesses. Engineers are employed by the national headquarters and easily transferred from the stagnating TV and audio-equipment plant in Toshigi to the expanding LCD facilities in Tenri and Mie. Workers are employed locally and are therefore less easily transferred. The company has to negotiate and consider individual cases, such as family and housing conditions.

NEW GROWTH PRODUCTS AND OLD MAINSTAYS

In several ways, Sharp was the happy exception during the first half of the 1990s. However, all consumer electronics companies were striving hard to find new growth products for the domestic market that could substitute for declining exports and production transfers. What *Nikkei Weekly* called 'a smattering of new gadgets' were announced to Japanese consumers in 1995: mini-disc players, digital camcorders, digital video-disks (late in 1996) and large, flat TV panels (to be launched in 1997). Actual or projected sales figures were small compared to the conventional mainstay products, however. Mini-disc players were expected to reach one million in 1995, sales of digital camcorders, which can be connected to PCs and printers, would probably total 400,000 in 1996. By comparison, Japanese companies produced 42 million TVs and 36 million VCRs in 1994. In spite of a high level of market saturation, TV sets sell at a stable annual rate of 8–9 million units per year in Japan, and thus remain a very important business. During the recession years 1993–5, the consumer electronics companies were able to upgrade this mainstay product by launching price-competitive wide-screen sets. Sales of wide screens increased from 400,000 in 1993 to a projected several millions in 1995 (Mitsusada, 1995g). The manufacture of wide screens is more technically demanding and labour intensive than conventional TV production, and thus supports domestic production. But as the case of Hitachi has demonstrated, this up-grading was not enough to safeguard Japanese employment and, moreover, overseas transfer of wide-screen production was only a question of time.

For several years, the electronics companies have pinned their hopes on HDTVs. The semi-national Japanese broadcasting company NHK commenced pilot broadcasting in the late 1980s, but the demand for the expensive sets was slow to take off; in 1993, sales only reached 15,000 units. More serious than flat sales, however, was the fact that Japanese makers had chosen a technical *cul-de-sac* – analogue instead of digital transmission. 'Hi-vision', the Japanese version of HDTV, is a fruit of a long-term co-operation between manufacturers, NHK and the post and telecommunications ministry. Both the USA and Europe have chosen digital transmission, however. Digital transmission is a key to interactive TV, an important part of the multimedia concept. As a result, the Japanese technology, promoted by the Japanese government as worthy of becoming a world standard, will become obsolete. When Akimasa Egawa in 1994 at the Ministry of Posts and Telecommunications publicly acknowledged that 'the world is going digital' and expressed his concerns about Japan's 'clinging to outdated technology', he was met by furore from the industry. At an emergency press conference, the top executives of 11 consumer electronics makers pressed for and were reassured of continued government support for the home-grown 'hi-vision'-system (Kageki, 1994).

Unwillingly, Japanese makers seem to be back to another game of catch-up. On the other hand, there is a long way to a common western digital standard. In the mean time, NHK continues the expansion of hi-vision broadcasting, and manufacturers are developing niche markets for their HDTV equipment: in industrial film-making, electronic publishing, medical training and for scientific uses (Forrester, 1993). In order to be really appreciated by consumers, high-resolution broadcasting requires big screens, 40 inches or so diagonally. With traditional cathode-ray tube technology such a size makes a TV set too bulky, especially for crammed Japanese homes. The challenge is to find ways to package high resolution on a flat, wall-hanging screen. LCD technology is not suitable for large screens. The most probable solution is plasma displays. In 1995, NHK launched a plasma-supporting group to promote large display panels in order to call renewed attention to its hi-vision system. The 1998 Winter Olympic Games in Nagano are seen as 'the perfect opportunity to dazzle viewers with movie-like quality . . . Their hope is that high-definition television broadcasting will be robust enough then' (Mitsusada, 1995d). A new 'kaisha race' for market share in this potential high-growth market had already started. Since plasma technology is quite different from conventional TV technology, the established makers were challenged by entrants from the computer industry. In 1995, NEC announced plans to release a 40-inch screen priced at 450,000 yen, and large-scale investments for the monthly production of 150,000 units later in the decade. Fujitsu planned to produce 20,000 42-inch panels a month by late 1996, and Sony to launch a smaller 25-inch panel at the same time. Hitachi too intended to market a TV with a plasma screen in 1996, but would probably start production at the low rate of 2,000 units per month. According to Hitachi managers, the technology was still difficult to master and the reject ratio very high, close to 100%. The price depends on how successfully this ratio can be reduced. If the reject ratio falls from 95 to 90%, for example, the price could be halved. Ultimately, plasma displays will be manufactured in a highly automated process, but in the mid-1990s the product had not stabilised and engineering development was so fast, that it was not possible to develop an automated process. Intensive competition for market share will certainly drive down reject ratios, production cost and prices. The question is how fast this process will be, and thus how rapidly the new technology will realise the hope of reinvigorating the entire TV business. According to estimates in Nikkei Weekly, this will happen around the year 2000, when a market of about 3 million large flat panels is expected (Mitsusada, 1995g). The problem for Japanese domestic production is the time-lag between the transfer of mature products and the advent of new technologies capable of creating a stable mass demand.

THE INSTABILITY OF DEMAND

A common trait in the automobile, machine tool and consumer electronics industries is the stability of corporate commitment and competition. In spite of several years of losses, there is no consolidation, no divestment, no mergers and no acquisitions. Companies are reorganising and adjusting, but they hardly ever withdraw from any important market. This is reflected in the CTV industry, where market share for different makers overall has been very stable during the recession. Below the surface however, important changes seem to be taking place. A case in point is Hitachi's image and information systems division. In 1993, the atmosphere at its Gifu plant was gloomy, but there was a determination to endure and to continue investment. A senior manager explained their position:

> If plants like Gifu cease investing in automation, the competitive position will deteriorate even further. When the market eventually picks up, they will not have the manufacturing strength. Thus the Gifu plant continues to invest in advanced equipment, even if this is not profitable. We are tacitly supported by high-ranking managers in the corporation, who think it is essential to maintain and upgrade the Japanese manufacturing base.

Two years later, and after another two years of losses, there seemed to be a reorientation of the company's basic production philosophy in consumer electronics. The production of conventional video products was in a decline beyond recall. Promising products based on radically new technologies were far from commercial breakthrough. In the mean time, Hitachi had entered into the production of several different consumer products. They could not substitute for the previously so predictable TV production, however. Technically and commercially, these product were quite unstable. One example are CD-ROM players, whose speed is constantly multiplied, from normal to double, to four-fold to six-fold. In September 1995, Hitachi produced 250,000 per month; at the end of the year it planned to produce 800,000 a month! However, output could also drop precipitously, as a manager explained: 'If we are behind in investment we will lose everything, and production will go from 400,000 a month to zero.' In 1994, the Takayama branch plant assembled Sega Saturn game machines. At the end of the year, its production peaked at 300,000 sets a month. Six months later production was zero.

Hubs in constantly shifting production networks

The volatility of production volume makes it very difficult to plan and assess investment. Previously, Hitachi had a very elaborate calculating procedure. A main goal was to secure enough production capacity for peaks in demand to avoid losses in market share. As a basis for depreciation, five years of manufacturing was assumed. According to Gifu managers, this calculation method is now more or less meaningless in consumer electronics. Plant utilisation has acquired crucial importance, so Hitachi will invest for an expected minimum level of production instead of the previous maximum. If demand is in excess of that, outsourcing will be used. The enormous increase in the output of CD-ROM players described above will be achieved by subcontracting the complete assembly to manufacturing companies in various locations. Takayama will only produce a fraction of the total volume. This is a radically new production philosophy. There is no guarantee that an outsourcing relationship will be stable. A new technology will probably lead to a different outsourcing structure. As a result of the minimum investment strategy, there will also be a policy of minimum employment in the future. Once the personnel structure has been reduced to the core minimum, through a several-years process of incremental adjustment, the company will minimise the hiring of regular employees. Subcontracting and outsourcing will be the major means for absorbing demand variation, and the Gifu plant, previously a centre of advanced automation, will instead be a hub in shifting outsourcing networks.

The characteristics of the new consumer products also affect relations between engineering and manufacturing. The mature TV business has a stable rhythm of the annual introduction of new models. The new products, such as CD-ROMs, are different. New models using new technology are introduced as frequently as every six months. There is no time for fine-tuning the process during the months after the start of production. Ramp-up has to be almost instantaneous, and process engineers have a crucial role. Incremental rationalisation at shopfloor level, at *gemba*, is of diminishing interest; the process must start with maximum yield from the beginning.

Union response – the need for voluntary mobility

On a more general level, Denki Rengo, the Japanese electrical, electronic and information union, also stresses the importance of changing the postwar Japanese employment system to increase flexibility. The hollowing-out of Japanese manufacturing is seen as the main problem. In an interview in September 1995, a representative of the executive committee emphasised this urgency:

> Management is very serious about change this time, especially changes in long-term employment and the *nenko* wage system. It is no longer taboo within the union to discuss these things. New markets are evolving and there is a need for different forms of working and of organising human resources, for example working at home and new forms of compensation.

These changes could spell an end to the existing unitary system in Japanese companies, where the same evaluation and compensation system applies for both white and blue-collar workers, since the new pay-for-performance principles will probably only apply to engineers and salesmen. The changes could also spell an end to the conventional

notion of life-long employment. Denki Rengo approaches the problems of
flexibility from the perspective of the individual employees, and emphasises
the need to increase voluntary labour market flexibility instead of accelerating the involuntary mobility involved in corporate adjustment. The union
argues that retirement allowances and fringe benefits, such as company
housing, should be re-examined, since they create obstacles for mobility.
These benefits should be socially provided, and not arranged by companies.
If an employee wants to move to another company, the current system
affects very negatively his economic situation. A special problem for white-
collar workers is the lack of a socially accepted qualification. Basically, all
systems are in-house ones. To increase flexibility it is very important to have
externally recognised certificates.

Another consequence of the new *endaka* might be a redefinition of traditional labour–management relations. The representative of Denki Rengo
formulated the problem in the following way:

> Until recently, unions always stressed co-operation with management,
> and accepted almost all proposals from management. So the industry
> developed, but salaries did not develop at the same pace. And the end
> result has been *endaka* and hollowing-out, and then once more ra-
> tionalisation and perhaps a new *endaka*. We still need co-operation be-
> tween management and unions, but perhaps a different form of co-
> operation . . .

A TRISECTED PRODUCTION STRUCTURE?

A comparison of the consumer electronics and the automobile industries
yields similarities as well as contrasts. Both are rapidly internationalising,
but consumer electronics firms are far ahead. At the same time, both industries are making strong efforts to preserve their Japanese operations. In the
consumer electronics industry, the rapid transfer of mass products such as
VCRs overseas puts a lot of strain on domestic employment. In the automobile industry, the same process is slower, with more time for incremental
adjustment. In both cases, companies are extremely reluctant to reduce their
Japanese manufacturing base in any drastic way. This again underlines how
deeply embedded 'life-time employment' is for regular, male workers employed in large firms. Compared to the automobile industry, the consumer
electronics industry is more technologically dynamic and there are greater
opportunities. New technologies emerge, mature products are reinvented.
On the other hand, market demand is very difficult to predict. In response, a
'trisected' production structure seems to be evolving:

1) Conventional mass products are manufactured in Asian locations, where
   market saturation is low and labour costs permit a continuation of export
   production.
2) New key technologies and products, from thin-film transistor LCDs to
   plasma-screen TVs, are developed and manufactured in-house in Japan.

3) Commercially and/or technically unstable 'intermediate products' are also produced in Japan, but in new production configurations. To cope with market volatility, core firms invest only in minimum capacity, and outsource the balance to shifting networks of manufacturing companies. Conventional long-term employment is restricted to the core. The tradition of incremental *gemba* rationalisation, building on high worker involvement is increasingly replaced by the efforts of production engineers who are responsible for the 'vertical production ramp-up' of new and possibly short-lived products.

SUMMARY

Consumer electronics has been the second most important industrial sector in Japan's postwar growth. Manufacturing organisation and competitive strategies display many similarities with the automobile industry. Structurally, however, there are important differences: The automobile industry is focused on a few basic products, whereas consumer electronics encompasses a huge and constantly growing product range. The basic technologies in the automobile industry are evolving incrementally; whereas consumer electronics are characterised by a cyclical pattern of technological breakthroughs, gradual refinement and then new periods of breakthroughs. The internationalisation of production started much earlier in the consumer electronics sector. The vast majority of Japanese automobiles are still produced in Japan, whereas 75% of Japanese colour television sets are assembled offshore, as are 60% of all video-tape recorders (as in 1994). The industry giant Matsushita has a much larger workforce outside Japan than any other company. Early on the consumer electronics firms focused on southeast Asia. The Asian plants have successively become export centres, including export back to Japan. During the Bubble Boom, companies had no difficulties in combining transfer of mature products offshore with an upgrading of domestic plants and products. After the onset of the recession and the new *endaka*, the industry faced a serious problem: how to preserve Japanese employment in the wake of accelerated internationalisation. The major makers are pursuing different strategies.

Matsushita has adopted a gradual, conservative approach: continued transfer of mature products to 'cash-cow' plants in Asia; cost containment and incremental personnel adjustment in Japan; diversification into non-consumer areas; and investments in advanced technologies, which can generate new mass products and replace old ones. Sharp was an early leader in the calculator market, but otherwise belongs to a second-tier category of appliance assemblers. By investing aggressively in LCD technology it has become the first player in this boom market, where fierce competition between all Japanese electronics firms is now evolving. The LCD case demonstrates that Japan's famous '*kaisha* dynamics' of growth, competition, repeated capacity doubling and cost reduction is not a thing of the past. As a result of its technological leadership, Sharp has been able to move much more of its conventional products to Asia than Matsushita, while upgrading its domestic manufacturing base at the same time. Hitachi, the most diversified of the companies within this sector, has complemented its offshore investments with a two-pronged production strategy in Japan: in-house investment in new high-technology 'future products', and outsourcing of unstable products to external manufacturing firms. In this way the company can minimise its core of regular employees. Similar to the automobile industry, process engineering and the instantaneous ramp-up of new products have gained in importance at the expense of traditional shop-floor improvement programmes. The need for an overall increase in labour market flexibility is also acknowledged by unions, but so far it is by no means clear how this mobility will be achieved.

8

MACHINE TOOLS: VICTORY, CRISIS AND NEW EXPANSION?

A SPECTACULAR GROWTH RECORD

In the early 1980s, Japan unexpectedly became the biggest machine tool builder in the world. To understand how dramatically this Japanese industry has developed, it is necessary to look back into history. (For an overview of the structure of the Japanese machine tool industry, see Box 8.1.)

Box 8.1 *Structure of the industry*

In contrast to automobiles and consumer electronics, the machine tool industry is characterised by a large diversity in firm size, from smaller than 50 employees to larger than 5,000. The smaller a firm, the more specialised its machine tools. Table 8.1 provides an overview of the industry. It is based on statistics from the Japan Machine Tool Builders' Association, which covered about 90% of the total production of machine tools in 1994.

Table 8.1   Structure of the machine tool industry in 1994 (JMTBA members; size of firm by no. of employers)

	–50	51–100	101–300	301–500	501–1,000	1,001–3,000	3,001–5,000	5,000+	Total
No. of firms	10	9	33	8	19	15	8	4	106
Production of machine tools per firm (million yen)	233	632	1,987	3,733	6,223	11,616	14,863	11,063	50,300
% of machine tools to total production	53.8	61.0	59.0	43.0	39.6	21.4	11.0	0.5	
Employees producing machine tools	278	555	4,912	1,732	6,860	7,905	6,129	1,831	30,202
Total no of employees	333	702	6,366	3,093	13,256	26,108	33,374	151,484	234,716

Note: Ratio of machine tools to total production is calculated in value.
Source: JMTBA Machine Tool Statistics Handbook, 1995: 236.

Among 106 members of the JMTBA, 75% are firms with fewer than 1,000 employees. Big firms are less specialised. The bigger the company, the more it diversifies its products. Altogether, 106 firms employ 234,716 employees, but employees producing machine tools number only 30,202.

Japanese machine tool builders produce a limited range of products. In 1994, lathes accounted for 26.2% of the total production, machining centres for 23.3%, followed by special-purpose machines at 14.2%, grinding machines at 12.3%, electric discharge machines at 6.5%, milling machines at 2.7% and others at 14.9%.

Export ratio (export/production in value), once down to 32.5% in 1992, jumped to 59.3% in 1994 because of the export offensive during the depression. The largest export market is the USA with 36.9%, then South Korea with 15.5%, EU countries with 11.0%, China with 7.0% and Taiwan with 6.3%. The ratio of imports to exports is only 7.7%. Japan is a big consumer of machine tools, but it seems Japanese customers prefer to 'buy Japanese'.

Japan was a latecomer to machine tool production. In the latter half of the nineteenth century, Japan produced almost no machine tools. It was the Russo-Japanese War (1904–5) that gave birth to the Japanese machine tool industry. The military ordered many simple machine tools. From the Russo-Japanese War to the end of the Second World War, the development of the machine tool industry has been closely connected to military demand. Every time the military undertook major campaigns against foreign countries, the machine tool industry stepped up: the First World War (1914–18), the establishment of colonial Manchuria in 1931, the Sino-Japanese War (1937–45) and the Second World War (1941–5). Especially during the Second World War, the machine tool industry developed very rapidly. Production value increased from 10.7 million yen in 1930 to 46.6 million yen in 1935, 407.8 million yen in 1940, and finally 488.1 million yen in 1942. From 1930 to 1942, real production value increased 21 times. Accordingly, the number of the employees increased rapidly, from 6,144 in 1930 to 18,400 in 1935, 98,141 in 1940, and 125,048 in 1942 (JMTBA, 1984: 51–2).

With the end of the Second World War, the Japanese machine tool builders started again under miserable conditions. The break-up of the military forces and the munitions industry not only meant the loss of the biggest customer but also flooded the market with cheap machines. Machine tools used in munitions factories were lent or sold to small and medium-sized companies which were expected to be the machine tool makers' main customers after the war. These small and medium-sized companies preferred old and cheap machines to buying new ones (Kato, 1960: 341–2). As any export was unthinkable at that time, the machine tool builders could not find a market. Imported machines further deteriorated their economic situation. This was the starting point for the industry after the war. Thus, the success of the machine tool industry should be considered as one aspect of the 'economic miracle' of postwar Japan. What are the major factors accounting for its spectacular rise to a world-leading position in only 30 years?

The main customer for Japanese machine tools was and is the Japanese machinery industry (automobiles, electrical and electronic machinery and general machinery). With the rapid growth of the machinery industry, the machine tool industry also developed rapidly.

Similar to the automobile and electronics industry, the machine tool industry utilises many smaller companies as subcontractors. In the late 1980s, one machine tool builder on average utilised 53 subcontractors for casting, machining, assembly and so on, according to data from the JMTBA. Furthermore, one subcontractor used 10–20 second-level subcontractors (MITI, 1989: 36). As machine tool builders themselves are very small compared to automobile or electronic companies, their subcontractors are tiny. In the mid-1980s, about 68% of the subcontractors at the first level had fewer than 19 employees. Subcontractors with fewer than four employees accounted for 24% of all subcontractors (Miyamoto and Hagiwara, 1993: 28). The utilisation of subcontractors has contributed to the competitiveness of machine tool builders. First, the wage level of subcontractors is lower than that of machine tool builders. Secondly, machine tool builders make use of sub-contractors to rationalise their production flow. Parts produced in small lots are outsourced, whereas high-volume main parts are manufactured in-house. Thus the subcontracting system improved the machine builders economies of scale. Thirdly, there are a number of specialist subcontractors who contribute to higher quality and lower costs.

Japanese machine tool builders emphasised customer orientation, especially quick delivery and good after-sales service. The customers took it for granted that machine tool builders would send service personnel any time they were needed. Good after-sales service and long working hours for employees were two sides of the same coin.

MITI's industrial policy protected and supported the machine tool industry. This policy began in the early 1950s. At first, in order to study high technology, MITI recommended that machine tool builders import machine tools. Subsidies were also supplied to machine tool builders who invested in R&D. Furthermore, MITI introduced a special depreciation system to boost the machinery industry by encouraging the replacement of old machine tools with new ones. Owing to the industrial policy of MITI from 1956 to 1970, the machine tool industry succeeded in modernising itself and increasing production runs. However, even the industrial policy of MITI could not help the machine tool industry diversify its products, though MITI wanted to stabilise competition among makers by introducing an appropriate product mix (Sawai, 1990: 161).

These factors are important, but not enough. After the first oil crisis in 1973, the market share for the machine tool builders changed (the five biggest companies are listed in Table 8.2). A big change occurred in the late 1970s. The market share of big, diversified companies like Toshiba Machinery or Hitachi Seiki declined and machine tool specialists like Yamazaki Mazak or Okuma became the industry leaders. One reason lies in the product strategy of big companies, which reduced the ratio of machine tools by diversifying their product mix. Toshiba Machinery was, for example, good at plastic injection moulding machines and printing machines. However, the major reason lay in computerised numerical control (CNC) machines and exports. Companies that have enjoyed high growth since the mid-1970s have two common features: a high ratio of CNC machines and a high and increasing ratio of exports (Sawai, 1990: 188–9).

Table 8.2 Market share of machine tools in Japan, 1975–85 (fiscal years)(%)

	1975		1980		1985
Toshiba Machinery	7.1	Yamazaki Mazak	7.2	Yamazaki Mazak	7.6
Yamazaki Mazak	4.5	Okuma	6.7	Okuma	6.8
Hitachi Seiki	4.4	Mori Seiki	5.2	Mori Seiki	5.4
Toyoda Machinery	4.3	Toyoda Machinery	4.8	Makino	4.8
Makino	3.9	Toshiba Machinery	4.6	Mitsubishi Heavy	4.3

Source: Sawai, 1990:187.

CNC machines

Small and medium-sized CNC lathes and machining centres accounted for nearly half the total Japanese machine tool production in 1994. As the president of Mori Seiki once said, 'about 70% of the total production of the Japanese machine tool industry consists of standardised, cheap CNC machines' (cited in Kobayashi, 1993: 151). The development of standardised small and medium-sized machines had already begun by the late 1950s. After the war, Japanese tool builders faced severe competition from abroad. As foreign contenders produced mainly expensive heavy-duty machines, Japanese makers developed so-called 'junior machines'. Their price was low and their functions and precision were of course limited, but not poor (Kato, 1960: 378). As major domestic customers were small and medium-sized firms, these machines were welcomed.

The early adoption of CNC machines was decisive for the competitiveness of the Japanese machine tool industry. The first numerically controlled (NC) milling machine in the world was developed by the US MIT group in 1952. Six years later Makino Milling Machine developed the first Japanese NC milling machine in co-operation with Fuji Tsushinki (now Fanuc). Numerical controllers progressed to CNC machines. The mass production of CNC machines by Japanese makers began in the 1970s. The proportion of CNC machines to total production (in value) in 1970 was only 7.8%. This increased to 17.3% in 1975 and 49.8% in 1980. In 1994 it was 79.2% (JMTBA, *Machine Tool Statistics Handbook*, 1994: 10). Japan had become the no. 1 country for CNC machines. This position was the result of several different factors. First, in the USA and Europe, machine tool makers viewed NC machines as an up-market segment. Big and expensive CNC machines were developed for the precision cutting of aeroplane parts. Japanese makers, on the other hand, produced small and medium-sized CNC machines at cheaper prices. In Japan, however, the aerospace industry did not develop after the war, mainly due to the policy of the US occupation authority which regarded the aerospace industry as a munitions industry. Instead, Japanese machine tool builders found their main customers in small and medium-sized companies within the machinery industry. These customers demanded cheap, standardised CNC machine tools, because they could not afford to buy expensive ones and because they also suffered from a shortage of skilled workers. The average price for CNC machine tools in Japan was half or one third compared to German or US counterparts.

The mass production of the computerised control device itself, which is one of the most important components of CNC machines, contributed to the machines' low price. One Japanese company, Fanuc, monopolised the market for CNCs. Between 1969 and 1975, Fanuc produced 73% of all CNCs. Though there are several machine tool builders who produce CNCs in-house, such as Okuma, their total share of the CNC market was only 12%. (Sawai, 1990: 180). Japanese machine tool builders could make 'high-tech' machines by purchasing cheap CNCs from Fanuc. The strategy to mass produce a limited range of products was very successful. However, on the other side of the coin, this resulted in excessive competition and sharp fluctuations in profit.

The profits of the machine tool industry fluctuated much more sharply than the manufacturing industry average. One reason for the sharp fluctuation is the character of the machine tool industry as a capital-goods producing industry. Foreign machine tool builders also suffer from sharper profit fluctuations than manufacturing industry as a whole. In Japan, however, the dominant product strategy aggravated losses. Because there is no substantial difference between various makers, they compete with each other by offering cheaper prices to maintain their market share during recessions. After the Bubble Boom, for example, top makers such as Okuma, Mori Seiki and Yamazaki Mazak offered their important customers half prices (Nikkei Sangyo Shinbun, 1992: 189). Once major makers lower their prices, smaller makers are necessarily involved in a price-down competition, which leads to deteriorating losses.

Exports

The Japanese machine tool industry, like many other successful industries, developed initially in response to a strong domestic demand. However, also common to other industries, it has repeatedly launched export offensives during the recession periods in order to secure production volumes. This was the case during the first oil crisis of the mid-1970s. The export ratio (export/production) jumped from 11.5% in 1973 to 44.4% in 1978. This has also been the case during the post-Bubble recession in the 1990s. The export ratio increased from 35% in 1990 to 59% in 1994. This time the strong increase was not enough to stabilise production. Because of the collapse of domestic demand, total output was cut back sharply, from 1,303 billion yen in 1990 to 554 billion yen in 1994, a reduction of 57%. The world market was also shrinking, but the Japanese maintained their export volume and increased their world market share.

The repeated Japanese export offensives have evoked the fear and anger of foreign competitors. Though the export ratio of the German machine tool industry (46.6% in 1990) is higher than that of the Japanese (35.0% in 1990), Germany has not faced trade conflicts with other countries. One important reason is that Germany practises a substantial intraindustry trade, both exporting and importing a great many machines. Japan, on the other hand, has increased exports, while keeping imports at a minimum. As a result, Japan's trade surplus is much higher than that of Germany. In 1990, the export/import ratio of the Japanese machine tool industry was 6.6 compared to 2.1 of Germany.

Trade conflicts over machine tools with the USA began in 1977. In that year, the US Machine Tool Builders' Association tried to appeal using anti-dumping laws. Since 1982, the US association has organized campaigns against the import of Japanese machine tools. They appealed to the US Trade Representative and the Department of Commerce to restrict imports from Japan. Finally in 1986, President Reagan formally requested that the Japanese government voluntarily restrict exports from Japan (Nyusu Daijesto, 1989: 96).

In 1987, a 'voluntary restriction agreement' (VRA) was agreed upon by the Japanese government. According to this agreement, the Japanese government would control the volume of exports to the USA for five years from 1987 to 1991. The upper limit of the market share of Japanese CNC lathes in the USA would be 57% and 52% for machining centres. MITI should forecast the US market trend and allocate an export volume to each Japanese machine tool builder (Kokumin Kinyu Koko Chosabu, 1989: 45). This VRA expired at the end of 1993. Because of the high yen and the recovery of the US machine tool industry, it was not expected that exports from Japan would increase. But a trade conflict will emerge once again if Japanese makers continue their export offensive.

EXTERNALISATION OF TAYLORISM

In many ways the ascendancy of Japan's machine tools resembles the rise of the automobile industry. The machine tool industry displays several peculiar traits, however. One is its system of intercompany labour division and externalised Taylorism. When Taylorism is discussed in Japan, the automobile and electronics industries are used as examples. The machine tool industry is seldom analysed. Perhaps Japanese researchers are only interested in big industries. For many researchers, 'big is beautiful'. But it is unfair just to criticise researchers. In contrast to the German machine tool industry, the social prestige of the Japanese machine tool industry is not high, which discourages research.

We will take a machine tool builder as a case study on work organisation in the machine tool industry. In 1989 this company produced CNC lathes (64.9% of total sales), conventional lathes (16.5%) and small machining centres (13.6%). The company had 435 employees, of which the number of production workers was 148 (for details of this case study, see Nomura, 1991). It is not possible to say how many of these employees were 'skilled workers' (*Facharbeiter* in Germany). In Japan there is no formal vocational training system for skilled workers. There is no clear distinction between skilled, semi-skilled and unskilled workers. There is no socially accepted qualification for a skilled worker.

To be able to pursue cost reduction and also be capable of responding quickly to diverse customer demands, the company adopts a 'module production system'. CNC lathes are broken down into several modules, such as headstock module, tailstock module, bed module and so on. Management forecasts demand for each model and prepares modules in advance. When the company receives orders, modules are assembled into final products. By combining different modules, the company produces a relatively wide variety of products.

In 1983 the company developed a flexible manufacturing system (FMS) for machining. There are two lines in the FMS, Line A and Line B. Line A consists of five machining centres and automated pallets changers, and can be operated for 20–24 hours without operators. Line B consists of five machining centres with multiple pallets and one CNC lathe. Workpieces are carried by the unmanned wire-in-the-floor robo-carrier. Workpieces are set by workers before they go home and unloaded the next morning. The maximum operating time without operators is 16 hours. In the FMS plant, there is a premachining shop for the machining of the datum level, which consists of four milling machines and two machining centres.

The company's hierarchy is broken down into divisions – *bu*, *ka* and *han*. In the production division there are five *bu*. The machining *bu* is responsible for machining, including the FMS. A *bu* is broken down into two *ka*, Machining I and Machining II. Under Machining II there is a *han* IV responsible for the FMS. *Han* IV consists of 14 workers, including a leader of the *han* and a worker who comes from a daughter company on *shukko*. Of these 14 workers, 3 workers are assigned to the premachining shop, 4 to Line A and 7 to Line B. There is no rotation between the premachining shop and Line A or Line B. The workers in the premachining shop specialise in premachining. The workers at Line A sometimes help Line B. The workers at Line A and Line B are responsible for workpiece setting, scheduling, tool maintenance and improvement, the checking of programming for trial products and the improvement of drawing sheets.

As a supporting section for the FMS plant, the production engineering *ka* carries out programming, preparation of jigs and tools and maintenance of machines in the FMS. Previously, scheduling was also the responsibility of the production engineering *ka*. As the know-how of scheduling was shared by the *han* leader (hancho) and some elder workers, this task was transferred to FMS workers. For programming there is division of labour between production engineering and the FMS workers. The FMS workers check the program made by the production engineers for trial production. Programs seldom have bugs.

Not all workers in Line A and Line B can perform all the jobs assigned to the FMS. For example, a young worker who has just entered the company can only carry out simple operations. Only a few workers can do the scheduling job. But this should not be interpreted as a fixed division of labour. Management expects that all workers can perform all jobs in the shop. The difference in knowledge and skill level among the workers is, so to speak, a 'time lag' which should be covered gradually by on the job training (OJT). The division of labour between the production engineers and the workers in the FMS is flexible. In principle, there should be no division of labour among the FMS workers, and consequently it is not possible to talk about Taylorism in this context. It is worth noting that the work organisation has not been a matter of negotiation between management and the enterprise union. The non-Tayloristic work organisation is realised 'unconsciously'. However, the company makes only 16% of the total value of the product in-house. The rest is produced by subcontractors and daughter companies. In 1990 the company used two daughter companies and 75 subcontractors. Simple tasks are subcontracted. For example, there is a daughter company for the assembly of electronic components. There are 35 regular employees and 70 female part-timers. Most of them are engaged in repetitive routine work. Non-Tayloristic work organisation in building machine tools is possible when repetitive work is subcontracted. There is a Tayloristic division of labour not within the company but between the company and its subcontractors.

CRISIS MANAGEMENT AND THE PLIGHT OF OKUMA

The Japanese machine tool industry reached its peak in 1990. During the next five years production dropped by half. Without doubt the machine tool industry is facing a struggle for survival. This is the second time the industry has had to think about its future. The first time was during the oil crisis in 1973.

The first oil crisis

Hit by the first oil crisis, the production of machine tools fell by 36% from 1974 to 1976. In the fiscal years 1974 and 1975 four members of the JMTBA went into bankruptcy. It was the hardest recession since the war. Japanese machine tool builders learned much during this recession. The present structure of the industry was shaped by the first oil crisis.

First, the ratio of owned capital in the major machine tool builders increased from 22.6% in 1975 to 41.9% in 1984. They tried to defend themselves by improving their financial situation. The ratio of owned capital in the machine tool industry is above the average of manufacturing industry as a whole, which is believed to be the most important reason why the bankruptcy of machine tool builders has been limited in the post-Bubble recession (interview with the JMTBA in September 1995).

Secondly, machine tool builders quickly increased production of CNC machines. The ratio of CNC machines to all production jumped in value from 17.3% in 1975 to 67.0% in 1985. This rapid change to CNC machines made Japan the world leader. Thirdly, Japanese machine tool builders ousted the Germans aside from the US market with their CNC machines. Especially in the market segment of small and medium-sized lathes and machining centres, Japanese makers were very competitive. Japanese makers also succeeded in penetrating the European market with their CNC machines. Fourthly, machine tool builders invested heavily in new production equipment but suppressed wage increases. Coupled with employment adjustment, labour's relative share of value added decreased from 87.9% in 1975 to 50.4% in 1980.

During the first oil crisis, employment adjustment was the focus of rationalisation. Machine tool builders practised all methods of employment adjustment: the reduction of overtime, stopping new recruitment, temporary transfers (*shukko*), and the reduction of part-timers and temporary workers. To maintain the employment of regular workers during the severe recession, the Ministry of Labour introduced a new system called 'employment adjustment subsidy'. A subsidy was given to firms who continued to employ regular workers by the use of *shukko*, training or temporary release from work. Machine tool builders utilised this system, but after all these softer methods proved to be insufficient, companies began to offer voluntary retirement (Table 8.3).

Table 8.3 Voluntary retirement in major companies

	Date of VR	Before VR (a)	VR (b)	(b)/(a) %
Hitachi Seiki	March 1976	1,900	411	22
Washino Machinery	March 1976	1,580	282	18
Ikegai	May 1976	2,020	333	16
Tsugami	Jan. 1975	1,680	462	28
Okuma	March 1976	2,230	403	18
Enshu	Feb. 1975 & 1976	2,050	757	37
OKK	Jan. 1976	1,890	270	14
Howa	Nov. 1974	1,560	316	20

Note: VR = voluntary retirement.
Source: Yoshida, 1986:128.

The first oil crisis taught the machine tool industry the need to prepare for a sudden and severe recession. They increased their retained profit and owned capital. It is partly because of this policy that machine tool builders were able to get over the next two recessions (the second oil crisis at the end of 1979 and the high-yen recession in the mid-1980s) relatively easily. In these two recessions, they were able to adjust employment using only soft methods (Heiwa Keizai Keikaku Kaigi, 1995: 126–9).

Heisei recession

The Heisei recession, however, surpassed all expectations. This recession is lasting much longer and is more serious than the industry had anticipated. According to a survey of 29 major machine tool builders (JMTBA, 1995c), the profit margin dropped from 10.8% in the fiscal year 1990 to 6.5% in 1991. In 1992, business recorded a negative margin of –3.4%, which dropped further to –12.3% in 1993, although it improved a little in 1994. In spite of the suppressed wage increases, labour's relative share rose from 55.28% in 1991 to 76.9% in 1992, and to 103.8% in 1993. It was 77.55% in 1994. The ratio of machine tool sales to total sales declined from 68.7% in 1990 to 52.1% in 1994. JMTBA interprets this as a sharper slump in machine tools compared to other machines and not the result of a successful strategy of product diversification. Despite declining profits, the ratio of R&D expenditure to total sales was stable: 3.7% in 1991, 3.3% in 1992, 3.1% in 1993 and 3.1% in 1994. Machine tool builders fear that there will be no future without R&D. As machine tool builders are reducing outsourcing, the situation for subcontractors becomes more serious. The ratio of outsourcing cost to the total manufacturing cost dropped from 15.7% in 1990 to 10.3% in 1994. One member company of the JMTBA went into bankruptcy in June 1993. Sharp cutbacks in production compelled other makers to adjust their workforce. To apply for the employment adjustment subsidy, JMTBA presented data on 66 major companies to the Ministry of Labour in October 1993. These data are summarised in Table 8.4.

Table 8.4 Employment adjustment in the 1990s

	Firms	Since
Curtailment of operation, reduction of overtime	61	Oct. 1991
Transfer to another workplace	44	Oct. 1991
Increase in holidays	22	April 1992
No renewal of contract or dismissal of temporary workers, part-timers	34	April 1992
Reduction or stoppage of recruitment	58	April 1992
Temporary release from work	40	Dec. 1992
Shukko	23	Jan. 1993
Voluntary retirement or dismissal of regular employees	11	Jan. 1993
Others (training, shutdown of plants, dismissal of specified employees)	6	Feb. 1993

Source: JMTBA (1993).

These data show the preferences of Japanese companies clearly. First they take softer methods while maintaining employment. Then they fire temporary workers and part-timers. If needed, they go further to the final method, voluntary retirement and dismissals. Yuka shoken hokokusho (annual report) reports the following employee reductions:

- *OKK*. Reduction of 147 employees mainly by transfer to daughter companies in the fiscal year 1993. Further reduction of 110 employees mainly by transfer.
- *Amada*. Reduction of 232 employees by *shukko* and early retirement in the fiscal year 1994.
- *Amada Washino*. Early retirement of 36 employees in December 1993.
- *Hitachi Seiki*. Voluntary retirement of 141 employees in March 1994.
- *Shoun Machine Tool*. 74 employees reduced mainly by voluntary retirement in the fiscal year 1994.
- *Okamoto Machine Tool*. Early retirement of 135 employees in May 1994.
- *Hamai*. Reduction of 157 employees mainly by voluntary retirement.
- *Nippei Toyama*. Reduction of 259 employees by a 'job change scheme' in May 1994.
- *Enshu*. Reduction of 232 employees mainly by an early retirement scheme in the fiscal year 1993.
- *Makino Milling Machine*. Reduction of 192 employees mainly by transfer to daughter companies.

Of course, other industries also reduced employment by using voluntary retirement or early retirement schemes. But it was Okuma's case that was reported sensationally by the mass media. What happened at Okuma?

Okuma

Okuma is one of the oldest machine tool builders in Japan. The company was founded in 1898 as a noodle-making-machine maker. From 1904 Okuma began to produce machine tools. Since the 1920s it has been a leading producer. At the end of 1993 and at the beginning of 1994, news about Okuma was a hot topic in the Japanese press. Newspapers reported that Okuma wanted to fire managers and lower the compulsory retirement age, meaning that all employees over 56 had to leave the company. Though it was not the first case in Japanese history of lowering the compulsory retirement age, nevertheless it shocked Japanese society. People realised that even a famous company like Okuma would not hesitate to use this final method. It seemed that an era of massive dismissal had begun. The target was middle-aged and older employees.

Before lowering the compulsory retirement age and introducing voluntary retirement, the company had tried to improve the situation by the following measures:

- Develop new models.
- Strengthen exports to Asia, especially to China.
- Reduce purchasing cost by lowering the price of materials and sub-contracted parts. Increase the in-house production ratio.
- Establish a 'Committee for Cost Reduction' and campaign for cost reduction.
- Release workers from work two days in every month during the first half of 1993. Temporary release from work is a system set by the Employment Adjustment Subsidy Programme. When an industry is labelled by the Ministry of Labour as a recession industry, a part of the wage compensation during the temporary release from work is covered by the Ministry of Labour. This system was introduced in 1974 to maintain the employment of regular workers during the first oil crisis. Further, *shukko* of 70 employees.
- Decrease the remuneration of board members. In 1992 compensation was lowered by 10%, in 1993 it was further cut by 15%.
- Reduce managers' salary (*bucho* and *kacho*) by 2.5% in 1993.
- All *shokutaku* had to leave in September 1992. (*Shokutaku* are those who are re-employed in the firm at lower salaries as non-regular staff after they have reached the compulsory retirement age.)
- Fire half the part-timers (December 1992).
- Reduce the 450 subcontract workers (*konai sagyosha*) working in Okuma's factories.
- Reduce overtime.
- Cut the number of board members by half.
- Offer voluntary retirement for managers until December 1993.

The company informed the enterprise union that these measures would not be sufficient for its survival. No recovery of business was expected in the next few years. In December 1993, the company lowered the compulsory retirement age from 60 to 56 years and formally proposed a programme of voluntary retirement. All employees 54–5 years of age were expected to leave the company voluntarily. An additional special allowance was paid to those who left the company under this scheme. The main goal of the proposal was to reduce the workforce, including managers, by 400.

The scheme is described as follows:

As many employees as possible coming under one of the following conditions are asked to apply for voluntary retirement:

(a) those who are planning to leave the company in the near future.
(b) those whose lives are less affected by retirement.
(c) those who have health problems that interfere with job performance (except the physically handicapped).
(d) those whose aptitudes are not suited for work in the company.
(e) those whose performance is relatively poor.
(f) those who cannot be transferred to another job within the company.

After a closed discussion, the union decided not to oppose voluntary retirement but demanded more generous special allowances. After the negotiations, the company accepted an increase in these allowances. At an extraordinary meeting, the union decided to accept the company's proposal with 150 voting for, 4 against and 3 abstaining.

The voluntary retirement scheme was valid for one and half months from the beginning of January 1994. But more employees applied than the 400 the company had planned for. Furthermore, up to the end of 1993, 116 managers left the company by means of the voluntary retirement scheme for managers. Including transfers to daughter companies and some employees who had reached the compulsory retirement age, the number of employees, including the daughter company Okuma Engineering, fell by 729.

The company helped retired employees find new positions. About 200 did not try to find another job; 40 received unemployment benefits; and 437 were able to find another job. Most of them were employed by Okuma's supplier's and subcontractors who had suffered from labour shortages during the Bubble Boom. It was an opportunity to hire skilled workers easily. In 1995, 220 subcontract workers were employed in Okuma's factories. A number were former Okuma employees who left as part of the voluntary retirement programme. Though these former Okuma's employees are doing the same job as before, their wage as subcontract workers is definitely lower. That is what voluntary retirement meant for them.

This drastic workforce reduction did have serious consequences. At management level, three top managers, the *shacho* (president) and the two *senmu* (senior managing directors) resigned immediately after having finished the voluntary retirement scheme. The number of board members was reduced from 13 to 10. In a Japanese context, the management took responsibility for the undesirable voluntary retirement. In the union, no top officers except one were re-elected in August 1994. The only officer to be re-elected had previously criticised the old leadership for being too co-operative with management.

Concerning future personnel policy, a leading union representative told us:

The company will not increase the number of regular employees. The Japanese machine tool industry has become a mature industry. Of course we expect a recovery in the coming three years. However, the recovery will not be substantial. In Europe there will be no recovery within the next two years. In Japan there will be more demand, but only for replacement, not really new demand. The boom in the USA will last only until the presidential election in 1996. If a recovery does come, our company will use *kyoryoku kaisha*, [subcontractors]. Units will be out-sourced. For assembly, the company will use subcontract companies.

(Interview in September 1995)

Mori Seiki

Mori Seiki which has its headquarters in the historic capital of Nara is a symbolic success story. Mori Seiki was founded in 1948 as a maker of textile machinery. The company pamphlet states:

It [Mori Seiki] started as a joint-stock company from the beginning, but its scale was small, and capital was raised by investing all mountains, woods, farmland and housing of the Mori family's native home. It faced the harsh postwar inflation economy, and its management was always in a difficult state during the first ten years.

In 1958, the company switched from textile machinery to high-speed precision lathes. Ten years later Mori Seiki began to produce NC lathes. This new strategy made the Nara company a leading producer of CNC lathes in Japan. Since the 1980s Mori Seiki has been one of the top three producers in the machine tool industry. Starting from scratch, in 1958 Mori Seiki had become in only two decades one of the biggest machine tool builders in the world. Apparently, the most important success factor was the introduction at an early stage of CNC machines. Asked by a journalist why Mori Seiki has grown up so rapidly, its president answered: 'We had a good eye for timing: the development of high productivity and high precision machine tools, the build-up of a system of mass production and mass sales, an early shift to CNC machines. And we were lucky' (Nyusu Daijesuto, 1989: 90).

Mori Seiki, a competitor of Okuma, had a quite different experience in the post-Bubble recession. In spite of a radical drop in production in the 1990s, the number of employees has remained surprisingly stable. In 1991 Mori Seiki had 1,853 employees and in 1994, 1,850. One reason was a strong corporate commitment to maintain stable employment. A manager explained: 'Our president has clear policies. We have no *nenko* system. Lifetime employment will be maintained. We do not use subcontractors.' As the philosophy of lifetime employment has often been openly upheld by the president of Mori Seiki, employees believe in it. It would not be easy for management to abandon this principle without evoking deep mistrust. The fact that there is no enterprise union in Mori Seiki might affect the company's philosophy. Among major machine tool makers, Mori Seiki is an exception in that it does not have a union. Instead, there is an employees' representative committee for communicating with management. But it is not qualified to negotiate on wages and other working conditions. Lifetime employment may be the cost of keeping the company ununionised.

Mori Seiki uses almost no subcontractors. In the fiscal year 1994 the subcontract cost accounted for only 1.6% of all production cost, while in Okuma it was 26.9% (Yuka shoken hokokusho). Unlike Okuma, Mori Seiki is a family-owned company. The owner's philosophy does not come in for resistance from bankers. A top manager said: Our company is strong in recessions. Both in the first and the second oil crisis we recovered by the second year of the recession. Though we experienced losses in two successive years this time [1993 and 1994], we expect profits in 1995. Further he said: We produce fewer numbers of models than Okuma. This means that we are oriented towards mass production. With mass production, we have an advantage in negotiations with suppliers. We can demand lower prices (Interview, September 1995).

There is also another difference in the strategy of Mori Seiki. Okuma has transplants abroad: one in Germany for electric discharge machines and another in the USA for CNC lathes and machining centres. Mori Seiki has no overseas production. No overseas production, no subcontracting, no voluntary retirement – these practices are supported by the Mori family.

However, there is one thing in common between Mori Seiki and Okuma. Neither company will increase the number of regular employees. A top manager of Mori Seiki said:

> Even if there is an upturn in sales, we will not hire more regular workers. Instead, we intend to hire more temporary workers. The machine tool industry used to see itself as a very male industry. But there are many housewives who are easy to recruit and are very good. This year we hired 50 women and next year we plan to hire more. We want to have at least 100 such workers as a buffer.
>
> (Interview in September 1995)

Takisawa Machine Tool

Takisawa Machine Tool is a family-owned, medium-sized company, founded in 1922 by the Takisawa brothers. Since then all presidents of the company have come from the Takisawa family. Business has been good since its foundation. During the war, the company was compelled to produce munitions (engines for ships, aeroplane parts). The number of employees jumped to about 1,000. The end of the war brought catastrophe to the company. All except 30 employees were fired. The Korean War in 1950 was a good opportunity to produce machine tools once again. With the rapidly growing Japanese economy, Takisawa grew as well. Takisawa began to produce NC lathes in 1968 and machining centres in 1981. Takisawa's main products are small and medium-sized CNC lathes and machining centres. In the post-Bubble depression, production dropped sharply from 21 billion yen in the fiscal year 1990 to 7 billion yen in 1993. Takisawa was fighting for its life.

To cope with the sharp production decrease, the company began fundamental restructuring. The main method was workforce reduction. The number of employees was cut from 524 in March 1992 to 423 in March 1993. Workforce reduction was carried out by transferring employees to new daughter companies such as Takisawa International (sales and import and export, 28 employees), Takisawa Systec (data processing, sales of the factory automation system and office automation system, 11 employees) and Takisawa Business Support (the subcontracting of daily business work, 17 employees). Another method was to dispatch workers to any company that could make use of Takisawa employees (e.g. food companies, housing companies). One of the main tasks of the personnel department was to find any company that could accept Takisawa's excess workers. Takisawa did not offer voluntary retirement until 1993. The company wanted to receive employment adjustment subsidies which were given only when the company did not offer voluntary retirement (interview in October 1993).

In 1993, production volume continued to fall. At last the company offered voluntary retirement. The number of employees decreased from 423 in March 1993 to 344 in March 1994, mainly because of voluntary retirement. The Tamashima plant was closed down and sold. Though production for the fiscal year 1994 was nearly the same as in the previous year, the huge loss compelled the company to restructure even further. The technical centre in the USA was closed down and sold. Not only the newly founded daughter companies but also old Takisawa Mechatronics, Takisawa Deutschland and Takisawa Benelux ceased their activities. Of employees of these daughter companies, 71 came back to Takisawa. But the company offered voluntary retirement once more. In the fiscal year 1994, 112 employees left the company, including 81 voluntary retirements. In March 1995 the number of employees was 303, including 38 *shukko* (Yuka shoken hokokusho for each year). In the three years from 1992 to 1995, the number of employees fell from 524 to 303, a reduction of 42%: 'I'm very sorry, but we can't give you a plant tour. This year we expect huge losses. We need to restructure even further. I can't say when we will recover.' This is the answer we received when we asked a manager for a plant tour in August 1995. The company is undergoing a severe struggle for survival.

STRUGGLE FOR SURVIVAL: WHO SURVIVES?

The Japanese machine tool industry enjoyed rapid development by concentrating its R&D on a limited range of machine tools. It targeted the middle segment of the market while the Germans and the Americans tried to keep their prestige as high-end makers. Middle-class machines equipped with CNC were the main Japanese products. The success of the Japanese makers was a result of this expanding market segment. Can this market segment grow once more in the future? Perhaps not. Asian countries are now enjoying the highest rate of economic development. This area will be the most important area for Japan. According to Nomura Research Institute the future market segments will be as presented in Table 8.5.

Table 8.5 Growth forecast of various CNC machine tool segments

Price (million yen)	Main producers	CNC machines (units) 5 years ago	1994	5 years later
30–200	Germany, USA	5,000	5,000	5,000
10–30	Japan	60,000	30,000	40,000
5–10	USA (new makers)	0	5,000	10,000
3–5	Taiwan	5,000	10,000	15,000
2–3	China	2,000	10,000	30,000

Note: This table covers countries relevant to Japan only.
Source: JMTBA, 1995b:105.

Though the middle market segment will recover a little bit, it is not expected to return to the 'good old days'. The only rapidly expanding segment is at the low end of the market. The most profitable segment is the upper segment. Now Japanese machine tool builders have three choices: upgrading, keeping the no. 1 position in the middle segment, and/or producing machine tools for Asia.

In March 1995, the Committee on Machine Tool Technology of the JMTBA presented a report which critically evaluated the position of the Japanese machine tool industry (JMTBA, 1995a). The report pointed out that the Japanese machine tool industry had developed by combining mechanics with electronics. But the 'mechatronics' technology seems to have matured. There is no large area for further development. Further, Japanese machine tool builders have no indigenous technology. There is no individuality and direction in R&D and different firms look similar to one another. In original and basic technology (special types, high-end functions and high-end precision), US and European competitors are more advanced. Japan leads in machine productivity, but the efforts to increase the speed of the main spindle, the feed shaft and the data processing of CNC have reached their limit, according to the report. Aggravating the problems is customer behaviour. Customers are seeking low prices and are not prepared to pay any more for higher value. Added functions and features do not result in better prices. As prices are declining, it is becoming difficult to make working conditions attractive for the younger generation, which will lead to serious shortages of good engineers and skilled workers. Without young engineers and skilled workers, production engineering skills will not be passed on to the next generation.

This self-critical assessment suggests that for the mainstream of Japanese makers the road to upgrading is not easy. Not only from the viewpoint of technology but also from the viewpoint of the style of competition between Japanese makers, an upgrading strategy will soon fail. In the history of the industry, many builders adopted a 'side-by-side policy'. Once a leading company succeeded in the development of a popular model, other companies soon followed. As a natural result, similar models competed on the market, which lead to excessive competition and reduced margins. The upgrading strategy of some makers will duplicate this situation. Moreover, such a strategy will result in increased competition with German and US makers. It is likely that the mainstream of Japanese makers will follow a strategy of keeping the no. 1 position in the middle segment and/or of entering into 'Asian machine tools'. To keep the no. 1 position in the middle-class segment, Japanese machine tool builders are working hard for further rationalisation. Mori Seiki, for example, has introduced new rationalisation policies (interview in September 1995):

- Machine designs are simplified while focusing on real customers' demands. During the Bubble Boom customers wanted very flexible machines, but later discovered that they did not really need so much flexibility. As a result price and costs can be reduced.
- Development times are compressed. Previously new models were only introduced at a 10-year interval. This interval can be shortened to five years by reducing the number of parts from 30 to 40%.
- The system of cost calculation has been changed. Previously, Mori Seiki operated on a cost-plus system. Now they are adopting a target-cost system as used by the automobile industry.
- Manufacturing efficiency is improved. Management surveyed actual assembly time, and found that only two out of three of the production workers at assembly shops were used efficiently. The rest of the time was spent finding parts. Now Mori Seiki is hiring a consultant to introduce a materials supply system as developed at Nissan. This is expected to reduce idle times and increase productivity considerably.

Such rationalisation policies once made the Japanese industries strong. When a recession hits, companies improve product design and production engineering. After the recession, foreign competitors find that the competitiveness of Japanese makers is stronger than before. This has been seen in the past. It is likely that this pattern will repeat itself after the post-Bubble recession. However, if the middle-class segment cannot expand as predicted, machine tool makers will be forced to play a zero-sum game which will inevitably create winners and losers. There is a need for a growing market segment. The segment is the lower-class segment, namely, Asian machine tools. To enter the expanding Asian market, Japanese makers have to consider a division of labour between domestic and overseas production. Because of the high yen it is very difficult to supply 'Asian machine tools' from Japan. They will have to increase production in Asian countries where the labour costs are much lower than in Japan.

Traditionally, the Japanese makers have been reluctant to start overseas production. In Asia there are only a limited number of transplants. Machine tool builders have recently started looking at the Chinese market with eager eyes. In 1993 Kira Machine Tool transferred its capacity to produce conventional drilling machines to China. In 1994 Koyo Machinery began knock-down production of centreless grinders in China. Sodic has two joint ventures in China for electric discharge machines. Tsugami, Yamazaki Mazak, Okuma and Fanuc are strengthening their ties with Chinese companies through the export of technology (Chogin Sogo Kenkyusho, 1995: 58). Yamazaki Mazak has gone a step further. Mazak announced that they will develop small CNC lathes by 1996 for assembly in their Singapore plant. Casting, electronic components and other materials will be purchased in Asia. To reach the price target of 5 million yen, the traditional quality level will be revised (*Nikkei Weekly*, 12 November 1995). This is a clear signal that Japanese machine tool builders are now going into 'Asian machine tools'. But it is probably only a beginning.

SUMMARY

In the 1970s, Japan's automobile industry overtook the US industry as world leader; in the 1980s, Japanese machine tools took the no. 1 position from the German industry. Machine tool manufacturing has a long history, with intimate links to military requirements in Imperial Japan. The modern development of the industry took place after the Second World War, and was closely related to the rapid growth of the automobile industry. Whereas US and German makers focused on high-end, customised machines, the Japanese producers developed standardised inexpensive machines for the thousands of small and medium-sized companies supplying automobile makers and other large firms. Computerised numerical control (CNC) was adopted and diffused early in its history. After the oil crises in the 1970s, firms specialising in mass production of CNC machines emerged as industry leaders. A peculiar trait of the Japanese machine tool industry is the 'externalisation of Taylorism'. Workers in core firms are extensively trained and acquire broad skills in advanced machining or assembly. The division of labour between workers and engineers is elastic and flexible. Repetitive and simple tasks are transferred to daughter companies and subcontractors, and chiefly performed by female workers. As a consequence of the crisis in the first half of the 1990s, a similar differentiation is also gradually evolving within the core firms.

The oil crisis in the mid-1970s unleashed the first wave of employment adjustment since the end of the war in the machine tool industry. The post-Bubble recession has been much more severe, however. In four years production fell by 50%. In contrast to the automobile and consumer electronics firms, machine tool makers have not been able to solve their problems of overmanning with conventional methods, such as the reduction of overtime, *shukko* and subsidised training. Many firms, including the industry leader Okuma, have been forced to lower the compulsory retirement age and introduce programmes of 'voluntary' or 'early retirement'. In several cases, this has involved re-employment by supplier companies at significantly lower wages. There are exceptions, however.

Mori Seiki, for several decades the most rapidly growing company in the industry, has maintained stable employment and has also continued to produce all its machines in Japan. Internationally, Japan's machine tool makers remain in a very strong position, and in spite of the surging yen, exports from Japan increased markedly during the recession. In contrast to consumer electronics firms, there is no tendency to hollowing-out. All manufacturers are striving to rationalise their operations. They are simplifying products and taking out expensive features; they are radically reducing development lead-times; and they are introducing methods from the automobile industry to increase manufacturing efficiency. Their main problem is to find new growth markets. 'Asian machine tools' is the only expanding segment in the market. These tools have to be designed specifically for Asia and are produced locally. Exports from Japan are not possible. In the long-term, no company expects an increase in regular domestic employment.

9

COMPUTERS AND SOFTWARE: THE WEAKNESS OF THE INTEGRATED GIANTS

In the 1980s, Japanese companies targeted and swiftly captured leadership of the vitally important semiconductor industry. Since then, the Japanese have steadily moved up the so-called technology ' food chain', quietly building market share in laptop computers, workstations, mainframe computers, supercomputers and software. Along the way, they have gained a stranglehold over key areas of advanced manufacturing technology . . . and they have become No. 1 in the huge global telecommunications equipment market.

(Forrester, 1993: ix–x)

After the international successes of Japanese producers of steel, cars, ships, consumer electronics and machine tools, Japan seemed poised for the next step – to take the leadership in the fast-growing information industries. Developments during the 1980s appeared to confirm this – which painted for the west a very threatening picture. Japanese electronics companies emerged as the world's premier producers of memory chips (DRAMs). Sharp and other companies developed and took complete control of liquid crystal display (LCD) technology. When laptop computers became popular, Toshiba and NEC quickly took the lead and, by 1989, the Japanese had more than 40% of the US market: 'A tremor shook the US computer industry . . . Silicon Valley would soon resemble Detroit. . . The most ominous sign was Japan's enormous success in laptop PCs' (Verity, et al., 1992).

By dominating critical technologies, memory chips and flat-panel displays, as well as semiconductor manufacturing equipment, Japanese makers were building a position in the computer industry that many observers believed was becoming impregnable. In the early 1990s, four out of the ten largest computer companies in the world were Japanese – Fujitsu, NEC, Hitachi and Toshiba. And according to authors such as Cusumano (1991), these very companies were building world-class capabilities in software development as well.

COMPETITIVE IN COMPONENTS – WEAK IN DESIGN?

Extrapolations from Japanese competitiveness in the automobile, machine tool and consumer electronics industries to the computer and communications industries overlooked several key points. First, they overlooked the domestic orientation of the Japanese computer and communications industry as a whole. NEC, Fujitsu, Hitachi, Sharp, etc. compete worldwide in semiconductors and other components, but their PCs, mainframes, software and telecommunications equipment have mainly been targeted at the Japanese market. This is strikingly different from the strong and early international orientation of the automobile and consumer electronics industries.

Secondly, the 'information industries' have developed and adapted a large part of their resources to unique Japanese standards, from operating systems to telecommunications networks. This is of course related to their domestic orientation. In automobiles and consumer electronics, low factor costs, tariffs, complex distribution systems as well as the outright prohibition of foreign production in Japan were major protective factors when these industries developed international competitiveness in the 1950s and 1960s. In the R&D-intensive computer and communications industries, unique standards and government procurement played a similar protective role, making adaptation to the Japanese market excessively costly or cumbersome for overseas suppliers. However, these forms of protection also rendered it much more difficult for Japanese companies to develop globally competitive products. During the 1990s, they have become increasingly ineffective in safeguarding the domestic market. A recent case is the unique Japanese Personal Digital Cellular-standard for digital cellular systems. This has not hindered European companies such as Ericsson and Nokia from competing on the Japanese market, but it has severely delayed the development of Japanese products for the emerging digital world standard outside Japan (and the USA) – the Global System for Mobile Communications system. (According to western industry sources in Japan, in 1995 the Japanese equipment suppliers were complaining 'Why did we not choose the GSM standard?' Previously Japan was a protected market. Now Japanese suppliers are exposed to a dual pressure. On their home market they meet western competitors who have adapted their products to the Japanese standard. At the same time the Japanese companies have to develop new and different products for the non-Japanese standards. Unique standards have become a burden instead of a means of protection. In Sweden and Finland, with their strong internationally oriented suppliers of mobile telecommunications, the penetration rate of cellular phones in 1993 was 8%; in Japan the rate was only 1%, measured as subscribers/population (Teldok, 1994: 96). In 1995, the penetration rate in Sweden had increased to more than 18% but had not reached 4% in Japan (*World Competitiveness Report*, DN, 16 November 1995).

Thirdly, in the information industries Japan has encountered much more formidable western competition than it ever did in consumer electronics. This point is strongly emphasised by Fransman (1995) who points to the early collapse of RCA, the dominant US TV producer, in the early 1960s, and the weaknesses of the major European contender, Philips. In the computer industry, however, the Japanese have had to face a range of powerful US competitors from IBM to Microsoft and Intel. In telecommunications, they encountered equally resolute rivals in the USA as well as Europe: AT&T, Northern Telecom, Motorola, Alcatel, Ericsson, etc. The tradition of unique standards supported the development of infant Japanese information industries in the 1950s and 1960s, but it also resulted in a high-cost domestic environment. This was the case both for PCs and telecommunications equipment, which were characterised by stability and 'harmony' between NTT and its major suppliers NEC, Hitachi and Fujitsu. The dominant role of NTT, whose engineers both specified and designed key components, reduced its suppliers to producers in important areas. This status assured them of domestic orders but it did not help them build international competitiveness.

In the mid-1990s it had become evident that the oversimple image of a Japanese juggernaut in the computer and information industries was grossly exaggerated. Japanese makers are minor suppliers of desktop PCs. Their US market share in laptops fell from 40% in 1989 to 25% in 1992; Intel reigns supreme in microprocessors; Hewlett-Packard and Sun dominate the workstation market worldwide as well as in Japan; Japanese software is an unknown product in western markets; and Japanese providers of telecommunications equipment are seldom strong competitors in the high-growth market for cellular systems. At the same time, they remain superior in a whole range of components and industrial equipment: memories, silicon wafers, ceramic packages for integrated circuits, flat panels, high-tech batteries, as well as in semiconductor manufacturing and testing equipment.

The uneven strength of the Japanese industry has prompted a 'revisionist reinterpretation' of its competitiveness. Ferguson and Morris (1993) have argued that its competitive edge is confined to capital and technology-intensive commodity production such as DRAMs, and that Japanese producers lack the ability to compete in markets where design and product architecture are of crucial importance. In the same vein, Lillrank (1994) differentiates between prowess in process management and product innovation. The argument that mastery of process will sooner or later lead to dominance in products became popular in the west in the 1980s. The problems in Japan's computer industry in general, and the software factories in particular, imply that this argument has to be reassessed. However, in industries characterised by incremental change, the argument still seems to hold true. The computer and software industries, on the other hand, are different. Here creative design and the power to establish and utilise standards are decisively more important than manufacturing prowess.

A recent study of the Japanese computer and communications industries takes on this kind of argument (Fransman, 1995). According to Fransman the complex system products delivered for the domestic market demonstrate that Japanese computer companies do not lack ability to develop advanced designs and architectures. Their 'selection environment', however, has been different from the automobile and consumer electronics industries, and as a result their capabilities in design and architecture are less well known in the west. This argument is not entirely convincing. Many countries have nurtured indigenous suppliers of telecommunications equipment, and thus demonstrated system design capabilities. The true test, however, is the ability to compete in world markets. The automobile and consumer electronics industries in Japan started with a domestic orientation, producing for a rapidly expanding home market. This allowed them to move up the learning curve, invest in new facilities, enjoy increasing economies of scale and hone their design capabilities in intense domestic competition. Japan's automobile exports did not take off until the 1970s. Why did the computer and communications industry develop differently, sticking to such a strong tradition of idiosyncratic standards? Missing further is a discussion of the role of the *keiretsu* structure, so important for the long-term competitiveness of consumer electronics and automobiles, but so destructive for the creation of an independent software industry and common software standards.

Basically Fransman has an important message, though. After the exaggerations of Japanese strength in the 1980s, it is important to avoid the now popular opposite extreme of discarding its staying power and second-strike capabilities in a range of information industries. Competitive advantage is not cast in concrete, but is a dynamic and evolving phenomenon. At the end of the chapter we will return to the importance of a balanced view. However, the chapter will start with an overview of the Japanese catch-up in mainframes and its tardiness in PCs and will then analyse the opening of the market and the PC wars of the mid-1990s. Finally, it interprets new trends in the software industry. Japanese software may be less well known in the west but it is a major industry in Japan.

A CATCH-UP IN MAINFRAMES BUT SLOW MOVES IN PCS

'It is thus no exaggeration to state that the history of the growth of IBM is itself the history of the development of the computer industry throughout the world' (Shinjo, 1988: 334). In the late 1950s, Hitachi, Fujitsu, NEC and Toshiba announced their entry into the nascent computer industry. They were soon followed by Oki Electric, Matsushita and Mitsubishi Electric. In western countries, International Business Machines dominated the markets completely. In Japan, industry and government were determined not to let that happen. To catch up with IBM became a national rallying call. MITI targeted the computer industry for protection and promotion. The launch of IBM's 370 Series in 1970 signified a major increase in R&D expenses in order to stay competitive in the industry. In the USA, General Electric and RCA withdrew; in Japan, Toshiba, Oki, Mitsubishi Electric and Matsushita did the same. Hitachi, Fujitsu and NEC were determined to respond to the US challenge, however. As Fransman has stressed (1995), these companies had not progressed up the 'food-chain' from components to computers. Their computer divisions developed out of their competencies in telecommunications, which had their roots in the interwar period. Of the three, Fujitsu had the weakest position in telecommunications and thus was most determined to become a major computer maker. Assisted by a technical tie-up with IBM's US competitor Amdahl, Fujitsu took over Big Blue's first place in the Japanese market in 1979.

In the following decade the Japanese mainframe makers emerged as international low-cost competitors. In Europe, they launched a conspicuous offensive. Hitachi signed a deal to deliver mainframes on an Original Equipment Manufacturer basis (OEM-basis) to German Siemens. NEC invested in the bleeding French Bull company. Fujitsu acquired the leading British computer maker ICL, which had previously absorbed Nokia's computer division, itself a result of a merger of computer industries in Scandinavia (including Swedish Ericsson's information systems). The Japanese threat triggered a large-scale but costly and ill-conceived automation effort in IBM, based on the erroneous assumption that IBM's main competitive problem was manufacturing cost (Carroll, 1993: 60). In terms of product technology in the early 1990s, the Japanese mainframes were basically on a par with IBM; they were superior in speed of performance but in other areas still dependent on technology licences. This was borne out in 1994, when Hitachi signed a licensing agreement with IBM to secure access to the US firm's CMOS-based mainframes and reduced instruction-set computing RISC technology.

While the Japanese industry was obsessed in catching up with IBM, a new market for PCs was rapidly evolving internationally. Here, the Japanese presence was much less noticeable. Hitachi and Fujitsu started manufacturing PCs in the late 1970s, but retained their focus on mainframes. NEC had a different tradition (stronger in communications and weaker in mainframe computing), and was more sensitive to the new market. In contrast to the other makers, NEC early understood the importance of software applications for PC sales, and assisted independent software vendors to develop packages for its popular desktop models, such as the PC 9800. The success of this strategy resulted in a complete dominance of the Japanese PC market. For a long period NEC's market share exceeded 50%. However, Japan's PC market as a whole was slow to develop compared with the USA or Europe. In the early 1990s, Japan's share of worldwide consumption of PCs was less than 10%, compared with 30% for western Europe and 40% for the USA (Fransman, 1995: 176). The PC penetration rate in Japan in 1992 stood at 60 installations per thousand capita, compared to 170 in the USA, with some of the smaller European states, such as Sweden, very close to the US figure. Of total hardware consumption in 1993, PCs and workstations accounted for 60% in the USA and Sweden, but only 30% in Japan where mainframes and minicomputers still made up the bulk of sales (McKinsey, 1995: Exhibits 7, 12). Can this difference be explained?

According to some observers, language is the major reason. *Kanjis*, the Chinese ideographs which form the basis of written Japanese, cannot be typed directly on a wordprocessor. Instead the Japanese have to use phonetic *kana* characters, which are converted to kanjis by a selection procedure. Fransman, for example, argues that this cumbersome indirect way of producing *kanjis* has been a chief obstacle in the diffusion of wordprocessing, and thus PCs, in Japan. Unfortunately his line of reasoning overlooks the rapid diffusion of so-called Japanese wordprocessors in the 1980s. These dedicated and easy-to-use machines, which could not run any independent software, became very popular among students as well as business people. In 1989, sales peaked at 2.7 million units (*Nikkei Weekly*, 30 October 1995). When they were first introduced, there were no PCs that could handle Japanese wordprocessing. In the mid-1980s, several software makers introduced wordprocessing programs for PCs, but the high price was an obstacle to rapid diffusion. Furthermore, PCs had the reputation of being difficult to handle, and PC usage was confined to high-end users. Another important factor was the fragmented and captive nature of the Japanese PC market. Supported by MITI, the Japanese industry had first tried to develop a family of new operating systems, including one for PCs (the TRON project). The argument was that MS-DOS was a deficient system in many respects, an argument which most computer programmers would subscribe to. The TRON project, and its inspirer, Professor Sakamura, completely ignored the importance of all software written for MS-DOS, however, and therefore the effort failed. When DOS was adopted as the standard international operating system for PCs, the Japanese makers started offering non-compatible DOS versions, such as 'NEC-DOS' for the NEC PC 9800 Series, 'Toshiba-DOS' for the Toshiba J3100 Series, 'Fujitsu-DOS' for its FMR Series and so on. These idiosyncratic versions protected the domestic industry from US competition in hardware, since no Japanese applications could run on US machines. At the same time they fragmented the Japanese software market and obstructed the evolution of an independent software industry and the diffusion of standard programs. Language was important in shaping the Japanese PC industry, but not as Fransman conceives it as a factor retarding interest in wordprocessing. Its importance lay elsewhere: in contributing to a rival technology, to the dedicated wordprocessor and to a protected market.

In the USA and Europe, the availability of low-cost software packages has been a major factor driving PC diffusion. The high cost of hardware as well as software on the fragmented and captive Japanese market is another reason for the low penetration of personal computing in Japan in the early 1990s. In terms of performance, US software, for example Lotus 1-2-3 and dBASE, enjoyed an early strong position in Japan. However, the US vendors utilised their position to charge premium prices rather than to expand the market. Moreover, sales of Japanese software were controlled by the developers. Once they had announced a price for a certain package, retail shops would observe it. This lack of discount competition among software outlets also contributed to the generally high price level. A further reason for the lagging diffusion of personal computing has been the low level of computer literacy. Until recently, there has been almost no education in computers, from elementary schools to universities. Teachers have not been trained to use computers at university, and find it hard to teach their use in schools. In firms, middle-aged and older managers have difficulties with computers. 'Keyboard phobia' among managers is a frequent topic in the mass media. Since managers tend to think that computers are a luxury, firms have frequently cut investment in computer systems during the recession.

Weak sales and high costs in Japan have been reflected in low international competitiveness. In stark contrasts to the successes of Japanese automobiles, machine tools and consumer electronics, the US market share of Japanese desktop computers did not exceed 7% in 1988–92 (Verity et al., 1992). In 1994, NEC, the leading Japanese maker, shipped 1.8 million PCs but only 0.3 million of these were sold outside Japan (Mitsusada, 1995e). Laptops are exceptional. Here Toshiba has been very successful in developing and marketing products for the international market. In the Japanese PC market Toshiba is weak, however. In 1995, the company decided to focus almost entirely on laptops, and signed a deal with Intel according to which the US microprocessor giant will produce the bulk of Toshiba's desktop models on an OEM basis (Mitsusada, 1995f). This decision is related to the price war being waged on the Japanese market after the end of the era of language and standards protection.

The wall had started to crack in 1991 when IBM introduced the bilingual DOS/V operating system. IBM-compatible machines could now run both English and Japanese-language programs. In 1993, Microsoft offered a front-end addition to DOS/V, a Japanese version of its graphical interface Windows 3.1. Previously, Apple Computers had introduced a Japanese-language version of its graphical operating system, which could run both US and Japanese applications. These events signalled the outbreak of 'the PC wars' in Japan. In 1992, Compaq launched the first PC in Japan for less than 200,000 yen, thereby introducing real price competition to the market for the first time. A few months later, Dell Computers escalated the marketing war by offering an entry-level computer for half the price of Compaq's machine. These moves pressured NEC to reduce the prices of main PC products by as much as 40%. Even more importantly, one after another of Japanese manufacturers have been forced to discard their proprietary systems and adopt standard MS-DOS. Fujitsu and Toshiba were among the first to announce such decisions. Epson, which had previously adopted the so-called NEC-DOS to become a clone-maker of NEC machines, also followed suit. Since 1995, Epson only produces DOS/V machines. In spite of the mounting pressure towards standardisation, NEC officially sticks to its policy of maintaining the separate PC 9800 operating system, for which there is a large supply of Japanese software. Thus there are still two DOS standards in Japan, DOS/V and DOS for NEC 9800. Accordingly, there are two versions of both Windows 3.1 and Windows '95, one for DOS/V and one for NEC PC 9800. However, applications for Windows are not affected by this difference. If users are only interested in using Windows applications they do not care if a machine is designed for DOS/V or DOS-PC 9800. The only concern is cost performance, and as a result hardware prices have been tumbling. The same has happened to software, both Japanese and American. In the late 1980s, Lotus 1–2-3 sold for 98,000 yen. In 1995, the same program plus several others included in the Lotus Super Office package (Lotus 1–2-3, Ami-Pro, Approach and Freelance) were sold at only 30,000–40,000 yen! As a result of price reductions and increasing unification of standards, PC sales finally took off in Japan. In 1994, 3.4 million units were shipped, a 36% rise from the previous year. Compared to the USA, where 18 million PCs were sold in 1994, this figure was still low (Ishizawa, 1995). In 1995, however, sales in Japan were expected to increase by a further 60% to 5.3 million units (Mitsusada, 1995h). At the same time, the home-grown 'Japanese word-processor' continued to slide, and shipments were projected to sink below 2 million units.

In 1993, Fujitsu still depended on mainframes for 65% of its computer sales. The combination of recession and an unfavourable product mix resulted in net losses in both 1993 and 1994. The company had prided itself in being called the 'IBM of Japan'. Now, when it no longer had any merit, Fujitsu and its Japanese rivals were 'beginning to look a lot like IBM – too fat, too slow-footed and cautious' (Schlender, 1993). The dramatically shifting structure of the computer market prompted decisive action. Fujitsu decided to discontinue the development of its FMR Series, a line of PCs with a proprietary architecture, and instead launched the DOS/V-compatible, low-priced FMV-series. This did not help its Japanese factories, however, since Fujitsu transferred most of its PC production to Taiwan. Fujitsu's very competitive pricing resulted in an increased market share, largely at the expense of NEC. NEC lost 5% between 1993 and 1994, but retained an impressive 48% of the market (*Nikkei Weekly*, 7 August 1995). US suppliers gained ground, and together Apple, IBM and Compaq reached a 30% market share. Compared to Europe, however, domestic firms remained very strong in Japan, and price and volume projections in 1995 demonstrated their resolve to keep the majority of the booming market for themselves. Their intensive '*kaisha* competition' for market share and the aggressive pricing and strategies of capacity doubling resulted in poor profitability, however. In spite of booming sales, a majority of Japan's PC makers were expected to book losses in the fiscal year 1995.

Ultimately, the Japanese PC market is becoming similar to western markets in terms of standards and volumes. The computer industry, however, is still very different. In the USA the technological transformation in the 1980s led to the disintegration of previously highly integrated corporations such as IBM, and the rise of specialised providers of components, PCs, workstations, operating systems, applications software/networking software, and so on. In Japan, on the other hand, the computer industry is still dominated by integrated giants such as NEC, Hitachi and Toshiba. In the USA, four out of five leading PC companies (in 1992) were highly focused, deriving more than 70% of their revenues from PC sales. In Japan, on the other hand, there were no specialists at all among the top five PC vendors. At NEC, the market leader, PC sales only accounted for 20% of total revenue (1991 figures). As the McKinsey Institute observes, this means that Japanese manufacturers had 'less incentive to push PCs, since they will only cannibalize their existing product lines' (McKinsey, 1995: Exhibit 16).

A major challenge remained for Japan's PC producers: to overcome their domestic orientation and to build an international presence. In 1995, NEC announced an alliance with Packard Bell, whereby NEC would acquire a 20% stake in the leading US supplier of PCs for home users. Together the two companies could challenge Compaq's no. 1 position in global PC sales. Integrating US and Japanese business cultures has seldom been very successful, however, and the prospect for the deals seems uncertain. The alliance with Packard Bell is an indication, however, that the leading Japanese PC maker no longer believes in building an internationally competitive position by itself.

THE MIXED BALANCE OF MICROPROCESSORS AND SEMICONDUCTORS

Behind the previous forecasts of Japanese supremacy in the information industries was Japan's onslaught in semiconductors. In 1981, Japanese firms held 27% of the world market, and US firms 57%. In 1987, the figures were almost reversed: Japanese firms commanded 51% of global sales and US firms 37% (Stewart, 1995). Only a few US companies, such as Texas Instruments and Micron Technology, remained in the DRAM business – the others had withdrawn. NEC had become the overall largest semiconductor maker in the world.

The enormous PC expansion in the late 1980s and 1990s resulted in a new shift. In 1995, US firms were estimated to occupy 43% of the global semiconductor market, compared to 40% for the Japanese. The semiconductor markets in Japan and the USA differ remarkably. In the USA, the computer industry accounts for 62% of semiconductor demand, compared to 33% in Japan; in the USA, consumer electronics account for only 5% compared to 40% in Japan (Fransman, 1995: 177–8). The regained leadership of the US semiconductor industry is closely related to the growth of US PC and workstation manufacturers. This is particularly true for the high value-added production of microprocessors. Here Intel has established a *de facto* standard and enjoys 70% of the total PC market. All its rivals are US companies: Advanced Micro Devices, Cyrix and Motorola (for Apple Computers).

NEC produces its own microprocessors but does not compete outside Japan. In stark contrast to their general confidence in the 1980s, Japanese manufacturers now acknowledge the extreme difficulty of taking on Intel: 'We have already given up on the PC microprocessor market [declares Hitachi]. . . There is no room for newcomers because almost all software titles are based on existing microprocessors.' (Ishizawa, 1994a). The beauty of logic chips, such as microprocessors, is that they are difficult to copy, and once a supplier has secured a contract to a PC maker, competitors are effectively locked out. Based on its strength in this market sector, Intel could unseat NEC as the world's largest chip maker in 1993 and is an increasingly dominant force in the PC industry. Intel not only produces processors but has also emerged as a major supplier of complete motherboards and, in some cases, complete PCs under OEM agreements.

As for workstations, Japanese makers produce their RISC chips on licence from US firms such as MIPS, LSI Logic and Sun. Matsushita once developed a RISC chip but it never took off. In this technology the reason for the Japanese weakness is not a US standard *de facto*. Rather it reflects the inferior position of the Japanese software industry. Processors are developed in an industrial context, where possible software applications play a major role. US processor technology is supported by the formidable US software industry.

The bulk of Japan's chip production consists of memory chips, such as DRAMs. They have rapidly become a commodity, subject to price competition from aggressive Korean rivals. Several observers predicted that the Japanese makers would be caught in the middle between US high-end producers of microprocessors and Korean mass manufacturers of low-cost memory chips (Lillrank, 1994). In 1991-2, the Japanese semiconductor industry was suffering from slumping sales and unprofitability and, in the following year, Samsung emerged as the largest DRAM manufacturer in the world. But the threat of the 'double squeeze' did not materialise. From 1993 Japan's semiconductor industry has been able to take advantage of the global surge in demand, driven by rapid diffusion and upgrading of PCs and laptops, by memory-devouring releases of operating systems, such as Windows '95, and by the worldwide expansion in telecommunications and cellular phones. There seems to be plenty of room for both Japan and its Asian rivals.

For the fiscal year 1994, NEC, Toshiba, Hitachi, Mitsubishi and Fujitsu all announced strong rebounds in revenues and profits, mainly as a result of expanding semiconductor sales (and cost-cutting in other sectors). During 1995, semiconductor growth accelerated. This year capital spending plans for semiconductor production at the top five chip makers totalled 850 billion yen, an increase of 50% from the previous peak year of 1990. Leading chip-equipment makers, such as Advantest Corporation, Nikon and Kokusai Electric, reported an even stronger trend with increases in earnings ranging from 200 to 460%. (Inoue, 1995). The expansionary cycle of semiconductors had obviously not been disturbed by the collapse of Japan's Bubble Boom. Furthermore, the introduction of 16 M DRAMs in 1993 did not hurt sales nor the price of the older 4 M chips, an indication that Korean competition had been offset by rising overall demand. In 1996, however, there was a marked price decline because of a temporary overproduction in this cyclical industry.

A most important factor sustaining this strong growth is the depth of the Japanese semiconductor fabrication cluster and the upgrading capabilities of its related and supporting industries. In these respects, the semiconductor

'industrial diamond', to use Michael Porter's terminology, has a close re-
semblance to the automobile cluster. The Japanese semiconductor cluster
encompasses a wide range of firms, from producers of chips, semiconductor
fabrication equipment, silicon wafers and specialised chemicals to ceramic
packaging sets. When automobile makers are encountering zero-growth
prospects in Japan, related and supplying industries in the automobile cluster are instead developing new product lines to cater for the need of the
booming semiconductor sector in the famous Japanese way of internal
diversification and upgrading. In 1996, the production value of
semiconductor-making equipment was expected to surpass that of machine
tools for the first time. Another case in point is Hitachi Metals Ltd. To
compensate for the decline of its speciality-steel line, which had been supplying the automobile industry, it is rapidly expanding production of com-
pounds for semiconductor manufacturers. Tokuyama Corporation is a
similar case. While the mainstay cement business was operating at a loss in
1995, Tokuyama intensified its upgrading process and planned to double its
production of polycrystalline silicon, a raw material for semiconductor
wafers (Mitsusada, 1996).

In contrast to consumer electronics, Japanese semiconductors have largely
been produced by domestic plants. In 1995, Fujitsu manufactured 75% of its
chips in Japan, NEC 85%, Mitsubishi 90%, and Toshiba had hardly any
overseas Integrated Circuit (IC) production at all. Companies are expected
to increase their ratio of overseas production in order to cut costs and come
closer to customers. NEC, for example has developed a global strategy,
balancing the three poles of Japan, the USA and Europe. Its expansion plans
in 1995 included a state-of-the-art plant in Scotland as well as in California.
The majority of its production, however, is likely to remain in Japan. NEC
has cited several reasons for this concentration in Japan: key production
equipment is made in Japan; the capital-intensive nature of investment
makes production costs basically equal in Japan and overseas; and highly
skilled engineers make it easier to raise production yield rapidly in domestic
plants – an important factor when demand is surging (Mitsusada, 1996).

SOFTWARE DILEMMAS: FOCUSED FACTORIES VERSUS OPEN SYSTEMS

Whereas Japanese manufacturers are maintaining strength in semiconductors and have built remarkable positions in several other component areas,
they are hardly visible outside Japan in the products which make computer
usage possible – software. And yet 'information services' constitute a huge
industry in Japan, and one which was very prosperous during the Bubble
Boom. From a total of 330,000 in 1988, employment rose by 50% to 490,000 in
1991, the peak year of the bubble. The number of system engineers and
programmers increased even more rapidly, from 150,000 to 240,000 (Table
9.1).

Table 9.1 Employment in Japan's information service industry (000s)

	1988	1990	1991	1992	1993
1994					
Total information industry	334	458	493	488	446
Total software	190	286	319	313	277
System engineers and programmers	147	220	242	239	208

Source: MITI, 1995; 1996. Tokutei sabisu sangyo jittai chosa hokokusho, Joho sabisu gyo hen (Research report on Information Service Industry).

One reason for the lack of visibility of Japanese software is that much of modern computer programs are embedded in manufactured products, in consumer goods as well as industrial equipment. We will return to this point later. Another factor is the weak international competitiveness of the Japanese software industry. There is one important exception, however, and that is the computer game industry. Capitalising on a huge and demanding domestic market, Sega and Nintendo have become world leaders in this field. Computer games software is in many respects different from the software discussed below in the way it almost exclusively consists of dialogues with the user, without any recourse to manuals or documented procedures. The organisation of the game software development process is beyond the scope of this chapter. Below we will concentrate on software for business customers, which are by far the most important segment of the software market.

The factory approach

During the 1960s and 1970s, all the major Japanese hardware producers established divisions to write operating systems and other basic software as well as a broad range of customised applications. These were delivered in bundles with the hardware, in the way of IBM before the historic 'unbundling decision' in the late 1960s. Since the publication of Brooks' '*The Mythical Man-Month*' (1975) based on the company's legendary problems in writing the operating system for its 360 Series in the 1960s, IBM had been doing a great deal of research on how to rationalise and possibly industrialise software engineering. The Japanese took this approach to its ultimate end and literally constructed software factories, the first being Hitachi's software works in 1969. According to Michael Cusumano (1991) these factories posed a formidable challenge to western management. By that time Toshiba was operating the Fuchu software factory, employing 2,300 people. Hitachi had two software works employing 4,000 programmers and systems engineers, plus 7,000 employees at subsidiaries and subcontractors. Fujitsu also ran two software factories, employing 3,500 engineers supplemented by 14,000 personnel at 56 subsidiaries and subcontractors. Finally, NEC operated five software works with a total headcount of 9,500. Cusumano argued that these large-scale operations had solved a classic problem in software engineering – how to overcome notoriously unpredictable time schedules and cost estimates by introducing strict factory discipline, statistical project planning and systematic quality control. Hitachi's software factory, for example, developed a comprehensive planning and performance measurement system based on standard training curricula, standard effort calculation (computed from quantity in lines of code, program type, development type, rate of reused code and type of language), standard staffing schedules for balancing time and effort, computer-aided production control systems, a software quality estimation system and a software quality assurance system (Hitachi, 1992).

The basis for the software factories was a strategy of market segmentation. The Japanese computer makers focused on basic software and semi-customised, medium to large-sized systems. They avoided both the high end of the market (innovative and unique custom designs) and the low end (cheaply priced packaged software, which could be distributed by independent dealers). By concentrating on the repetitive production of similar programs, Japanese management skills in manufacturing could be applied, including systematic productivity measurement and emphasis on standards and the reusability of program source code. In contrast to the USA, in Japan the market for customised software was much more important than packaged software. In 1985, the ratio of customised to packaged software in the USA was 0.31; in Japan the corresponding ratio was 9.95, implying that the relative importance of customised software in Japan was 30 times its importance in the USA! (Fransman, 1995: 185). In 1991 packaged software still only accounted for 10% of total sales of software and services (a slight increase since 1982, when it accounted for 8%). In the USA packaged software was estimated to account for 46%, a dramatic increase from 21% in 1982 (McKinsey, 1995: Exhibit 9).

The strategy of fragmenting the market by selling proprietary systems, bundled to hardware, worked excellently in providing computer makers with captive customers. Once a bank or insurance company had acquired a mainframe and the accompanying operating system and applications program from Hitachi, for example, it had no real opportunity to choose another vendor in the future. The proliferation of customised computer programs is also very much in the Japanese business tradition of competing by differentiation. Conservatism of customer organisations is another reason. Individual organisations have their own document formats and work flows, and don't want to change them when introducing a computer system. Work structure is not adapted to the new computer system; it is the other way around, the computer system is adapted to the existing work structure. Professor Matsumoto at ASTEM has given a telling example (interview in September 1995): 'There are nine power utilities in Japan. Technically their plants are all the same [and there is no competition between them]. Nevertheless, the equipment suppliers have to develop different control software for each of them because of their desire to differentiate.' Power utilities were by no means unique. All Japanese banks, for example require their own specific software for automatic teller machines. This generates problems for an ATM producer such as Toshiba. The structure of the systems is difficult to understand and tends to be accessible only to experienced engineers. Toshiba's solution to the problem was characteristic: to develop a Computer-Aided Software Engineering (CASE) tool for the more cost-effective development of the customised systems! Another response would have been to introduce a low-priced packaged system and educate the customers to accept standard solutions. Excessive differentiation, however, has been stimulated by the policy of the equipment suppliers to bundle software and hardware, which means that customers have not been paying the full cost of software. The software factories prospered in this market environment.

They could also take advantage of the dualism of the Japanese labour market. Hitachi, Toshiba and their peers hired 'personnel unskilled in software and then [trained] them to use a standardized methodology and tool set as well as reusable designs' (Cusumano, 1991: 39). The prospects of lifetime employment and long-term careers within these large firms guaranteed that system engineers and programmers did not quit, as many would probably have done in the USA. But the software factories also utilised a large substructure of subsidiaries and external low-wage software houses. The division of labour and personnel skills between the developers and their suppliers tends to be strict. Developers take responsibility for requirements specifications and system design, and then again, system test and plant site commissioning. These tasks require skills in operation analysis, control theory and a broad array of specific domains. Therefore the developers recruit high-level graduates from a variety of different university departments. Some suppliers enjoy domain-specific competence, in hotel booking systems, for example. Most of them, however, are assigned low-level tasks such as programming, debugging and module testing. They recruit from lower-status computer schools (the so-called *senmon gakko*) and employ a much higher proportion of female workers than their parent firms. According to Lillrank (1994: 47), the 'software groups' in Japan are different from the stable pyramids in the automobile industry: 'There is no software keiretsu really. It's all cut-throat competition; there is no loyalty between players, no long term views, very little joint development . . . In bad times, subcontractors are cut off without remorse.'

These supplier relations were only briefly referred to in Cusumano's (1991) book. His study focused on the four big computer and software companies: Hitachi, Fujitsu, NEC and Toshiba. After comparing their performance with US software vendors, he claimed that the Japanese factory approach in software development had resulted in superior lead-times, better quality (defined as absence of program bugs) and higher productivity (measured in lines of source code per programmer). In the early 1990s, these claims of superiority were consistent with other accounts of Japan's manufacturing prowess. Were the software centres of Hitachi and Fujitsu to become another 'machine that changed the world'? Actual development took a route very different from these confident predictions.

The onslaught of US packages in the post-IBM era

The software factories were built during a process lasting 20 years, involving enormous investments in systems and standards. In the 'post-IBM era' of the early 1990s, their fundamental assumptions have been called into question. In a world of downsizing from mainframes to PCs and networks operated by servers, the factory approach was no solution. Their strength was the incremental improvement of large semi-customised systems for main-frames, using old-style programming languages such as Fortran and Cobol. In the rapidly growing market for packaged software for workstations, PCs and networks, their 'platoons of disciplined software specialists' are ill-adapted (Lillrank, 1994: 64). Cusumano (1991) noted the striking difference between the US and Japanese software markets in the 1980s, but treated this difference as a permanent phenomenon and missed the dynamics and where the market was heading and how this would affect the factory system of software engineering. During visits to the software centres of Hitachi, Fujitsu and Toshiba in September 1995, the author encountered criticisms of the 'old-style software factories' concerning several key aspects – internal organisation, relations to customers, labour market image and the problems of performance measurement in the era of open systems:

1) The factories were organised on the basis of a detailed division of labour, where project managers played a key role. They defined the tasks in detail, in the case of Toshiba using so-called Unit Workload Operating Sheets (Matsumoto, 1992). Managers allocated the minutely divided tasks to each member in their teams and had responsibility for close monitor-ing of progress. In a rapidly changing market this vertical structure has become too rigid and inflexible.
2) The software factories were of a closed nature. Each corporate group had its own proprietary tools and systems. Users could not access the soft-ware factory development environment. This was a serious obstacle in the case of new and complex programs, when the software factory needed user participation to specify the requirement correctly. In-creasingly, large customers criticised this closed nature, and required open access as well as the possibility of using their own tools.
3) In the tight labour market of the Bubble Boom, the software factories suffered from an image problem. Young people did not want to work in factories any more! Companies responded by renaming their divisions as software development centres, dropping the factory terminology.

The efficiency of the software factories was based on their ability to measure and standardise performance, and use that as a basis for product calculation, scheduling and operational improvement. In the new software environment, distinguished by open systems, the established forms of measurement be-came much less effective. The traditional unit of measurement was KLOC (kilo-lines of code). This was used to estimate program size as well as pro-grammer productivity, for example, KLOCs per programmer and month.

The ratio of KLORCs/KLOCs (RC for reused code) measured program re-use, which was the most important productivity predictor. In open systems development, commercially available packages, such as operating systems and database handling programs, are part of the final solution. In this environment, skilful integration of external program components in a customised control system may not produce many lines of code, but are of the utmost importance for the functionality and reliability of the system. By the same token, the repeated application of source code from old programs is no longer a very potent productivity driver. There are numerous other problems with the usage of KLOC as a measurement of productivity. One of the fascinating aspects of software is its plasticity, as Frederic Brooks (1975) remarked: 'Finally, there is the delight of working in such a tractable medium . . . Few media of creation are so flexible, so easy to polish and rework, so readily capable of realizing grand conceptual structures.' As we shall see later, this very tractability has its own problems. However, this means that raw-size measurements have a rather remote relation to functionality. This was illustrated in the ill-fated collaboration between IBM and Microsoft to develop the OS/2 operating system. When system engineers from Microsoft found short cuts that eliminated tens of thousands of code written by IBM programmers they were severely criticised by managers at IBM: 'Measured in lines of code, they said, Microsoft was actually doing *negative* work, meaning Microsoft should have been paying IBM for the condensing it was doing' (Carroll, 1993: 101).

The performance of the software factories, however, is only a minor part of the picture. The basic problem confronting Japan is the lack of an independent software industry as such. For a long period software was seen as additional to hardware and often sold below cost price. This impeded the development of a vigorous industry, as did the fragmentation of the market where each major group pursued its own proprietary operating system. The difficulties to agree on common standards are vividly described by insiders, such as the president of Novell Japan, who previously worked at the Japan Electronics Industry Development Association: 'Watanabe fought hard for an industry software standard but felt that he did not get anywhere. At meetings everyone would say "Yes, yes, let's have open systems". But then they would go back to their companies and get severely criticised for betraying the company architecture' (Holyoke, 1995).

The problems have been noted by the Japan Information Processing Development Centre: 'in Japan, there has been a low recognition of the value of intellectual creations to begin with, and there are trade practices which discount software as just an accessory of hardware' (Kishi, 1993: 17). A basic condition for the development of an independent industry is to create a functioning market and a price mechanism for software. These issues are addressed in a report from MITI's Information Industry Committee (1992): *Urgent Proposal: The New Age of Software*. Among other things, the proposal requested the promotion of transparent trade rules, standardised contracts (instead of different rules within each *keiretsu*), the promotion of software independence and packaged software.

In the mid-1990s, the situation had started to change. Standards had started to emerge, albeit from external players – the US firms. Increased cost-consciousness and a *de facto* unification of the PC market spurred interest in software packages at the expense of proprietary customised solutions:

> For years, Japanese software houses prided themselves on writing custom programs for large business users. For each client, legions of programmers would string together specially developed lines of code, creating monster programs that were unique – and often unwieldy. These days, . . . individuals and business users alike want to buy their computer software off the shelf in tidy packages with clear instructions and proven quality. This trend goes hand in hand with the shift among businesses from using mainframe and minicomputers to smaller workstations and personal computers. Because they're spending less on their computers, customers don't want to make as hefty investments in software.
>
> (Ishizawa, 1994b)

In 1993, the market for packaged software totalled US$2.1 billion, up 12%. In 1994 the growth rate increased to 28% owing largely to the fast acceptance of the Windows 3.1 operating environment (*Japan Economic Almanac*, 1995: 88). The new market opportunities were rapidly seized upon by foreign software vendors. In 1995, Novell Inc. had 60% of the market for network software, with the rest largely held by Microsoft, IBM and Oracle (Holyoke, 1995). In spreadsheets, Lotus 1–2-3 and MS Excel commanded 65% of the market. MS Word marketed the most popular wordprocessor, followed by a package from Japan's Just Systems (an independent software house headquartered in the southeast island of Shikoku). Among Europeans, German SAP also experienced strong Japanese growth for its systems integration software for client-server networks.

According to John Stern at the American Electronics Association in Tokyo, the structural problems of the Japanese software market are deeply rooted, and a rapid emergence of strong Japanese competitors is not very likely:

> Software developers have low status. They are treated as assembly workers – take a look at their facilities, where engineers work on crammed impersonal desks in huge open rooms. There are no folk heroes among them, as in the US. The major equipment makers are still very powerful and exert strong pressure on their traditional customers. There is a lack of venture capital and entrepreneurial risk-taking in the software industry. The business culture is radically different from the start-up climate of California, which in itself differs drastically from the rest of the US.
>
> (Interview, Tokyo, 13 September, 1995)

The difficulties of starting new high-tech businesses in Japan are addressed in an interview with the Japanese turned US venture capitalist, George Hara (1995). According to Hara, the situation for new start-ups is better in the

USA in all respects, not only the availability of venture capital. Among other things it is much easier to recruit talented personnel: 'Also, it is much easier in the USA to get fresh new graduates. The best and brightest from Stanford and MIT all want to go into small companies. In Japan, this is almost impossible. Everyone wants to work for large corporations or the government.' The minuscule interest of Japanese venture capital for software firms is also emphasised by Baba et al. (1995: 478), quoting a study from 1989 which showed that 11% of US venture capital went to the US software industry compared to only 0.04% in Japan.

On one point John Stern was mistaken, however. Actually, there is one 'folk hero' among Japanese software developers. His name is Kazunobu Ukikawa, president of Just Systems, which produces Ichitaro, the best-selling Japanese wordprocessing program. It is no coincidence that the only Japanese 'software hero' is in the closed market of Japanese wordprocessing.

Downsizing in the software industry

The new business climate – competition from packages and an emphasis on cost – has had important consequences for the system divisions of the integrated computer manufacturers. Downsizing has become a general trend in several areas. In the late 1980s, a dominant share of Fujitsu's software business, for example, consisted of large projects, defined as 500,000 lines of code or more per project. The recession meant a marked decline in project size. Instead of large profitable orders the company had to take on a great many small low-margin projects, requiring only a few weeks or a few months to complete. Hitachi and the other major companies had the same experience. This trend also had serious repercussions among their suppliers. All in all, recession, downsizing and increasing imports of packaged programs resulted in reduced employment. From 1991 to 1994, the number of system engineers and programmers in the information services industry fell by more than 20%, from 241,000 to 187,000 (see Table 9.1). Small firms with fewer than 100 employees expanded rapidly during the bubble. They were the first to adjust their staffing level downward and reduced their total employment (including sales and administration) by 26,000 in only two years. Large firms were more cautious, in line with their tradition of permanent employment policies. Total employment at eight of the largest software firms – Hitachi Information Systems and Hitachi Software Engineering Corporation, CSK Corporation, Toshiba Information Systems, Fujitsu Facom Information Processing Corporation, NTT Data Communications Systems Corporation, Intec Inc. and NEC Software – only decreased from 36,600 in 1991 to 35,300 in 1995.

Some firms, like NTT Data Communication Systems (a spin-off from NTT), prospered, mainly because of strong public demand, and increased their workforce considerably. CSK, the biggest independent service company, was less successful and had to reduce employment from 8,200 in 1991 to 5,400 in 1995. The brunt of workforce reduction was borne by the smaller subcontractor firms, however. In contrast to consumer electronics, this adjustment has not been related to any offshore moves. Software development has traditionally been an entirely domestic affair for Japanese firms. This might change in the future. In 1992, Hitachi established a subsidiary in China. In its first years this operation employed 100 people and was only entrusted with coding and debugging. The high skill level of the Chinese soon impressed Japanese managers and, in 1995, Hitachi had increased the workforce to 500 and expanded the scope to include system analysis and testing. The Beijing venture is important for a successful penetration of the Chinese market, which is viewed as having enormous potential, but it also helps Hitachi to cut costs in Japan.

In Japan's automobile and consumer electronics industries, stagnating or shrinking employment in domestic operations is no sign of eroded competitiveness, since this is matched by a rapid increase in international operations. The situation in software is different and more serious. However, it is important to take a nuanced perspective. In an open systems environment, a very substantial part of software is not and will not be delivered in commercial packages. Much software is embedded in consumer products. A modern camcorder for example, cannot operate without its advanced embedded software. Other software is part of complex industrial and technical equipment, from power plant controls to telecommunications systems. In 1994, Ericsson, the Swedish telecommunications equipment and systems provider, employed 20,000 engineers undertaking research, development and system adaptation in various markets. About 75% of them were engaged in the development or maintenance of software. Traditional electrotechnical products, such as rail systems and locomotives, are also becoming increasingly software intensive, and companies such as ABB and Siemens define software development as one of their future core competencies. In these areas of complex technical system engineering, where discipline and consistency are of prime importance, there are no signs of a Japanese software lag. 'The notion of a Japanese software crisis is a myth', say western sources in the telecommunications industry in Tokyo: 'In our field they are certainly not behind.' The dichotomy suggested by Lillrank (1994) between manufacturing skills, process management and constant incremental improvement, and software skills, design creativity and radical innovations, only captures part of the picture.

Transformation at the software factories

The integrated Japanese computer and communications companies may remain competitive in software for technical and industrial systems. Nevertheless, a process of change is transforming the major software centres. One of the most important aspects affects the traditionally closed character of the software factories. For many years, they cultivated not only a mainframe mind but also a more 'proprietary mentality': everything, from hardware to basic software, development tools and application packages were developed in-house or by captive suppliers. The momentum of change was described by managers and system engineers during visits to several centres in September 1995. At Fujitsu's Makuhari laboratory the following account was given:

In the 1980s, we were programming in assembler and machine language, now the high-level C-language is increasingly popular. We used to have mainframe terminals to develop mainframe applications. In the last few years UNIX, Windows running on workstations and PCs are becoming the new tools. Previously all equipment was made by Fujitsu and all languages developed by Fujitsu. Now we want to use the best tools available. Previously the total system was developed by us. Now many products are provided by outside companies, for example MS Windows. However, a difficult issue in this development is quality assurance, since [the source code of] Windows is, for us, untouchable.

According to engineers at Toshiba's system and software engineering in Kawasaki, urgent customer demands are driving the change:

The other big companies, Hitachi, Fujitsu, etc., are in the same situation. There are a few new competitors delivering systems based on integration of external components, but they are not very strong. The pressure to change comes from the users. They do not want proprietary systems any more. They want open systems, Windows NT, graphical-user interfaces, etc., and they want reduced costs. A steel plant customer, for example, recently asked us: use PC, use UNIX, please use . . . ! But at the same time they also want tailor-made applications. We need to use visual types of languages. We have to train people in object-oriented design. We know the need for rapid change, we need to rush, but in reality change is slow. It is a difficult and confusing situation.

At Fujitsu, the role of the 'software factory department' has changed. Previously it was churning out tailor-made programs. Now the main tasks are to re-engineer old programs and to experiment with new tools, to identify risks and problems and to guide the field engineers. There is also a different view on the reuse of programs. In the 1980s, the design teams reused fragments of source code in order to increase productivity as measured by KLOCs/time units. Detailed coding was at the centre of this. In the laboratory's new approach, the focus is on business rules, which generate the structure of the programs. Fujitsu has also been revamping its quality assurance system. The company has a tradition of devoting itself to high software reliability, inspired by the TQM approach of its manufacturing departments. However, this turned out to be too hardware oriented and, in the changing environment, the company felt a need for a more software-oriented method. In 1993, Makuhari's quality systems department started an ambitious project to develop a customised version of CMM (capability maturity measurement) (Miyazaki et al., 1994). This is a method for evaluating software developers which was originally commissioned by the Department of Defence, and has become a standard assessment tool in both the USA and

Europe (Humphrey, 1989). Initially, Japanese firms did not show any strong interest in CMM, but in 1995 Fujitsu's CMM exercise had already covered 400 projects. Previously, high quality had been secured by rigorous testing. The CMM approach to quality assurance is much more process oriented. This may sound familiar to students of the Japanese automobile industry, but nevertheless has not been common among software developers.

Fujitsu also spent considerable efforts on re-educating its workforce. Because of general economic difficulties, the company hired very few new graduates in the years 1992–5. Instead of recruiting people with new skills, which is a common approach in western firms that want to catch up with rapid technical change, Fujitsu has been retraining older people. At the same time, the pay system has been reformed. Before the 1990s, Fujitsu had a conventional seniority pay system. In 1994 a new system was introduced, in which employees have to formulate yearly achievement plans. At the end of the year, the results are checked and individual salary increases decided. The system applies to people older than 30, and the main intention is to increase productivity and performance among the company's white-collar employees.

Hitachi was the pioneer of the factory concept in software engineering. Here too a wind of change is blowing. According to managers at its Totsuka 'Software development centre' (renamed so in 1992), the 'factory' is now trying to transform its line-staff hierarchy to a flat project-oriented organisation to become like a small company. Instead of the traditional strictly sequential development model (commonly referred to as the 'waterfall model'), concurrent methods are introduced for new product types of medium size. The main goal is to shorten development lead-time. In the factory approach, detailed specifications of requirements played a crucial role in calculating project size, allocating tasks and establishing time schedules. This kind of 'manufacturing planning' has become much less effective. As explained by one manager: 'In modern PC-based software, graphical-user interfaces play an important role, but it is very time-consuming and difficult to write specifications for interfaces. Rapid prototyping is preferred here – develop a crude graphic prototype, evaluate it, revise it, evaluate the new version, and so on.' Another challenge is to identify alternative measures to the traditional KLOCs, which were so important in the factory system. The centre has developed new product-oriented measurements for speed performance, usability, portability and flexibility, but similar to other Japanese software centres, Hitachi experiences great difficulties in defining new process-oriented standards and measurements. A further challenge for the Totsuka centre is to increase productivity. The target is a 200% increase in five years, although many engineers seem to doubt both the possibility of achieving this and the measure of productivity, which is the traditional one – lines of code. The stringent productivity target is a reflection of the intense cost pressure on the company's software operations.

The role of software suppliers is also in a state of transition. In the 1980s, their skills were homogeneous. Basically, they constituted a pool of human resources for coding, testing and debugging. The suppliers were sent lists of specifications and were supposed to code according to these. The majority were exclusively dependent on the parent firms for new orders. During the boom many were using local second-tier software houses, but these contracts have not been extended. Low-skilled subsidiary companies have been cut off too. In the new situation, some supplier firms try to differentiate themselves and develop and sell expertise in particular computing areas, such as Oracle, or develop domain-specific types of skill. Others are still part of the traditional division of labour, but tight communication and early participation in the design phases are now much more important. This also involves closer management control from the customer firm. In order to secure long-term survival, the development of independent and genuine software skills seems to be of vital importance.

SUMMARY

Of the four industries focused on in this book, computers and software present the most contradictory case. On the one hand, Japan has displayed formidable strengths. As the only country in the world, it staged a successful catch-up struggle with IBM and nurtured several integrated computer makers, such as Fujitsu, NEC, Hitachi and Toshiba. Further, Japan became a leading player in semiconductors in the mid-1980s. On the other hand, Japan largely missed the transition from mainframes to PCs in the late 1980s. As a result its semiconductor manufacturers are weak in microprocessors and the US industry has been able to dominate this field completely. Japan's integrated computer makers also made an attempt to apply their manufacturing skills to software. In their software factories the development process was streamlined by means of standardisation, rigorous quality control, statistical planning methods and systematic reuse. The approach was efficient in the repeat production of semi-tailored programs for mainframe customers. Japanese software was only successful in the captive domestic market, however, and a history of market fragmentation, proprietary systems and bundled sales debilitated the growth of independent software houses.

In the early 1990s, US companies launched bilingual operating systems for PCs, which suddenly opened up the Japanese market for international competition. Prices of PC hardware and software in Japan started to tumble. Belatedly, the PC market took off in 1994–5. Taking advantage of offshore production operations, Japan's integrated computer companies were determined to take the lion's share of this boom market. For their economic recovery, the surge in semiconductor demand was very important. This market has also been very important in stabilising domestic employment. For a majority of the new semiconductor plants, the computer industry remains firmly committed to Japan.

The strong semiconductor exports are a polar opposite to Japan's weak performance in software. In the new 'post-IBM world', the software factories have lost their edge. Their proprietary mentality, strict division of labour and closed nature hindered a transition to open systems and the development of low-cost packages which customers increasingly demand. Moreover, the 'factory' concept has a negative image in the Japanese labour market, especially with young people. The software development centres are back in a phase of catch-up with perceived best practice in the USA. From NEC to Fujitsu, Japanese software divisions are teaming up with US start-ups to obtain access to new products and software services. Overall there has been a reduction in employment, but the brunt has been carried by the many small subcontractors and subsidiaries. Different from the west, leading firms such as Fujitsu have not been able to recruit workers skilled in new technologies from the external labour market. Instead, they have invested in major retraining programmes. The uneven performance of Japan's computer and communications industries as a whole will probably continue for a long time in the future.

—— PART 3 ——

CONCLUSION

10

THE RESILIENCE OF ALLIANCE CAPITALISM

The introduction to this book outlined two principal purposes:

1) To analyse the adaptation of major Japanese companies to the competitive realities of the mid-1990s, after the long post-Bubble recession.
2) To probe into the prospects of Japan's specific personnel practices in the new low-growth economy.

These two themes can be collapsed into one major question: is the era of Japanese exceptionalism, of unparalleled competitiveness and unique employment policies, drawing to a close? Is Japan finally approaching 'normal' (Anglo-Saxon) capitalism?

Chapters 2–4 added background to this question by presenting the trends and problems of the early 1990s that, taken together, reshape the environment of Japanese corporations:

- The end of four decades of almost uninterrupted high growth.
- The end of Japan's 'full-set industrial structure', a unique industrial compact that emerged after the war, now eroded by the accelerated transfer of productive operations to offshore locations.
- The end of four decades of political stability and economic-bureaucratic governance: the dissolution of the iron triangle made up of LDP politicians, big business and élite administrations.

The economical and political problems in Japan have coincided with a powerful resurgence of the US economy, from beleaguered sectors such as steel and automobiles, to computer and information industries. This revived US dynamism plays a major role in the current European debate on the reasons for Europe's lagging performance in innovation and industrial competitiveness. US labour market flexibility, deregulation and economic liberalism are becoming increasingly important models. For substantial sectors within Europe, however, there are mixed feeling towards this new americanisation, in view of the highly contradictory nature of the US experience: innovation is prospering but so is economic inequality and polarisation; new jobs are created on a massive scale, but real wages have been falling for a majority of workers; and entrepreneurship is flourishing but the social fabric is disintegrating. Is this the necessary price for technological and economic success in the global competition of the 1990s? Or are there other ways of responding to the new competitive pressures and imperatives to innovate? In Chapters 2–4 we analysed the challenges Japan is encountering. Chapters 6–9 explored the response to these pressures in four different sectors. The dominant pattern can be summarised in two words: revival and resilience – efforts to restore competitiveness while at the same time preserving vital elements of the Japanese employment model.

MANUFACTURING COMPETITIVENESS REVIVED

Japan's recession and macroeconomic stagnation, aggravated by the crises in its banking system, financial institutes and real-estate sector, have been highly publicised in the western media. The four industries studies in this book tell a different story, about the fundamental strength of Japanese manufacturing, in spite of all its financial mismanagement; and about the perseverance and staying power of its established labour market practices. Manufacturing companies did indeed suffer from high costs, low growth and diminishing profits during the recession; they suffered from a loss in business confidence and a revitalised foreign competition. However, they did not panic, and only very seldom took recourse to dramatic acts of restructuring, such as plant closing, industry consolidation and sell-offs. In a systematic and gradual way they adjusted to unfavourable currency relations and new competitive pressures. The loss of the supreme business confidence, bordering on arrogance, of the Bubble Boom, unleashed new spirals of learning and new waves of rationalisation, and in this way helped companies to refocus after the excesses of the bubble. Tables 10.1–10.4 summarise the main features of the four industry studies. The basic format and content of the tables are as follows (but the order within each column varies somewhat):

Bubble Boom (or 1980s broadly)	Recession	Response	Outlook
Market conditions	Demand changes	International moves	Industry structure and competitiveness
Overseas activities	Western competition	Manufacturing strategies	Role of Japanese manufacturing
Japanese invest-ment pattern		Product strategies	New rationalisation patterns
Labour market		Workforce adjustment	Employment practices

Table 10.1 is a summary of the development of the automobile industry from the contradictory conditions of the Bubble Boom in the late 1980s, to the outlook in terms of competitive position and personnel policies in the mid-1990's. Table 10.2 presents a similar brief on consumer electronics: from the combined domestic and international expansion of the 1980s to the increased offshore investments *and* domestic *kaisha* race of the 1990s. Table 10.3 treats the machine tool industry according to the same formula: Bubble Boom expansion, recession, strategic response and industry outlook. Table

10.4, finally, is divided into two sections, computer hardware and software. Their trajectories are summarised by means of a similar four-phase structure, albeit their starting point in the 1980s was very different from that of the world-leading positions of the other three sectors. The industry summaries point to six important components in the efforts of Japanese industry to regain competitiveness and vitality.

Streamline Japanese manufacturing operations

Streamlining means lowering break-even levels, reassessing costly automated systems and increasing volume flexibility to cope with volatile markets. Plants are 'deautomated' and simple solutions are sought after. In certain parts of the consumer electronics industry, this stress on reduced break-even levels has meant that previously integrated plants are turned into hubs of rapidly changing outsourcing networks. So far, this is a minor trend.

Relocate mature products to offshore plants

This process is most evident in the consumer electronics industry. In automobiles, all further expansion of production capacity will probably take place overseas. In machine tools, the internationalisation of production has started only recently. The design and production of low-cost 'Asian machine-tools' will accelerate this process, but for the companies' mainstay products no significant shift offshore is expected.

Continue the upgrading of domestic production

Industrial relocation has inspired fears of hollowing-out in Japan, but so far the island country retains a solid and dynamic manufacturing structure. Offshore moves are combined with the expansion of Japanese capacity for advanced components and new products. Japan's high-cost domestic environment makes production plants, (from automobiles to machine tools) hot-houses for cost-saving devices. All industries surveyed maintain a unique degree of competitive intensity in Japan, and this further contributes to driving product and process innovation.

Invest aggressively in new technologies and growth markets

During Japan's high-growth decades, economic expansion in new areas was driven by 'kaisha dynamics' (see Chapter 2): the massive entry of new and old competitors struggling for market share; price reductions and repeated capacity doubling; and the constant search for new applications and ways of widening the market. The same dynamics still apply in the 1990s, from computer components to novel consumer electronics. In a way unparalleled

Table 10.1   Automobiles – from Bubble Boom to reborn competitiveness

Bubble Boom (1980s)	Recession	Response	Outlook
Volume expansion driven by strong domestic demand	Decline in both domestic and export markets	Accelerated expansion in Asia and the USA	Japanese production maintains a crucial role for cost and product engineering; 'third wave' of competition; global manufacturing, products in every market segment
Trade friction because of huge surplus; increasing investments overseas	Western catch-up in manufacturing productivity and development lead-time	Cost-cutting in Japanese manufacturing: 'deautomation'	Strong companies use reduced cost base to lower price and gain market share; weakest companies lose autonomy
Heavy investments in automation; construction of new 'worker-friendly' plants in Japan	Overcapacity, no growth prospects in Japan; Nissan closes plant	Reduction of product and development costs, shorter lead-times, more common parts; 'decontenting' - elimination of costly features	
Profits squeeze because of model proliferation, increasing production costs and 'fat design'	Workforce adjustment: *shukko*, reduced overtime and hiring, no more temporaries; hard-hit firms offer 'early retirement', suppliers also 'voluntary retirement'	Broader product programmes and new component technologies; 'instant' ramp-up of new models	*Personnel*: basic stability of employment practices, but increasing age, diminishing career prospects, prompt company interest in wage reform and new promotion options
Acute shortage of young male workers, excessive overtime, heavy use of temporary and foreign workers (at suppliers)			Process planning is key, traditional *kaizen* loses relevance
			New hiring remains low, but importance of interfirm network for concurrent engineering limits company interest in short-term specialist contracts

Table 10.2 Consumer electronics – increased internationalisation and revived *kaisha* dynamics

Bubble Boom (1980s)	Recession	Response	Outlook
Strong demand in Japanese and western markets of VCRs, camcorders, CTVs, etc. following the *endaka* of mid-1980s; firms move mature products overseas	Steep decline in exports and domestic demand	Surge in southeast Asian investment: in 1995 a majority of colour television sets and VCRs produced outside Japan	No Japanese industry consolidation; imports from transplants maintain competitive intensity also among mature products
Productive capacity in Japan maintained by help of new or upgraded products	Potential western lead in new high-tech areas, such as digital HDTV	Reassessment of production strategy for volatile consumer products, e.g. CD-ROMs, minimum investment and large-scale outsourcing rather than advanced in-house automation	'*Kaisha* races' emerge in new areas such as plasma screens, LCDs and other components; fierce rivalry and massive investments reinforce Japanese dominance in high-tech areas – and safeguard Japan as a manufacturing base
Massive investment in automated machinery in domestic plants to safeguard competitiveness and ease labour shortage	Workforce adjustment without layoffs a major problem in Japan, *shukko*, reduced overtime and hiring, no more temporary contracts; are preferred measures	Diversified business structure and international strength help firms recover and sustain R&D and capital spending for new products	Compressed core employment in sectors with volatile demand; trend towards different categories and plural pay systems within the core
			Shorter product life-cycles make 'instant' mass production critical; preplanning and process engineering gain in importance relative to incremental shopfloor improvement

Table 10.3 Machine tools – global supremacy unchallenged, but no growth in regular employment

Bubble Boom (1980s)	Recession	Response	Outlook
Heavy investments in standardised CNC tools propel Japanese makers into world leadership, automobile industry expansion triggers strong domestic demand	Unprecedented slump in Japan, when orders from the automobile industry practically disappear	No move offshore; some bleeding firms close overseas operations, and concentrate all manufacturing in Japan	Japan's tool makers reign supreme in the middle segment of the market: competitive intensity within its industry is unabated; production continues to be concentrated in Japan; neither technological breakthroughs nor expansion are expected
Trade friction force companies to set up shop in major western markets, USA, UK, Germany	Despite high costs, Japanese makers increase export sales; but this cannot compensate for domestic short-fall; industry faces overcapacity and severe losses for several years	Aggressive cost-cutting in manufacturing by means of production control methods from automobile industry	Growth is at the low end of the market; 'Asian machine tools'; to compete with makers in China and Taiwan; Japanese firms set up production offshore to make simplified machines using local materials
In Japan, competition among 'big eight' is relentless; industry leader Okuma expands capacity aggressively; advanced factory automation, FMS systems, etc. is a general trend	Financial plight aggravated by price discounting and fierce competition between firms offering look-alike products	Reduction of product content; expensive options and features are taken out	
		Lead-times in product development shortened to speed up model renewal	
Machine tool makers employ male workers with broad skills and responsibilities; unskilled, repetitive work is transferred to subcontractors employing female labour	Industry trend is to adjust employment gradually by soft measures; hard-pressed companies go further; lower compulsory retirement age, and offer 'voluntary retirement'		*Personnel:* no future increase in regular employment; peak demand will be met by female *paatos* or subcontract workers; position of core workers remains stable

Table 10.4 Computers and software – uneven performance and rapid shifts

Bubble Boom (1980s)	Recession	Response	Outlook
Hardware			
Strong efforts to catch up with US mainframes and supercomputers, world-leading position in semiconductors	Downsizing in computer world belatedly hits Japan; US firms break 'language wall' and set *de facto* software standards; outbreak of 'PC wars', prices tumble	Firms compensate for sliding mainframe sales by aggressive expansion in PCs. In spite of US attacks, Japanese suppliers keep lion's share of domestic market; price competition drives firm to outsource components (excl. chips) assembly to Taiwan	Efforts to build an international presence in PCs by means of alliances and acquisitions
Slow diffusion of PCs in Japan because of high costs, fragmented markets, no recognised standard, rival specialised technology	Japanese PC demand takes off: 2.5 million in 1993, 5.3 million in 1995		In semiconductors and components leading firms expand global networks, but keep bulk of production in Japan to benefit from advanced equipment makers and process engineering
Domestic orientation of PC producers, no international presence except for laptops	US firms regain lead in semiconductors on the back of microprocessor strength	Japanese remain strong in memories, boom in semiconductor sales major factor in the recovery of integrated electronics firms	Component strength stabilises employment; firms push for performance pay instead of seniority
Software			
Major growth sector in the Bubble Boom, total employment up 50%	Demand for large custom programs for mainframes rapidly declining; increased interest in packages	Rush to create alliances with US firms to learn new skills in development, distribution and services	Diffusion of PCs and general standards 'westernise' computer market; Japanese software vendors remain domestically focused, trying to catch up with US competition
Focus on customised programs for domestic clients; undeveloped market for packaged software; no international presence, except for computer games	Exploiting new *de facto* standards, US vendors make rapid inroads in packaged, software market	Reorganisation of software factories to increase flexibility, cut costs and enhance use of commercial standards instead of proprietary languages and systems	Absent external recruitment, firms invest heavily in retraining to enhance use of modern programming tools and methods
Hardware producers operate 'software factories' to make use of manufacturing skills; high productivity and quality low level of innovation; recruitment problems in the late 1980s	Falling employment in information sector; most large firms keep a stable level; restructuring and downsizing among subsidiaries and subcontractors	MITI seeks to establish an independent software market, and unbundle software from hardware, but meets resistance	Flexible employment and limited time contracts for specialists of potentially great interest; key issue: establish creative work forms and upgrade status of software engineers

elsewhere, Japanese companies compete in establishing new plants for LCD and plasma screens, high-tech batteries or semiconductor equipment manufacturing. A similar logic applies to new automobile components from more fuel-efficient engines to advanced navigation systems.

Reorganise product development and compress lead-time even further

Engineering departments are revamped to cope with multiproduct management with a strong emphasis on time and cost reduction. The 'fat designs' of the Bubble Boom are pruned. Automobile and machine tool makers are simplifying products, using common parts across models and eliminating excessive features ('decontenting'). The resulting price reduction on new models, combined with a stabilisation of the dollar–yen exchange rate at a lower level compared to the peak of 1995, has restarted the battle for market share, which US competitors started to experience in 1996.

Set new standards for 'ramp-up rapidity'

In automobiles, the ramp-up to full production rate is accomplished within days of model changeovers; the ideal is an instant, 'vertical', ramp-up. In the manufacture of high-tech components, there is a similar pressure to accelerate process yields very rapidly. In this way, Japanese producers adapt to increased market volatility and can recoup their plant investment in spite of shortening product life-cycles. 'Ramp-up skills' play an important role for total R&D-efficiency, and for justifying continued plant investment in Japan. To achieve this, manufacturers tend to focus on advance process engineering at the expense of their traditional *gemba* approach with its emphasis on low-cost improvements by plant managers and workers. Toyota-style just-in-time production control remains of crucial importance, but its classical Ohnoism and the incremental *kaizen* approach are losing much of their relevance.

The situation in software is different in several respects. Here the Japanese companies never achieved an international standing, with the exception of the computer games industry. The PC revolution, and the concomitant spread of packaged software instead of bundled hardware-software deliveries, have forced the Japanese companies to rethink their technologies, organisation and products. After a long struggle to compete in large mainframe systems by means of productive but slow-moving software factories, Japanese computer and software companies are back in a catch-up mode, and have to learn anew from the US industry leaders. Their difficulties to keep pace in software illustrate a weakness of the diversified business structure of Japan's electronics giants. Their broad product range helped them to weather the long recession and offset slumping demand in one area with brisk sales in another, for example semiconductors. However, the very same structure contributed to the lack of an independent software industry with its own organisational and management models. Japan's software vendors remain predominantly domestically oriented, but the market is rapidly westernising and becoming much more competitive than before, and this could create new business openings.

Overall, the industrial dynamics described above are working powerfully to restore and increase the international competitiveness of major Japanese corporations. However, it does not mean a return to the 1980s, when Japanese superiority in some sectors was extrapolated to nearly all advanced industries in a general forecast of Japan becoming 'no. 1'. The US resurgence in the 1990s has provided two important caveats: first, extrapolations of trends, for example Japanese output growth during a particular period, are a very poor guide to the future. Secondly, the variation of key competitive factors across industries does not allow for one corporate or management model. Japanese skills in manufacturing management have been decisive in automobiles, machine tools and advanced component fabrication, but so far failed in achieving any advantage in software development.

THE APPROACHING END OF JAPAN, INC. – BUT NOT OF ALLIANCE CAPITALISM

Does our insistence on regained Japanese competitiveness imply that its macroeconomic difficulties and political turbulence are of no consequence for corporate performance? To some extent the answer is yes. During the 1960s and 1970s, makers of machine tools as well as semiconductors strongly benefited from MITI's research programmes and industrial policies. In the 1990s, major Japanese corporations are operating internationally. They are less dependent on the domestic economy and in less need of political support and bureaucratic protection. Thus they do not seem to be directly affected by the decomposition of Japan's 'developmental state', signified by the decline of MITI. (In some emerging technology areas, such as high-definition TV or telecommunications standards, they are still very much affected by public policy-making.) The political and bureaucratic turbulence in Japan has certainly affected domestic business and consumer confidence, however, and prolonged the recession. It has also possibly eroded managers' mental inhibitions to relocating production overseas. There is also a more ideological consequence. The notion of 'Japan, Inc.', which gained currency in the 1970s, was never a very accurate way of conceiving the Japanese economy, since it grossly underestimated the elements of corporate competition and rivalries between industry and bureaucracy in Japan. The erosion of the postwar power triangle, and the demise of the two élite ministries, MITI and MOF, have rendered this concept even less effective in explaining Japanese industrial dynamics.

Another consequence of the decline of once-powerful state agencies and the intensified international competition is an increasing level of variation within individual industries. Previously, MITI and the Ministry of Finance had a basic policy of preserving balance and equilibrium in major industries and no important player was allowed to fail. In the financial sector this was called the 'armed convoy' principle. In the future, the two ministries will not have the power to maintain this principle. This will reinforce a trend towards increasing diversity within industries. The widening gap between strong and weak players is already evident in several of the industries studied in this book. In the automobile industry, Toyota has staged a formidable come-back after a few difficult years, resuming its pursuit of global market share growth. At the other extreme, Mazda has lost its corporate autonomy and is becoming dependent on Ford's global decisions. In machine tools, the previous industry leader, Okuma, was forced into a humiliating programme of restructuring, redundancies and change of chief executive. Family-owned Mori Seiki, on the other hand, weathered the recession without any reorganisation or reduction in employment. In the future it will become more and more important for outside observers to focus on individual firms, but without neglecting the differences in the structural environment between Japanese and western industries.

The erosion of Japan's developmental state does not mean an end to Japanese exceptionalism. This becomes clear if we look at its system of corporate governance and employment. In the USA, the 1990s have witnessed a series of boardroom revolts. Shareholders assert their interests against corporate managers, forcing low-performers out of the executive suites. A similar trend is on its way in Europe. Not so in Japan. Its system of 'alliance capitalism', characterised by stable corporate cross-ownership organised in cohesive but competing groups, remains virtually intact, and shareholder interest is as subdued as before the crisis. Foreign investors and several Japanese financial institutions have argued that there is a need for a greater transparency of corporate practices and for more generous cash payouts to shareholders. Their success has been very limited. Management remains in firm control of Japanese corporations. This was symbolically illustrated at the annual shareholders meetings held on 27 June 1996. Nearly all the 2,241 meetings ended within an hour; only 11 lasted more than two hours. Efforts by foreign investors to use this opportunity to wield influence had no impact (Yokoyama, 1996).

Thus Japanese companies have not experienced the same impatient pressure for profit improvements as their western counterparts. There is no equivalent to the enormous gap between executive and employee compensation that has become such a striking feature in the USA and parts of Europe. No market for corporate control, for mergers and take-overs, has emerged. In spite of the long recession there have been remarkably few instances of industry consolidation. In all the industries studied in this book, the group system of corporate control has preserved the same basic competitive structure as before the recession. No major player has retreated, not even in the machine tool industry, where sales fell to more than half at the bottom of the recession. The competition between its 'eight big makers' remains as intense as ever. In the automobile industry, Ford's take-over of management control at Mazda could be viewed as an instance of international consolidation, but within Japan, the Hiroshima company remains an independent player. In all four sectors, the resilience of established practices has been remarkable. Thus the prediction of Mark Fruin (1992) of a fundamental robustness of the Japanese enterprise system, beyond the high-growth postwar period, seems to be substantiated.

Despite the rise of institutional economics, there is in the economics literature only a scant interest in the phenomenon of resilience of industrial structures and social values. The few exceptions to the rule mainly deal with economic institutions in southeast Asia (for example, Tang, 1995). Within the social sciences, psychology and sociology have been much more inclined to explore and interpret resilience: in studies of how children survive stress and abuse, or how schools could foster resilience in inner-city youth; in investigations of cultural resilience in ethnic minorities; and in studies of union resilience in troubled times. Thus there is no established or defined meaning of resilience in the context of industrial and economic dynamics. The above-mentioned sociological studies provide some important clues, however. Resilience is not about rigidity or resistance to change. In the understanding of Dore (1986), it is about *flexible rigidities*, a capability to absorb external shocks and adverse circumstances by processes of incremental adaptation while preserving the core of social beliefs, norms and organisational relationships. It is about a perseverance mood, a determination to weather it out. It's about a capacity to 'spring back' or in military terms, a second-strike capability. During the last recession, this perseverance mood was demonstrated in many ways: by the very low rate of capacity reduction in suffering industries (see Chapter 3); and by the refusal of the consumer electronics companies to withdraw from any major business, in spite of cut-throat competition, and by their determination to preserve and gradually transform physical as well as human resources, instead of closing plants and cutting personnel. The 'second-strike capability' is a *leitmotiv* of the automobile industry story in Chapter 6 but the ability to spring back and catch up seems to be strong in the computer industry as well. In spite of a serious market lag and a weak international position, Japanese PC makers have weathered the onslaught of US competition. They have increased their share in the booming domestic market (in 1995, the big three domestic PC makers controlled 70% of Japan's home market; a stark contrast to the situation in Europe), and are prepared for the next competitive wave, new net-computers, integrated 'entertainment PCs', etc.

Further, resilience does not mean bland consensus and complacency. The crisis-consciousness and the public soul-searching in Japan concerning its industrial future (as exemplified by 'the new weakness debate' in Chapter 3, and the fear of hollowing-out discussed in Chapter 4) indicate that it is rather the opposite: the staying power of Japan's corporate governance, industrial organisation, horizontal competition, internal labour markets and employment practices is strongly related to a constant awareness and discussion of potential threats and adaptation requirements. This again, underlines that Japanese resilience is not an unchanging, static industrial system;

however, the mode of change is different from the west. This brings us back to the discussion of divergence–convergence briefly touched upon in Chapter 5. There we introduced a force-field figure presenting forces driving convergence (discussed in Chapters 2–4) and forces sustaining diversity between Japanese and Anglo-Saxon capitalism. We did not discuss the relative strength of the various factors, and the forces preserving diversity were presented only very sketchily in order not to pre-empt the industry studies. The figure is reproduced here in an amended format (see Figure 10.1). The upper half of the figure – forces driving convergence – is the same as in Chapter 5; in the lower half, the factors of resilience have been fleshed out in more detail, integrating some of the evidence of Chapters 6–9.

The Japanese industrial fabric is a complex web of social and corporate values, long-standing political, economical and managerial relationships (within as well as between firms) and stable yet plastic practices. During recession times, Japanese companies tend to develop an acute crisis-consciousness, which helps them to modify and adapt without sacrificing basic elements. This lay at the heart of Japan's corporate resilience in the crisis of the early 1990s, and it is in sharp contrast to the 'west': Japan's subtle but consistent accommodation, compared to the bold moves, the drama, the vigorous entrepreneurialism but also the 'slash and burn' approach of contemporary US industry. Will this difference remain?

It is not possible to quantify the individual factors in the convergence/diversity field of Figure 10.1, but the net effect so far is that diversity, not convergence, carries the day. In key sectors Japan's 'alliance capitalism', its system of corporate governance, competition and employment prevails, although the core of the standard employment system seems to be slowly declining. Perhaps most importantly, there is no equivalent in Japan to the sharply expanded role of US financial markets and their pressures on corporate behaviour and personnel practices. Thus, it might even be argued that in the medium term the difference between the two systems of capitalism will increase, in spite of similar global competitive pressures.

EMPLOYMENT PRACTICES – THE DIFFERENCE OF JAPAN PREVAILS

The pattern of resilience and perseverance which emerged out of the studies of industrial competitiveness also applies to Japan's employment practices. The end of the era of constant growth has not implied the expected convergence to Anglo-Saxon personnel policies. Japanese practices are often simplistically treated, so it is important to present a nuanced picture. It has been known for a long time that the standard image of life-time employment and careers does not encompass the many small firms in the service and supplier industries. However, as we have pointed out in Chapter 5, this picture also has to be qualified for large firms. There have been several waves of employment adjustment in Japan's core corporate sector during the postwar period: in the 1940s, in the late 1970s, and again during the post-

Forces driving convergence

Pressure from **financial markets** because of eroding *fukumieki* and increased profit demands from low-performing banks and insuring companies	Long recession **low growth** in Japan force companies to reduce permanent employment	**Kudoka** transfer of manufacturing because of *endaka* and trade friction	New informa**tion technology** and networking reduce need for administration and human relations-oriented management	Reborn **US competitiveness** fuels employer interest in flexible employment and downsizing	**International pressure** on Japan to open up and deregulate protected sectors; **declining domestic power** of industrial policies and élite bureaucracies
Cross-ownership controlled by corporate management still rules, because of benefits of long-term, reciprocal and multiplex interfirm relations; efforts by foreign investors to increase their influence have failed	Stable ownership permits **piecemeal adjustment;** upgraded products and stream-lined production safeguard manufacturing in Japan; rush to invest in new technologies repeats postwar *kaisha* dynamics; reduced hiring affects young and temporary workers, but brunt of adjustment borne by middle-aged and older workers	**In-company networks** remain crucial for simultaneous engineering; **retraining** supports incremental adjustment; for manufacturing of complex products these networks are more important than ever	**Strong consumer and employee expectations** that companies honour obligations; end of Bubble temporarily strengthens traditional values	**Dogged resistance** to foreign pressure; Japan reduces international imbalance by moving production abroad, not by internationalising its own markets	

Forces sustaining diversity

Figure 10.1. Japanese capitalism versus Anglo-Saxon forces of convergence and divergence

Bubble recession. The Japanese system is by no means rigid and there is certainly an element of hypocrisy, but beyond the euphemisms important differences to the pattern of personnel adjustment in the Anglo-Saxon countries do remain. First, there has been a distinct trend from blunt to subtle, from direct to indirect methods of workforce adjustment in Japan: from the outright dismissals in the late 1940s to the programmes for early retirement in the early 1990s. In the USA and several European countries, there is a trend in the opposite direction, from soft and slow to harsh and hasty methods of downsizing. Further, redundancies are always the last resort in Japan, after a series of other measures have been applied and found inadequate. If a division of a major corporation is bleeding, it is the corporate responsibility to take care of its employees as long as group finances are healthy. The fragmentation of corporate responsibility in the west in the wake of divisionalisation and decentralisation has no equivalent in Japan. In the USA, and increasingly also in Europe, labour shedding is appreciated by the stock market as proof of strong and determined management. Redundancies are accompanied by soaring stock prices. In Japan, redundancies are seen as management failures and imply a loss of public confidence and trust.

During the Bubble Boom there seemed to be an erosion of Japan's standard employment system. The status of manufacturing jobs declined, and labour turnover increased significantly. Companies resorted to temporary employees, immigrant workers and mid-career entrants to an unprecedented degree. The short-term result of the post-Bubble recession has been a return to Japanese normalcy, and the traditional focus on regular male employees. The reinforcement of Japan's established labour market practices unfortunately also includes a continuation of its entrenched gender segregation. Demographic changes and educational achievement – rising marrying age, declining birth rates, a constant increase of female university graduates – raised hopes for a less circumscribed role for female employees in Japan. Educational advancement has been slow to translate into any serious extension of female job opportunities, however. The particular economic role of women in Japan seems to be firmly entrenched in its structure of employment, education competition and lack of public welfare. Aggravating the situation, the general difficulties for university students to find good jobs after graduation have been particularly severe for female graduates.

Our stress on robustness and resilience does not imply that the Japanese labour market and employment relationships are static structures. *Nenko*, the seniority-based pay system, is increasingly challenged by performance-oriented principles. Productivity problems among white-collar employees and the costs of a rising medium age because of reduced hiring are driving companies to reassess their seniority systems. This change could probably also imply an end to the unitary treatment of white and blue-collar workers – a trend opposite to that in western Europe, where companies stress the need to eliminate previous differences between categories. Further, there is a gradual shrinking of the core of standard employees with a prospect of long-term, stable employment. During the recession, Japanese companies have been extremely reluctant to dismiss these employees, but on the other hand in the future they will try hard to limit recruitment of new permanent workers. At least that is the case in sectors such as automobiles and machine tools. On the other hand there seems to be only a weak support for Nikkeirei's insistence on the need for an external labour market involving limited hiring contracts for specialists. In automobiles, for example, stable intrafirm networks are more important than ever to succeed in concurrent engineering and 'instant' production ramp-up. In other sectors, such as software and telecommunications, however, there might be a stronger interest in professional mobility. Thus there is no general convergence of Japanese practices with the west, but rather a pattern of increasing differences within Japan. If current tendencies remain important in the future, the result might inadvertently also be a levelling of working conditions between many men and women. Most women will continue to be excluded from the male world of permanent employment and long-term careers in large companies, but this world will become more difficult to enter for young male graduates too.

During the long post-Bubble recession, the need for more drastic measures to deal with corporate overmanning was a recurrent theme in the business press. By and large, however, companies used the previously established repertoire for incremental workforce adjustment. On sum, the balance of the recession and the new economic situation is that Japanese companies have honoured their implicit social contracts. The principles of JIT production have not been linked to JIT employment. An increasing proportion of the population will probably not be offered stable employment and long-term careers in the future, but key groups will continue to be integrated into Japan's intensively relational corporate organisations. Traditional standards will remain very important for the popular ideals and perceptions of various labour market practices.

The specific Japanese pattern of intra and interfirm relationships makes companies less agile in manufacturing and management restructuring. A turnaround of a bleeding firm normally takes more time to achieve than in the west. In the long recession, the difficulty for Japanese companies to reduce excessive employment quickly was a financial burden, but at the same time a crucial driver for their efforts to upgrade technologies and retrain workers. The development of the Sharp company in the 1980s and 1990s is a case in point. Its conventional products, such as colour television sets, are mature and cannot be produced in Japan at competitive prices any more. The response of many western companies to such a situation is to reduce employment in the domestic high-cost economy, move production abroad and possibly take over competitors to establish a dominant position in the slow-growth market. This, for example, has been the strategy of the Swedish white-goods company Electrolux. Sharp has followed a part of the recipe, and moved most of its production of CTVs offshore. However, the workforce in Japan has not been reduced. Instead Sharp has invested heavily in new technologies, such as LCD screens and built new growth products around these technologies, and this has absorbed any excess employment. From a pin-sharp pen (the origin of the company name) to pin-sharp screens, the Sharp company illustrates the trajectory of corporate innovation and upgrading in a system of sharp competition but stable ownership and employment. The Sharp story thus demonstrates the power of some of the basic aspects of Japan's alliance capitalism.

INTERCULTURAL LEARNING: FROM RECIPES TO REFLECTION

Between Japan and the west, especially the USA, there has been a cross-flow of ideas throughout the postwar period. First, from the USA to Japan in the wake of defeat and occupation; then from Japan to the USA following the island country's rise to world leadership in key sectors; and in the 1990s, both a new wave of influences from the USA to Japan (in, for example, the software industry), and from Japan to the west (concerning, for instance, its eminent production accelerating capacity). Considering the vast cultural and social differences, this cross-flow has been remarkably effective in diffusing 'best practices' in managerial techniques in various sectors. Would an extended agenda of institutional learning also be feasible? Several students of Japan have advanced such possibilities, a recent case being Carl Kester (1996), and his plea for a synthesis of US and Japanese forms of corporate governance and interorganisational exchange. According to Kester the US system is effective in exposing corporate management (the 'agents' in the principal agency theory) to market discipline and making it accountable to shareholder interest. The Japanese system, on the other hand, is superior in the way it minimises transactions costs in intrafirm relationships, and thus stimulates long-term relation-specific investments. Kester attempts to identify changes in the USA and Japan that might indicate a convergence to a common 'best practice', but in the end he is not very successful. The problem of course, is that structures of corporate governance and interfirm relations could not be reduced to techniques and organisational set-ups, which are easily transferred and copied. A new synthesis requires a profound process of reflection and a rethinking of established institutional practices. In a situation where one model is ideologically dominant and economically successful, as was the case of the USA in the mid-1990s (at least according to conventional indicators), such a rethinking is a precarious proposal. The situation in Europe is different, however. Here many models of corporate governance coexist and compete (Woolcock, 1996), and so do various variants of labour law, employment practices and management traditions. At the same time there is a widespread acknowledgement of the need for change to cope with problems of unemployment and innovation. This European reorientation has mainly been influenced by the new *défi americain*, and its accompanying economic orthodoxy. The message of this book is that it is time for a more sophisticated reflection on Japan, including systematic comparisons of how Japanese and European industries have responded to the recession of the early 1990s: a new reflection on Japan's forms of firm governance, horizontal competition and vertical co-operation, personnel practices and corporate responsibilities; and a new agenda for exchange and learning, beyond the three-letter techniques and quick-fix consultancies of the 1980s. The essence of such a reflection is to explore the alternatives, the different ways of restructuring and repositioning, of combining economic imperatives and social responsibilities; without such knowledge there is little freedom of social choice.

In the decades succeeding the Meiji revolution in the 1860s, and then again after the defeat in 1945, Japanese companies and society were constantly watching technical and managerial developments in the west, but selective and consistent in their adoption and application practices. The 1990s has meant an increasing interchange with both the west and Asia in the form of global investment strategies, networks of international company alliances and to some extent more open markets. Japan's learning behaviour of the past will probably remain unchanged. What will be the European pattern?

APPENDIX: A NOTE ON SOURCES

The general framework of this book builds on the authors' previous research in the automobile, consumer electronics and machine tool sectors as detailed in the author presentation. The empirical analysis of changes within Japanese industries is based on four specific sources (the last two sources being listed in the reference section):

1) Industrial field studies, plant visits and interviews with managers, in some cases also with unionists. The majority of these field studies were conducted jointly in October–November 1993 and September 1995 (see details below).
2) Discussion with various experts: academics, consultants and government officials. In the automobile industry – Professor Fujimoto at Tokyo University, September 1995, May 1996; Yoshida Nobumi at Jidosha Keiei Kaihatasu Kenkyu-sho, September 1995. Computer and software: John Stern, American Electronics Association, Tokyo, September 1995; Professor Matsumoto, ASTEM in Kyoto, September 1995; Bengt Asker, Ericsson Telecomm, co-organiser of the Swedish industrial study tour to Japanese software development organisations in 1993; Toru Maegawa, Director of the Information, Computer and Communications Policy Office at MITI, November 1993.
3) Japanese trade magazines and business journals. The single most important of them is *Nikkei Weekly*, which is also published in an English weekly edition.
4) Statistics and reports from MITI, Ministry of Labour, etc.

Plant visits and interviews, 1993–5

Car companies
1) Mitsubishi Motors, Mizushima Plant, 18 October 1993. Interviews with managers at production engineering and human resources development departments.
2) Mizushima Machinery and Metal Industry Co-operative – Soya Industrial Park, 15 October 1993. Interviews with general manager at Hiruta Kogyo Co., and officers at the Industry Co-operative.
3) Nissan Kyushu (Kanda) plant, 4 November 1993. Interviews with managers of general affairs; production engineering and personnel administration
4) Toyota Kyushu Plant visit, 6 November 1993. Interview with manager of general affairs.
5) Toyota Tahara, 29 October 1993. Interview with manager in the administration division.
6) Toyota Tsutsumi, 28 October 1993. Interview with public relations officer.

7) Kanto Auto Works, Yokosuka, 26 November 1993. Interview with managers at personnel department.
8) Kanto Auto Works, Yokosuka, 18 September 1995. Interviews with production and personnel managers.
9) Daihatsu, Ikeda headquarters and main plant, Osaka, 20 September, 1995. Interviews with managers from various departments.
10) JAW, Hamamatsu-cho, 29 September 1995. Interviews with director of industrial affairs bureau, assistant general secretary, deputy director, international affairs bureau.

Electronics companies
Plant visits and management interviews at:
1) Hitachi Gifu. Colour television plant, 22 October 1993.
2) Hitachi information and image systems division, Gifu, 26 September 1995.
3) Matsushita overseas planning department, Osaka, 20 October, 1993.
4) Matsushita Ibaraki CTV plant, 26 October 1993.
5) Matsushita overseas planning department, Osaka, 19 September 1995.
6) NEC semiconductor plant, Yamagata, 12 November 1993.
7) Fujitsu Yamagata hard-disk plant, 11 November 1993.
8) Sharp, Osaka headquarters, 21 September 1995.
9) Denki Rengo, Japanese electrical, electronic and information union, Hamamatsu-cho, 30 September 1995. Interviews with members of the executive committee.

Machine tools
1) Takisawa Machine Tools, Okayama 14 October 1993. Interviews with personnel managers.
2) Mori Seiki, Iga plant and Nara headquarters, 22 September 1995. Interviews with director of the board, manager at the corporate planning and administration department, production managers.
3) Okuma Corporation, Shimooguchi, 25 September 1995. Interviews with the president and vice-president of the Okuma Machinery Labour Union.

Computers and software
1) Fujitsu Makuhari Laboratory, 14 September 1995. Interviews with managers from quality systems department, systems business group; SE systems business group; research department, research and planning division, Kawasaki.
2) Hitachi System Plaza Shinkawasaki, 27 September 1995. Interviews with managers from information systems division; Hitachi Software Development Centre, Totsuka; Hitachi Institute of Advanced Business Systems, Shin Yokohama; Hitachi System Engineering Ltd., Shin Yokohama.
3) Toshiba Systems and Software Engineering, SSEL laboratory, Kawasaki-shi, 12 September 1995. Interviews with managers at the information and control system group and managers and specialists at development departments.

BIBLIOGRAPHY

Abegglen, J. (1958) *The Japanese Factory. Aspects of its Social Organization*. Glencoe, IL: Free Press.

Abegglen, J. and Stalk, G. (1987) *Kaisha. The Japanese Corporation*. Tokyo: Charles F. Tuttle.

Adler, P. (1992) The 'learning bureaucracy'. New United Motor Manufacturing, Inc. In B. Staw and L. Cummings (eds) *Research in Organizational Behavior*. Greenwich, CT: JAI Press.

Alexander, A. J. (1994) Comparative innovation in Japan and the United States. In W. H. Tan and H. Shimada (eds) *Troubled Industries in the United States and Japan*. London: Macmillan.

Amsden, A. (1990) Third world industrialization – 'global Fordism' or a new model? *New Left Review* 182: 5–31.

Baba, Y., Takai, S. and Mizuta, Y. (1995) The Japanese software industry: the 'hub structure' approach, *Research Policy* 24: 473–86.

Baker, S. (1994) Why steel is looking sexy. *Business Week* 4 April.

Bosch, G. (1995) Working time and operating hours in the Japanese car industry. In D. Anxo et al. (eds) *Work Patterns and Capital Utilisation*. Dordrecht: Kluwer Academic.

Bremner, B. and Updike, E. H. (1995) Cash is king in corporate Japan. *Business Week* 1 May.

Brooks, F. P. (1975) *The Mythical Man-Month*. Reading, MA: Addison Wesley.

Carroll, P. (1993) *Big Blues*. New York: Crown.

Chogin Sogo Kenkyusho (1995) Nihon no kako kumitate kikai no kokusai kyoso kankyo no henka – Kosaku kikai, sangyoyo robotto, purasutikku kako kikai wo chushin ni (The changing environment of the international competition for Japanese machining and assembly machines with a focus on machine tools, industrial robots and plastic moulding machines). *Soken Chosa*, July.

Chogin Sogo Kenkyusho (1996) *Kudoka suru sangyo shinai sangyo (Industries that are Hollowed Out and those that are not Hollowed Out)*, Tokyo: Toyo Keizai Shinposha.

Clark, K. and Fujimoto, T. (1991) *Product Development Performance. Strategy, Organization and Management in the World Auto Industry*. Boston, MA: Harvard Business School.

Cole, R. (1971) *Japanese Blue Collar*. Berkeley, CA: University of California Press.

Cusumano, M. (1985) *The Japanese Automobile Industry*. Cambridge: Harvard University Press.

Cusumano, M. (1991) *Japan's Software Factories – A Challenge to US Management*. New York and Oxford: Oxford University Press.

Denki Rengo, (Japanese Federation of Electrical Machine Workers' Unions) (1995a) *The Fifth Industrial Policy of Denki Rengo*. Tokyo: Denki Rengo.

Denki Rengo (1995b) *Chosa Jiho* (research report). Tokyo: Denki Rengo.

Dertouzos, M., Lester, R. and Solow, R. (1989) *Made in America – Regaining the Productive Edge*. New York: HarperPerennial.

Dore, R. (1986) *Flexible Rigidities*. London: The Athlone Press.

Dore, R. (1987) *Taking Japan Seriously*. Stanford, CA: Stanford University Press.

Eberts, R. and Eberts, C. (1995) *The Myth of Japanese Quality*. Englewood Cliffs, NJ: Prentice-Hall.

EIAJ, (The Electronics Industries Association of Japan) (1995) *Facts and Figures on the Japanese Electronics Industry*. Tokyo: EIAJ.

Ellison, D., Clark, K. B., Fujimoto, T. and Huyn, Y.-S. (1995) *Product Development Update* (working paper). Cambridge, MA.: Harvard Business School.

Endo, K. (1995) Densan chingin taikei ni okeru noryokukyu to jinji satei (Ability pay and personnel assessment in the Densan wage system).*Ohara Shakai Mondai Kenkyusho Zasshi* April: 1–38.

EPA (1992) *Economic Survey of Japan 1990–1991*. Tokyo: EPA.

EU (1994) *The European Report on Science and Technology Indicators*. Luxembourg: European Commission, Directorate General XIII.

Farrell, C., Mandel, M. and Weber, J. (1995) Riding high. Corporate America now has an edge over its global rivals. *Business Week* 16 October.

Fassbender, H. (1993) and Cooper-Hedegaard, S. The ticking bomb at the core of Europe. *The McKinsey Quarterly* 3: 127–42.

Ferguson, C. H. and Morris, C. R. (1993) *Computer Wars: How the West can Win in a Post-IBM World*. New York: Time Books.

Fingleton, E. (1995a) *Blindside. Why Japan is Still on Track to Overtake the US by the Year 2000*. New York: Houghton Mifflin.

Fingleton, E. (1995b) Jobs for life: why Japan won't be giving them up. *Fortune* 20 March.

Forrester, T. (1993) *Silicon Samurai – How Japan Conquered the World's IT Industry*. Cambridge, MA: Blackwell.

Frank, R. H. and Cook, P. J. (1995) *The Winner-Take-All Society*. New York: Free Press.

Fransman, M. (1995) *Japan's Computer and Communications Industry*. Oxford: Oxford University Press.

Friedman, D. (1988) *The Misunderstood Miracle. Industrial Development and Political Changes in Japan*. Ithaca, NY: Cornell University Press.

Fruin, M. (1992) *The Japanese Enterprise System: Competitive Strategies and Cooperative Structures*. Oxford: Oxford University Press.

Fucini, J. and Fucini, S. (1990) *Working for the Japanese. Inside Mazda's American Auto Plant*. New York: Free Press.

Fujimoto, T. (1995) Lean Product Design versus Exchange Rate. Unpublished research note. Tokyo: University of Tokyo, Faculty of Economics.

Fujimoto, T. and Takeishi, A. (1994) An international comparison of productivity and product development performance in the automobile industry. In R. Minami, K. S. Kim, F. Makino and J. Seo (eds): *Acquiring, Adapting and Developing Technologies*. New York: St Martin's Press.

Fulford, B. (1996) Jusen probe to hit broad swath of society. *Nikkei Weekly*, 22 January.

Fushimi, S. (1995) Japan's VCR output rapidly moves offshore. *Nikkei Weekly* 31 July.

Garrahan, P. and Stewart, P. (1992) *The Nissan Enigma*. London: Mansell.

Gerlach, M. (1992) *Alliance Capitalism. The Social Organization of Japanese Business*. Berkely, CA: University of California Press.

Gross, N. and Carey, J. (1994) Japan's liquid-crystal gold rush. *Business Week* 17 January.

Hara, G. (1995) Advice to Japanese entrepreneurs. Go west, young man. *Computing Japan* September/October.

Hayashi, H. (1995) Danjo koyo kikai kinto ho 10 nen to kongo no kadai (Ten years of Equal Opportunity Law and problems to be solved). *Juristo* 1079: 4–15.

Heiwa Keizai Keikaku Kaigi (The Association for the Peace Economy) (1995) *Seizogyo no risutorakucharingu to koyo mondai (Restructuring and Employment Problems in the Manufacturing Industries)*, Tokyo: Koyo Sokushin Jigyodan.

Hitachi (1960) *Hitachi Seisakusho shi (History of Hitachi), Vol. 2*, Hitachi: Hitachi.

Hitachi (1992) *Outline of the Software Factory Approach*. Hitachi: Hitachi.

Holyoke, L. (1995) Sweet on software. Americans rush in where Japanese makers feared to tread. *Business Week* 12 June.

Humphrey, W. (1989) *Managing the Software Process.* Reading, MA.: Addison-Wesley.

Iida, M. (1994) Government study addresses excessive work habits. *Nikkei Weekly* 17 January.

Ikeya, A. (1995a) No mass unemployment. *Nikkei Weekly* 12 June.

Ikeya, A. (1995b): Hints of recovery – choppily. *Nikkei Weekly* 9 October.

Ikeya, A. (1995c) Surplus down for fourth half in a row. *Nikkei Weekly* 13 November.

Inoue, T. (1995) Chip-equipment profits soar: top earner sees 450% leap. *Nikkei Weekly* 30 October.

Inoue, T. and Ehara, Y. (eds) (1995) *Josei no deta bukku (Women's Data Book)* (2nd edn). Tokyo: Yuhikaku.

Isaka, S. (1995a) Japanese style rated with pluses and minuses. *Nikkei Weekly* 22 May.

Isaka, S. (1995b) New models put Nissan back on track. *Nikkei Weekly* 6 November.

Isaka, S. (1996) Automakers, moving into black, give green light to capital outlays. *Nikkei Weekly,* 3 June.

Ishibashi, A. and Iida, M. (1995) Foreign banks cash in on Japan premium. *Nikkei Weekly* 30 October.

Ishizawa, M. (1994a) Hitachi to manufacture product lines based on IBM's mainframe brain. *Nikkei Weekly* 2 March.

Ishizawa, M. (1994b) Software houses latecomers to downsizing. *Nikkei Weekly* 7 July.

Ishizawa, M. (1995) NEC growth slips in booming PC market. *Nikkei Weekly* 20 February.

Japan Commission on Industrial Performance (JCIP) (ed.) (1994) *Meido in Japan: Nihon seizogyo henkaku eno shishin (Made in Japan: Guiding Principles for the Innovation of Japanese Manufacturing Industry)*. Tokyo: Daiyamondosha.

Japan Economic Almanac (1995) Tokyo: Nihon Keizai Shimbun.

Japan Productivity Centre (1994) *Shushin koyo seido no shorai yosoku chosa hokokusho (Report on the Forecast of Lifetime Employment)*. Tokyo: JPC.

Japan Productivity Centre (1995) *21 seiki ni okeru nihon no jinji chingin seido. Seijuku shakai ni muketa jinji chingin seido no tenbo to saihensaku (Japanese Personnel and Wage Systems: Towards the 21st century. Perspective and Reorganization of the Personnel and Wage Systems for a Matured Society)*. Tokyo: JPC.

Japan Productivity Centre (1996) *Katsuyo rodo tokei (Practical Labour Statistics)*. Tokyo: JPC.

JAW (Confederation of Japan Automobile Workers' Unions) (1989). *Genki no deru Jidosha Sangyo Anketo Hokokusho (Report on the Consciousness of Union Members)*. Tokyo: JAW.

JAW (1992) *The Japanese Automobile Industry in the Future. Towards Coexistence with the World, Consumers and Employees*. Tokyo: JAW.

JAW (1994) *Transition of Annual Working Hours in JAW: 12 Major Unions*. Tokyo: JAW.

JAW (1995) *Koyo yojo ni taisaru jidosha soren tositeno taiosaku ni tsuite. (The Policy of JAW on Workforce Redundancy)*. Tokyo: JAW.

JMTBA (Japan Machine Tool Builders' Association) (1984) *Kosaku kikai kogyo sengo hattensi (Postwar Development of the Machine Tool Industry), Vol. 1.* Tokyo: JMTBA.

JMTBA (1994) *Nihon no kosaku kikai 1994 (The Japanese Machine Tool Industry 1994)*, Tokyo: JMTBA.

JMTBA (1995a) *Kosaku kikai gijutsu no genjo to kadai hokokusho (Report on the Present State and Problems of Machine Tool Technology)*. Tokyo: JMTBA.

JMTBA (1995b) *Chugoku oyobi ajia shuyokoku no kosaku kikai shijo doko (The Market Trend of the Machine Tools in China and Major Asian Countries)*. Tokyo: JMTBA.

JMTBA (1995c) *Kosaku kikai kogyo keiei chosa jokyo 1994 nendo (Survey on the Business Situation of Machine Tool Builders for the Fiscal Year 1994)*. Tokyo: JMTBA.

Johnson, C. (1982) *MITI and the Japanese Miracle. The Growth of Industrial Policy 1925–1975.* Stanford University Press.

Johnson, C. (1995) *Japan: Who Governs?* New York: Norton.

Johnson, R. (1994a) The re-leaning of Japan. *Automotive News* 5 December.

Johnson, R. (1994b) Toyota stresses 4-year cycle. *Automotive News* 2 May.

Johnson, R. (1995) Mazda tries to find a place in Ford's future. *Automotive News* 28 February.

Kageki, N. (1994) HDTV shift stuns industry. *Nikkei Weekly* 28 February.

Kajiwara, K. and Tokudazji, A. (1992) *Jidosha Sangyo Bokoku Ron – Toyota Nissan no 'Seigi' ha Nihon no Tsumi (The Auto Industry Destroys the Country – the 'Justice' of Toyota and Nissan is the Sin of Japan.* Kobunsha: Kappa Business.

Kajiwara, K. and Tokudazji, A. (1993). *Mesaki no Riekishugi Kaikaku Ron – Nippon Kigyo Mionikusa kawa no Shuppatsu (Reforms of the Short-Term Profit Orientation – Japanese Enterprises Departure from Ugliness.* Kobunsha: Kappa Business.

Kamata, S. (1973) *Japan in the Passing Lane.* New York: Random House.

Kamata, S. (1993) *Zosen hukyo (The Shipbuilding Industry in Recession).* Tokyo: Iwanami shoten.

Kato, H. (1960) Kosaku kikai kogyo no hatten katei (The development of the machine tool industry). In H. Arisawa (ed.) *Gendai nihon sangyo koza (Contemporary Japanese Industries), Vol. 6,* Tokyo: Iwanami Shoten.

Kato, H., (1993a). Wake up to crises, IBJ tells car industry. *Nikkei Weekly* 23 August.

Kato, H. (1993b) Job losses raise hollowing-out debate but economic strength tempers fears. *Nikkei Weekly* 4 October.

Kato, H. (1994) *Henkakuki no nihon sangyo. Kaigai seisan to sangyo kudoka (Japanese Industries in Transition. Overseas Production and Hollowing Out),* Tokyo: Shinhyoron.

Kenney, M. and Florida, R. (1993). *Beyond Mass Production. The Japanese System and its Transfer to the US.* New York: Oxford University Press.

Kester, C. (1996) American and Japanese corporate governance: convergence to best practice? In R. Dore and S. Berger (eds) *National Diversity and Global Capitalism.* Ithaca, NY: Cornell University Press.

Kinutani, H. (1993) Modular Assembly in Mixed Model Production. Hosei University: Workshop on Assembly Automation. Mimeo, Tokyo, 19 November.

Kishi, H. (1993) Towards an appropriate software trade. *JIPDEC Information Quarterly* 95: 17–25.

Kitagawa, K. (1995) Danjo koyo kikai kintoho no genkai (The limitations of the Equal Opportunity Law). In: Kiso keizai kagaku kenkyusho (ed.) *Nihongata kigyo shakai to josei (Japanese Corporate Society and Women)* Tokyo: Aoki Shoten.

Kobayashi, M. (1993) Nihon kosaku kikai sangyo no gijutsu hatten no tokeiteki bunseki (Statistical analysis of the development of Japan's machine tool industry). In Y. Takeoka, H. Takahashi and T. Nakaoka (eds) *Shin gijutsu no donyu (The Introduction of New Technology).* Tokyo: Dobunkan.

Koike, K. (1981) The inner workings of Japanese diligence, *Japan Echo* 8: 30–43.

Koike, K. (1982) *Skill Formation on the Shop Floor – Foundation for Development.* Kyoto: Kyoto University.

Kokumin Kinyu Koko Chosabu (1989) *Nihon no chusho kikai kogyo (The Small and Medium-Sized Machinery Industry in Japan).* Tokyo: Chusho Kigyo Risachi Senta.

Komiya, R., Okuno, M. and Suzumura, K. (eds) (1984) *Nihon no sangyo seisaku (Industrial Policy in Japan),* Tokyo: University of Tokyo Press. English translation (1988). *Industrial Policy in Japan.*

Kroll, J. (1993) From capitalism without cost towards competitive capitalism. *Nikkei Weekly* 25 October.

Larsson, G. (1995) Banksjukan har nått Japan. (The bank disease has come to Japan). *Dagens Industri* 14 November.

Lashinsky, A. (1995) Nissan's gentle exit eases town's pain. *Nikkei Weekly* 27 March.

Lashinsky, A. and Sumiya, F. (1995) Nissan struggles to staunch losses. *Nikkei Weekly* 13 March.
Lillrank, P. (1994) *The Software Society (discussion paper)*. Stockholm: The European Institute of Japanese Studies.
Lincoln, E. J. (1993) *Japan's New Global Role*. Washington, DC: The Brookings Institution.
Lincoln, J. R. and Kalleberg, A. L. (1990) *Culture, Control and Commitment*. New York: Cambridge University Press.
MacDuffie J. P. and Pil, F. K. (1996) *Performance Findings of the International Assembly Plant Study*. Philadelpia: The Wharton School of Management, University of Pennsylvania.
Matsumoto, Y. (1992) Japanese Software Factory, In *Encyclopedia of Software Engineering*. New York: Wiley.
Matsuzaka, T. (1994) Matsushita shrinks 'bloated' management. *Nikkei Weekly* 13 December.
McKinsey Global Institute (1993) *Manufacturing Productivity*. Washington, DC. McKinsey Global Institute.
McKinsey Global Institute (1995) *Sweden's Economic Performance: Computer Industry Case Study*. Stockholm: McKinsey Global Institute.
Ministry of Labour (1995a) *Nihonteki koyo seido no genjo to tenbo (The Japanese-Style Employment System and its Perspective)*. Tokyo: Ministry of Labour.
Ministry of Labour (1995b) *Rodo hakusho 1995 nenban (White Paper on Labour for 1995)*. Tokyo: Ministry of Labour.
Mishina, K. (1994) Seeing is believing, believing is doing and doing is learning. Lessons from Toyota Motor Manufacturing, USA. Mimeo, Harvard Business School.
MITI (1980) *80 nendai no tsusan seisahn bijon (Vision of International Trade and Industry in the 1980s)*. Tokyo: Tsusho Sangyo Chosakai.
MITI (1989) *21 seiki no sagyo kikai bijon (A Vision of Industrial Machinery in the 21st Century)*. Tokyo: Sangyo Tsusho Chosakai.
MITI (1990) *90 nendai no tsusan seisaku bijon (Vision of International Trade and Industry in the 1990s)*, Tokyo: Tshusho Sangyo Chosakai.
MITI (1992) *Urgent Proposal: The New Age of Software* (draft), Tokyo: Information Industry Committee of the Industrial Structure Council.
MITI (1993) *Statistics on Japanese Industries*. Tokyo: Tsusho Sangyo Chosakai.
MITI (1995) *Statistics on Japanese Industries*. Tokyo: Tsusho Sangyo Chosakai.
Mitsusada, H. (1995a) Advanced LCD makers look beyond PCs. *Nikkei Weekly* 20 March.
Mitsusada, H. (1995b) Bucking industry trend. NEC opts for domestic production. *Nikkei Weekly* 24 April.
Mitsusada, H. (1995c) Mitsubishi faces grim choices after Rockefeller failures. *Nikkei Weekly* 15 May.
Mitsusada, H. (1995d) TV makers aim to fatten profits with flat-panels. *Nikkei Weekly* 3 July.
Mitsusada, H. (1995e) NEC–Packard Bell alliance holds promise, bodes conflict. *Nikkei Weekly* 10 July.
Mitsusada, H. (1995f) Toshiba puts desktop fate in Intel's hands. *Nikkei Weekly* 31 July.
Mitsusada, H. (1995g) Will electronics spark general recovery? *Nikkei Weekly* 16 October.
Mitsusada, H. (1995h) Price-war specter haunts PC surge. *Nikkei Weekly* 23 October.
Mitsusada, H. (1996) Chips recharge materials suppliers. *Nikkei Weekly* 29 January.
Miyamoto, K. and Hagiwara, S. (1993) Kosaku kikai seizogyo (The machine tool industry), *Kokumin kinyu koko chosa kiho*, November.
Miyazaki, Y. (1992) *Hukugo Hukyo (Complex Recession)*. Tokyo: Chuko Shinsho.
Miyazaki, Y., Ohtaka, Y., Kubono, K., Fujino, A. and Muronaka, K. (1994) *Software*

Process Assessment and Improvement Based on the Capability Maturity Model for Software. Chiba: Fujitsu Ltd, Quality Systems Dept, Systems Group.

Mori, K. (1995) Industry leader looks for auto recovery in spring. *Nikkei Weekly* 9 October.

Mori Seiki *The Mori Seiki History*. Nara: Mori Seiki.

Morris, J., Munday, M. and Wilkinson, B. (1993) *Working for the Japanese. The Economic and Social Consequences of Japanese Investment in Wales*. London: Athlone Press.

Morris, K. (1994) The town watcher. How Haruo Tsuji of Sharp, a one-time producer of cheap television sets and calculators, has set the pace in Japanese electronics. *Financial World* 19 July.

Nakamoto, M. (1996) New driver takes the wheel. *The Financial Times* 22 April.

Nakano, M. (1993) *Nihon no seiji rikigaku: Darega seisaku o kimerunoka (Power Dynamics in Japan: Who decide policies?)*, Tokyo: Nihon Hoso Kyokai.

Namiki, N. (1989) *Tsusansho no shuen (The End of the MITI)*. Tokyo Daiyamondosha.

National Defence Council for Victims of Karoshi (1990) *Karoshi. When the 'Corporate Warrior' Dies*. Tokyo: Mado-Sha.

Neff, R., Shatu, M., Barnathan, J., Dawson, M. and Updike, E. (1995) Japan's new identity. *Business Week* 10 April.

Nihon Keieisha Dantai Renmei (Nikkeiren) (1995) *Shin jidai no nihonteki keiei (Japanese-Style Management in a New Era)*. Tokyo: Nikkeiren.

Nihon Keizai Shinbunsha (Nikkei) (ed.) (1990) *Gendai kigyo nyumon (Contemporary Enterprises. An Introduction)* (1st edn). Toyko: Nihon Keizai Shinbunsha.

Nihon Keizai Shinbunsha (Nikkei) (ed.) (1994a) *Kanryo: Kishimu kyodai kenryoku (Bureacrats: Shaky Huge Power)*, Tokyo: Nihon Keizai Shinbunsha.

Nihon Keizai Shinbunsha (Nikkei) (ed.) (1994b) *Yomigaere seizogyo: 'Sozoteki hakai' ga kigyo wo kaeru (Revive, Manufacturing Industry! 'Creative Destruction' Changes Enterprises)* Tokyo: Nihon Keizai Shinbunsha.

Nihon Keizai Shinbunsha (Nikkei) (ed.) (1995) *Gendai kigyo nyumon (Contemporary Enterprises. An Introduction)* (2nd edn). Toyko: Nihon Keizai Shinbunsha.

Nikkan Jidosha Shinbunsha (1995) *Jidosha sangyo hando bukku 1996 (Handbook of the Automobile Industry for 1996*. Tokyo: Nikkan Jidosha Shinbunsha.

Nikkei Business (ed.) (1992) *Kaisha no kaizo: Nippon Saikochiku heno taido (Reforms of Enterprises: The Beginning of Japan's Restructuring)*. Tokyo: Nihon Keizai Shinbunsha.

Nikkei Sangyo Shinbun (1990) *Za shea 1991 (The Share 1991)*. Tokyo: Nihon Keizai Shinbunsha.

Nikkei Sangyo Shinbun (1992) *Shijo Senyuritsu, 1993 (Market Share, 1993)*. Tokyo: Nihon Keizai Shinbunsha.

Nikkeiren (1994) *Shin nihonteki keiei sisutemi to kenkyu purojekuto. Chukan hokoku. (Interim Report of the Study Project on New Japanese Management)*. Tokyo: Nikkeiren.

Nikkeiren (1995) *Shin jidai no nihonteki keiei. Chosen subeiki hoko to sono gutaisaku. (Japanese Management in a New Era. Principles and their Concrete Policies)*. Tokyo: Nikkeiren.

Nihon Keieisha Dantai Renmei (Nikkeiren) (1995) *Shin jidai no nihonteki keiei (Japanese-Style Management in a New Era)*, Tokyo: Nikkeiren.

Nippon – A Charted Survey of Japan (1994) Tokyo: Tsuneta Yano Memorial Society.

Nishiguchi, T. (1994) *Strategic Industrial Sourcing – The Japanese Advantage*. Oxford: Oxford University Press.

Nohara, H. (1991) Some Notes on the Japanese Work Experience: Toyota – A Case Study. Working Paper, The Michael Harrington Center, Queens College, City University of New York.

Nomura, M. (1991) Social conditions for CIM in Japan. A case study of a machine tool company. In E. Hidebrandt (ed.) *Betriebliche Sozialverfassung unter Veraenderungsdruck*. Berlin: Edition Sigma.

Nomura, M. (1993a) *Jukuren to bungyo. Nihon kigyo to teira shugi (Skill and the Division of Labour. Taylorism in Japanese firms)*. Tokyo: Ochanomizu Shobo.

Nomura, M. (1993b) *Toyotizimu – Nikongata Seisan Sisutemu no Seijuku to Henyo (Toyotism – Maturity and Metamorphosis of a Japanese Production System)*. Kyoto: Minuruva Shobo.

Nomura, M. (1994) *Shushin koyo (Lifetime Employment)*. Tokyo: Iwanami Shoten.

Normile, D. (1995) Sharp – sticking to the basics. *Electronics Business Asia* June: 34–8.

Nyusu Daijesuto (1989) *Quarter. FA sangyo 25 nen no ayumi (Quarter. 25-year History of the FA Industry)*. Nagoya: Nyusu Saijesuto Sha.

Ohmae, K. (1990) *The Borderless World*. London: Collins.

Ohta-ku (1995) *Ohta-ku kogyo no kozo henka ni kansuru chosa hokokusho (Research Report on Changing Structure of Ohta-ku Industries)*, Tokyo: Ohta-ku.

Oishi, N. (1994) Low-growth era seen after recession. *Nikkei Weekly* 17 January.

Okamoto, M. (1995) There is no underestimation of unemployment. *Nikkei Weekly* 18 November.

Okamoto, Y. (1994) The Tokyo report. The changing political and economic landscape in Japan. *Nikkei Weekly* 25 July.

Okazaki, T. (1994) The wartime planned economy. In M. Aoki and R. Dore (eds) *The Japanese Firm: Sources of Competitive Strength*. Oxford: Clarendon Press.

Okimoto, D. (1989). *Between MITI and the Market*. Stanford, CA: Stanford University Press.

Ono, G. (1992) *Jissenteki sangyo seisaku ron. Nihon no keiken karano kyokun (Practical Industrial Policy. Lessons from Japanese Experiences)*, Tokyo: Tsusho Sangyo Chosakai.

Osawa, M. (1993a) *Keizai henka to joshi rodo. Nichibei no hikaku kenkyu (Economic Changes and Female Work. A Comparison between Japan and the USA)*. Tokyo: Nihon Keizai Hyoronsha.

Osawa, M. (1993b) *Kigyo chushin shakai wo koete. Gendai nihon wo jenda de yomu (Beyond the Company-Centred Society. An Interpretation from the Viewpoint of Gender)*. Tokyo: Jiji Tsushinsha.

Ouchi, W. (1981) *Theory Z*. New York: Avon.

Porter, M. (1990) *The Competitive Advantage of Nations*. London: Macmillan.

Power, C. (1995) The Business Week global 1000. *Business Week* 10 July.

Reading, B. (1992) *Japan – The Coming Collapse*. London: Weidenfeld & Nicolson.

Rechtin, M. (1994) Lexus sets a new norm in initial quality study. *Automotive News* 30 May.

Rechtin, M. (1996a) Decontenting: when there's no cost left to cut. *Automotive News* 22 January.

Rechtin, M. (1996b) Japanese plan major price cuts in the US. *Automotive News* 10 June.

Rengo (1995) *Koyo tenken anketo shukei kekka 2ji shukei (Questionnaire on Union Activities Regarding Employment Practices, Second Edition, July 27)*. Tokyo: Rengo.

Robertson, D., Rinehart, J., Huxley, C., Wareham, J., Rosenfeld, H., McGough, A. and Benedict, S. (1993) *Japanese Production Management in a Unionized Auto Plant. Willowdale*. Ontario: CAW-Canada Research Department.

Rogers, J. and Freeman, R. (1994) *Worker Representation and Participation Survey: First Report of Findings*. Princeton, NJ: Princeton Survey Research Associates.

Rogers, J. and Freeman, R. (1995) *Worker Representation and Participation Survey: Second Report of Findings*. Princeton, NJ: Princeton Survey Research Associates.

Rosei Jiho ('Labor Policy Journal') (1993) Shinbun Hodo ni miru Gorika, Kogyo Chosei no Doko. (Newspaper articles on Rationalization and Trends of Adjustment, August 1992–February 1993), 12 March.

Samuelson, R. (1993) Japan as number two. *Newsweek* 6 December.

Sato, M. (1995a) Conservative employee attitudes. Class of '95: new blood, old attitudes. *Nikkei Weekly* 24 April.

Sato, M. (1995b) As cold war ends, hot economies bloom. *Nikkei Weekly* 26 May.

Sawai, M. (1990) Kosaku kikai (The machine tool industry). In S. Yonekawa, K. Shimokawa and H. Yamazaki (eds) *Sengo nihon keieishi (Business History in Postwar Japan), Vol. 11.* Tokyo: Toyo keizai shinposha.

Schlender, B. (1993) Japan – hard times for high tech. *Fortune* 22 March.

Scott, G. (1994) *The Chrysler Corporation. MIT IMVP New Product Development Series.* (International Motor Vehicle Project, working paper). Cambridge, MA: MIT Press.

Seki, M. (1993) *Huru setto gata sanngyo kozo wo koete. Higashi ajia sinnjidai no nakano nihon kigyo (Beyond the Full-Set Industrial Structure. Japanese Industries in a New Era of the Asian Economy).* Tokyo: Chuko shinsho.

Seki, M. and Hitokoto, N. (eds) (1996) *Chiho sangyo shinko to kigyoka seishin (Promotion of Local Industries and Entrepreneurship).* Tokyo: Shinhyoron.

Sekiguchi, S. (1994) An overview of adjustment assistance policies in Japan. In W. H. Tan, and H. Shimada (eds) *Troubled Industries in the United States and Japan.* London: Macmillan.

Servan-Schreiber, J. J. (1969) *The American Challenge.* Harmondsworth: Penguin Books.

Sharp, M. (1995) The role of private companies and the state in the promotion of biotechnology: options for government. In M. Fransman, G. Junne and A. Roobeek (eds) *The Biotechnology Revolution?* Oxford: Blackwell.

Shinjo, K. 1988. The computer industry. In Komiya, R. et al. (eds) *Industrial Policy in Japan.* Tokyo: Academic Press.

Shinmura, T. and Ishizawa, M. (1994) Redundant workers falling through cracks in the lifetime-employment system *Nikkei Weekly* 24 January .

Smitka, M. (1991) *Competitive Ties: Subcontracting in the Japanese Automobile Industry.* New York: Columbia University Press.

Stewart, H. (1995) Foreign semiconductor makers enter the electronics industry. *Journal of Japanese Trade and Industry* 3: 52–5.

Sumiya, F. (1994a) Strong yen: weak demand hit automakers. *Nikkei Weekly* 30 May.

Sumiya, F. (1994b). Small manufacturers face survival fight. *Nikkei Weekly* 13 June.

Sumiya, F. (1995a) More closures foreseen in bloated auto industry. *Nikkei Weekly* 27 March.

Sumiya, F. (1995b) Toyota rolls out strategy to snare Asian market. *Nikkei Weekly* 28 September.

Tabb, W. (1994) *The Postwar Japanese System.* New York: Oxford University Press.

Taira, K. (1983) Japan's low unemployment. An economic miracle or statistical artifact. *Monthly Labour Review,* 106.

Takenaka, E. and Kuba, Y. (1994) *Rodoryoku no joseika. 21 seiki heno paradaimu (Feminization of the labour force. A Paradigm for the 21st century).* Tokyo: Yuhikaku.

Tang, S.-Y. (1995) Informal credit markets and economic development in Taiwan. *World Development* 23: 845–55.

Teldok (1994) *Yearbook on Telecommunications and Information Technology in Sweden – In an International Perspective.* Stockholm: Teldok.

Thurow, L. (1995) America's other problems pale beside falling wages. *Asahi Evening News* 14 September.

Toga, M. (1995) Showcase plant boxes in Mazda options. *Nikkei Weekly* 2 October.

Tokunaga, S., Nomura, M. and Hiramoto, A. (1991) *Nihon kigyo. Sekai senryaku to jissen (Japanese Firms. World Strategy and Practices).* Tokyo: Dobunkan.

Toyo Keizai (1994) *Toyo Keizai data bank. Chugoku shinshutsu kigyo soran 1995 (List of Firms Operating in China, 1995),* Tokyo: Toyo Keizai Shinposha.

Tsuru, S. (1993) *Japan's Capitalism: Creative Defeat and Beyond.* Cambridge: Cambridge University Press.

Updike, E., Armstrong, L., Kerwin, K., Naughton, K. and Woodruff, D. (1996) Japan is back. *Business Week* 19 February.

Verity, J. W., Gross, N. and McWilliams, J. (1992) The Japanese juggernaut that isn't. *Business Week* 31 August.

Vital Statistics on American Politics (1993) Washington, DC: CQ Press.

Vogel, E. (1980). *Japan as No. 1*. Tokyo: Charles Tuttle.

Wada, Y. (1994) Japan's export-pinching yen. *The Asian Wall Street Journal* 14 July.

Wernle, B. (1995) Japanese again top J.D. Power quality survey. *Automotive News* 29 May.

Wolferen, K. van (1990) *The Enigma of Japanese Power. People and Politics in a Stateless Nation*. London: Macmillan.

Womack, J. P., Jones, D. T. and Roos, D. (1990) *The Machine that Changed the World*. New York: Rawson Associates/Macmillan.

Woolcock, S. (1996) Competition among forms of corporate governance in the European Community: the case of Britain. In R. Dore and S. Berger (eds) *National Diversity and Global Capitalism*. Ithaca, NY: Cornell University Press.

Yahata, S. (1993) Relocation arising from the gradual close of Nissan's Zama plant production line. *Japan Labour Bulletin* 1 July.

Yokoyama, K. (1996) Most quiet on the shareholder front. *Nikkei Weekly* 1 July.

Yoshida, M. (1986) *Sengo nihon kosaku kikai kogyo no kozo bunseki (Analysis of the Machine Tool Industry in Postwar Japan)*. Tokyo: Miraisha.

INDEX

DATE DUE